Counting People in the Information Age

Duane L. Steffey and Norman M. Bradburn, *Editors*

Panel to Evaluate Alternative Census Methods

Committee on National Statistics

Commission on Behavioral and Social Sciences and Education

National Research Council

NATIONAL ACADEMY PRESS
Washington, D.C.   1994

This project is supported by funds provided by the Bureau of the Census, U.S. Department of Commerce, under contract number 50-YABC-1-66032.

Library of Congress Catalog Card No. 94-68466
International Standard Book Number 0-309-05178-9

Additional copies of this report are available from:

National Academy Press, 2101 Constitution Avenue, N.W., Box 285, Washington, D.C. 20418
Call 800-624-6242 or 202-334-3313 (in the Washington Metropolitan Area)

B482

PANEL TO EVALUATE ALTERNATIVE CENSUS METHODS

NORMAN M. BRADBURN (*Chair*), National Opinion Research Center, University of Chicago
ROBERT M. BELL, RAND Corporation, Santa Monica, California
GORDON J. BRACKSTONE, Statistics Canada, Ottawa, Ontario
CLIFFORD C. CLOGG, Departments of Sociology and Statistics, Pennsylvania State University
THOMAS B. JABINE, Statistical Consultant, Washington, D.C.
KATHERINE S. NEWMAN, Department of Anthropology, Columbia University
D. BRUCE PETRIE, Statistics Canada, Ottawa, Ontario
PETER A. ROGERSON, Department of Geography, State University of New York, Buffalo
KEITH F. RUST, Westat, Inc., Rockville, Maryland
NORA CATE SCHAEFFER, Department of Sociology, University of Wisconsin
EDWARD A. SCHILLMOELLER, A.C. Nielsen Company, Northbrook, Illinois
MICHAEL F. WEEKS, Battelle Memorial Institute, Durham, North Carolina
ALAN M. ZASLAVSKY, Department of Statistics, Harvard University

DUANE L. STEFFEY, *Study Director*
ANU PEMMARAZU, *Senior Project Assistant*
MEYER ZITTER, *Consultant*

Contents

Preface

In response to the Decennial Census Improvement Act of 1991 and at the request of the U.S. Department of Commerce and the Bureau of the Census, the National Research Council in 1992 began two studies on the census in the year 2000. The studies are being conducted by two panels under the Research Council's Committee on National Statistics. One study, being conducted by the Panel on Census Requirements in the Year 2000 and Beyond, is considering what purposes a decennial census serves and whether alternative data collection systems can meet these objectives. The interim report of that panel was published in May 1993 (Committee on National Statistics, 1993a); its final report is scheduled for completion in late 1994.

The second study, being conducted by the Panel to Evaluate Alternative Census Methods, has focused on *how* the census should be taken. The panel includes members with expertise in statistics, survey methods and design, decennial census operations, field organization of large-scale data collection, demography, geography, marketing research, administrative records and record linkage, small-area statistics, and respondent behavior (see the Appendix for biographical sketches of panel members and staff).

The panel has conducted much of its work through four working groups that were formed to consider different aspects of alternative census designs: (1) response and coverage issues, including alternative enumeration methods; (2) sampling and statistical estimation; (3) administrative records; and (4) alternatives for small-area data collection. In preparing this report, working groups and staff drafted material for review by the full panel and subsequent revisions were made in response to members' comments. Thus, the report represents the collective thinking of the panel on the issues we have addressed. Nonetheless, we recognize the substantial contributions of individual panel members through their working group affiliations.

Nora Cate Schaeffer was convenor of the first working group, which includes Katherine Newman and Michael Weeks. This group examined response and coverage issues and reviewed research on methods to improve census response and reduce differential coverage. Topics studied by the group include questionnaire design and implementation, census rostering and residence rules, methods for hard-to-enumerate populations, and census outreach and promotion. This working group was primarily responsible for drafting Chapter 3 of this report.

Robert Bell was convenor for the second working group, which includes Clifford Clogg and Alan Zaslavsky. This group examined how problems of coverage and differential coverage could be assessed and improved with sampling and statistical estimation methods. Topics investigated by the group include sampling and truncation of nonresponse follow-up, alternative methodologies for coverage measurement, and the integration of sampling and estimation with other census operations to produce final population totals. This working group was primarily responsible for drafting Chapter 4 of this report.

Thomas Jabine was convenor of the third working group, which includes Gordon Brackstone and Peter Rogerson. This group studied current and potential uses of administrative records in censuses and other components of the Census Bureau's demographic data systems. The group considered technical, legal, and administrative issues—as well as such factors as cost and public acceptability—regarding new uses of administrative records and future research and development. This working group was primarily responsible for drafting Chapter 5 of this report.

Keith Rust was convenor for the fourth working group, which includes Norman Bradburn, Bruce Petrie, and Edward Schillmoeller. This group studied two proposed alternatives—continuous measurement and matrix sampling—for collecting the detailed sociodemographic data that are currently gathered on the decennial census long form. The group examined methodological and operational issues associated with the implementation of these proposals. The group also considered other factors in its evaluations, including accuracy, costs, acceptability to census data users, and effects on the decennial enumeration. This working group was primarily responsible for drafting Chapter 6 of this report.

The panel transmitted its first brief report to the Census Bureau in December 1992 (Committee on National Statistics, 1992). That letter report offered general comments on the design selection process and made several recommendations regarding further consideration of the use of administrative records for the nation's censuses in the future. In September 1993, the panel transmitted an interim report, which presented the panel's findings and conclusions to that date, many of which concerned plans for the 1995 census test (Committee on National

Statistics, 1993b). We have excerpted relevant material and integrated earlier recommendations in preparing this report.

The panel has endeavored to deliver a timely and thorough report. Although the primary audience for this report is the Census Bureau, we have also tried to include sufficient technical background so that the report is of value to a wider audience. We have offered a generous number of recommendations, and we hope the Census Bureau will find this report useful in planning for the 1995 census test and the 2000 census. We have been heartened by the responsiveness of Census Bureau staff to recommendations in our earlier report. This report reflects our general satisfaction with the direction of the census research and development program, although we note exceptions and suggest modifications or shifts in emphasis of the program.

At the time of this report, the major components of the 1995 census test have been identified, but details of field operations and estimation procedures are still being determined. Therefore, the plans for the 1995 census test discussed in the report are tentative and are subject to change. We believe that one major contribution of the 1995 census test, if it is properly designed and executed, will be cost data on the innovations under consideration—e.g., nonresponse follow-up sampling and truncation, application of the planning database and tool kit, and new approaches for integrated coverage measurement. Accurate information on cost and operational effectiveness will be essential for making sound decisions in December 1995 on the final design for the 2000 census.

We thank the Census Bureau staff for their accessibility and cooperation in providing information and materials for deliberations of our panel and its working groups. We would like to thank Harry Scarr, acting director of the Census Bureau, for addressing the panel at numerous panel meetings during the past two years. We would like to give special thanks to Robert Tortora, Susan Miskura, and Mary Mulry for providing regular briefings on 2000 census research and for responding promptly to requests for documentation. Also, we thank the following members of the Year 2000 Research and Development Staff, who were extremely generous with their time: Solomona Aoelua, Bob Bair, LaVerne Collins, Arthur Cresce, Jim Dinwiddie, Catherine Keeley, Jay Keller, Joe Knott, Charlene Leggieri, Sandy Lucas, and Violetta Vasquez. Other Census Bureau staff with whom the panel consulted include Charles Alexander, Leslie Brownrigg, Jon Clark, Tom DeCair, Gregg Diffendal, Don Dillman, Jerry Gates, Deborah Griffin, Susan Knight, John Long, Elizabeth Martin, Lawrence McGinn, Laurie Moyer, Gregg Robinson, Rajendra Singh, John Thompson, Signe Wetrogan, David Whitford, and Henry Woltman.

Federal agency representatives who provided information include Bruce Johnson and Jack Kaufman of the U.S. General Accounting Office; Katherine Wallman of the U.S. Office of Management and Budget; Fritz Scheuren, Ellen Yau, and Peter Sailer of the Internal Revenue Service; and Jim Scanlon, John Fanning, Dale Hitchcock, and Jim Kaple of the U.S. Department of Health and

Human Services. The panel is also grateful for discussions with several congressional staff members, including TerriAnn Lowenthal, Shelly Wilkie Martinez, David McMillen, and George Omas.

We are grateful to Johnny Blair, associate director of the Survey Research Center, University of Maryland, College Park, for preparing a technical paper that evaluated, summarized, and analyzed data from the Internal Revenue Service taxpayer opinion surveys and other relevant sources. The paper also evaluated the design and methodology used in the surveys and other research. We also thank Edwin Goldfield for preparing two background papers reviewing innovations in the decennial census and previous studies of the decennial census of population and housing.

There are many staff members of the Committee on National Statistics who provided guidance and advice, particularly Miron Straf, Constance Citro, and Barry Edmonston. The panel also appreciates the editorial work of Eugenia Grohman, associate director for reports, and Christine McShane, editor of the Commission on Behavioral and Social Sciences and Education. Their efforts have greatly improved the report's structure and presentation.

We especially thank our panel staff. We thank Meyer Zitter, consultant to the panel, for his part in drafting the material in Chapter 5 on the use of administrative records in other demographic programs of the federal statistical system. Anu Pemmarazu, senior project assistant, competently prepared summaries of panel meetings and draft documents, and handled myriad administrative matters with efficiency and professionalism. Her keen ability to anticipate project needs and to manage the often challenging logistics of panel meetings, as well as her unflagging willingness to take on diverse assignments, kept our day-to-day operations running smoothly.

No greater blessing can be given to a panel than to have a study director with the depth of understanding, sense of organization, felicity of expression and willingness to put in long hours possessed by Duane Steffey. He gently, but firmly, kept us on track, made certain that we always had the next milestone in sight, and turned our often rambling prose into an integrated and readable document. Our gratitude to him truly knows no bounds. A special place in the pantheon of National Research Council study directors is reserved for him.

Finally, I would like to thank the panel members for their generous contribution of time and expert knowledge. They gave unstintingly of their expertise and never faltered in their assignments. The report is truly a collaborative effort. Working with them was both a great pleasure and a learning experience for me.

Norman M. Bradburn, *Chair*
Panel to Evaluate Alternative
Census Methods

Counting People in the Information Age

Summary

Throughout the history of the United States, and indeed in democracies throughout the world, censuses have been key sources of information to facilitate governance and improve public understanding of nations and their communities. An evaluation of alternative census methods involves a major component of a national statistical system that produces knowledge for many purposes.

The U.S. Census of Population and Housing serves two distinct functions. First, there is a constitutional mandate (Article 1, Section 2) to conduct an enumeration of the national population every 10 years for the reapportionment of congressional seats. The population counts are also used for the redistricting of political jurisdictions at all levels of government and the allocation of federal program funds.

In addition to counting people, the decennial census serves as a linchpin of the federal statistical system by collecting data on the characteristics of individuals, households, and housing units throughout the country. The census is uniquely positioned to gather comprehensive and comparable information for communities and population groups, small and large, that cannot be obtained from any other source.

THE CHALLENGE FOR 2000

The broad challenge facing the U.S. census in the year 2000 is to continue to meet information requirements for the country in an environment in which it is increasingly difficult to collect good information by traditional methods.

The two strongest criticisms leveled against the 1990 census are that unit costs increased significantly, continuing a trend that began with the 1970 census, and that the problem of differential undercount by race persisted and possibly worsened, despite a large investment in programs that were intended to improve coverage (see, e.g., U.S. General Accounting Office, 1992). These criticisms have contributed to the growing momentum and advocacy for fundamental change in census operations.

In constant (1990) dollars, the unit costs of counting a household have increased significantly in the past 30 years: less than $10 in 1960, $11 in 1970, $20 in 1980, and $25 in 1990. These increases in expenditures have been accompanied by the persistent problem that the people missed by the census are not representative of the population as a whole: the Census Bureau estimates that the net undercount in the 1990 census was 1.6 percent of the U.S. population, or about 4.0 million people, and the estimated difference in the undercount rates for blacks and non-Hispanic whites was 3.9 percentage points (Hogan, 1993)[1]. Differential coverage by certain characteristics, such as race and geographic location, has significant implications for political representation and allocation of federal program funds.

Measures of gross census error are also important indicators of census data quality. Such measures consider not only omissions (that produce undercounts) but also erroneous enumerations (that produce overcounts). The 1990 census included approximately 11 million erroneous enumerations, the largest number recorded to date (Bryant, 1993). All undercounts and overcounts complicate the task of accurately measuring census net coverage. Undercounts and overcounts that are nonuniformly distributed among particular areas or types of people lead to misdistribution of the estimated population, even when such errors balance at larger levels of aggregation.

Some advocates of census reform have also questioned the collection of detailed sociodemographic data as part of the decennial census. Since 1960, this additional information has been gathered by distributing a census "long form" to a national sample of households. One current argument is that the accuracy of the decennial population figures would be improved if long-form data collection is eliminated, reduced, or displaced in time from the effort to enumerate the population. Others have suggested that some of the data gathered in the 1990 census could be collected through alternate methods and made available for use in a more timely manner (see, e.g., Sawyer, 1993; U.S. House of Representatives, 1993). Still others have challenged the quality of data collected on the long form, noting the high rates at which this information is gathered indirectly (relative to

---

[1] These results were obtained by analysis of data from the 1990 Post-Enumeration Survey. The estimated undercounts for blacks and non-Hispanic whites were 4.6 and 0.7 percent, respectively. Independent estimates based on demographic analysis were similar: the net undercount was estimated to be 1.8 percent of the population, and the estimated undercounts for blacks and nonblacks (the latter category includes Asians and Hispanics) were 5.7 and 1.3 percent, respectively (Robinson et al., 1993).

the decennial short form), either by imputation or from someone outside the household, particularly for minority populations (see, e.g., Ericksen et al., 1991).

The panel's work emphasizes those aspects of census methodology that have the greatest potential effect on two primary objectives of census redesign: reducing differential undercount and controlling costs. In particular, we focus on processes for the collection of data, the quality of coverage and response that these processes engender, and the use of sampling (and subsequent estimation) in the collection process. Our field of examination is not restricted to the 2000 census: a significant number of our findings and recommendations look beyond 2000 to future censuses, relate to other Census Bureau demographic programs (current population estimates and sample surveys), and discuss the collection of small-area data from administrative files. Redesigning the nation's census should not be carried out without due consideration of other components of the Census Bureau's demographic program and the larger federal statistical system.

The census data collection processes involve four key steps: (1) the construction of an address frame, (2) an initial process to obtain responses that can be linked to the address frame, (3) a follow-up process to obtain responses from those not covered in the initial process, and (4) a coverage assessment process that estimates the size of the population not covered through the initial and follow-up processes. In the 1990 and earlier censuses, the first three steps led to the official census estimates; whether or not to incorporate the estimates from the fourth step into the official census estimates became the "adjustment issue." For the 2000 census, the Census Bureau is proposing a fundamentally different approach, called a "one-number census," in which this fourth step is an integral part of the census process that leads to the official estimates.

The design of a census data collection process in essence amounts to deciding which methods of identification, enumeration, response, and coverage improvement should be applied at each of the steps; whether sampling methods (and the corresponding estimation methods) should be used at any of the four steps; and, if sampling methods are used, which methods and at which steps. These decisions should be based on information about the effectiveness and costs of the various alternative methods; the 1995 census test should be a prime source of such information.

In subsequent sections of this summary, we list key recommendations, numbered in order of appearance within the report chapters. A complete list of recommendations appears at the end of the report.

MAJOR INNOVATIONS FOR THE 2000 CENSUS

The panel found much progress in census research and development since the 1990 census, and this progress reflects new and creative thinking at the Census Bureau. The two main areas in which innovation in census design is taking place are response and coverage improvement and expanded use of sampling and estimation. Research on response and coverage improvement has led to potentially important changes in questionnaire design and implementation. Sampling and statistical estimation methods are being explored to close the remaining differentials in census coverage while controlling, or even reducing, overall cost.

The Census Bureau will test a variety of innovative design features in the 1995 census test. Collection of reliable information in the 1995 census test about the costs and effectiveness of census design components will be essential for their proper evaluation—in particular, to inform decisions about allocating resources between efforts to improve primary response and efforts to use sampling and estimation methods to correct the counting operation.

The operational constraints on the 1995 census test underscore the importance of learning as much as possible from other research. For example, simulation studies using 1990 census data can investigate the effects of truncating nonresponse follow-up operations at different points in time, using different rates of sampling nonrespondents for follow-up, and applying different coverage measurement methods. Similarly, not all methods need to be tested in large-scale field settings. To ease experimental complexity, certain methods might be excluded from large-scale field testing in 1995 when such an exclusion would not disrupt the research and development program or if smaller experiments (e.g., questionnaire research) conducted simultaneously with the 1995 census test will provide useful information.

Sampling, Estimation, and the One-Number Census

A key panel finding concerns the validity of the use of sampling and estimation in census-taking. The panel concludes that sampling and associated statistical estimation constitute an established scientific methodology that must play a greater role in future censuses in order to obtain a more accurate picture of the population than is provided by current methods. For this reason, the panel endorses the Census Bureau's stated goal of achieving a one-number census in 2000 that incorporates the results from coverage measurement programs, including programs that involve sampling and statistical estimation, into the official census population totals. The panel also recommends continued methodological research, development, and testing in pursuit of this goal.

Recommendation 4.2: Differential undercount cannot be reduced to acceptable levels at acceptable costs without the use of integrated coverage measurement and the statistical methods associated with it. We endorse the use of integrated coverage measurement as an essential part of census-taking in the 2000 census.

One proposed method for integrated coverage measurement, CensusPlus, involves intensive enumeration methods and highly trained interviewers with the objective of obtaining a complete enumeration of the population in a sample of census blocks. Tentative plans call for the CensusPlus operation to be carried out concurrently with mail and follow-up operations, and data from this coverage measurement survey would be used in producing the final, official population totals. Because it is a fundamentally new approach to measuring census coverage, the CensusPlus operation will require thorough testing and evaluation prior to approval of its use in a decennial census. Estimation methods that might be used in integrated coverage measurement will require further study using simulations of 1990 census data and field data from the 1995 census test.

> **Recommendation 4.3: The Census Bureau should investigate during the 1995 census test whether the CensusPlus field operation can attain excellent coverage in CensusPlus blocks without contaminating the regular enumeration in those blocks. If substantial problems are identified, CensusPlus should not be selected as the field methodology for integrated coverage measurement in the 2000 census unless clearly effective corrective measures can be implemented within the research and development schedule.**

The panel's position on this issue is similar to the view expressed by the National Research Council's Panel on Decennial Census Methodology, convened prior to the 1990 census, which argued for balance between efforts to achieve a complete enumeration and efforts to improve the accuracy of census results through coverage measurement methods (see Citro and Cohen, 1985).

The follow-up of households that do not return the mail questionnaire is one of the most costly and labor-intensive operations in the traditional census. Sampling during nonresponse follow-up offers the potential for saving hundreds of millions of dollars, but it also would increase the variability of population estimates, especially for small geographic areas. The panel recommends research, development, and testing of nonresponse follow-up sampling in the 1995 census test. On the basis of results of the 1995 census test, the Census Bureau should make a careful and thorough determination of the data quality and cost implications of this promising approach to the long-standing problem that not everyone responds to the mail questionnaire.

> **Recommendation 4.1: Sampling for nonresponse follow-up could produce major cost savings in 2000. The Census Bureau should test nonresponse follow-up sampling in 1995 and collect data that allows evaluation of (1) follow-up of all nonrespondents during a truncated period of time, combined with the use of sampling during a subsequent period of follow-up of the remaining nonrespondents, and (2) the use of administrative records to improve estimates for nonsampled housing units.**

Response and Coverage Improvement

A second major panel finding is that problems of cost and differential coverage should also be addressed directly at the primary response stage of the census. Ongoing research at the Census Bureau is focused on improving coverage within households by changing the census form. The panel strongly supports the continuation of this research through and beyond the 1995 census test because of its potential for yielding a cost-effective means of improving the initial count and possibly reducing differentials in coverage.

> **Recommendation 3.1: A program of research extending beyond the 1995 census test should aim to reduce coverage errors within households by reducing response errors (e.g., by using an extended roster form). This research should also evaluate the impact of these new approaches on gross and net coverage errors, as well as assess the effects on coverage of obtaining enumerations using different instrument modalities (e.g., paper and computer-assisted) and different interview modes (e.g., paper instrument completed by household respondent and by enumerator).**

Recently tested improvements in census questionnaire format and implementation procedures could increase mail response rates, thereby saving money on the follow-up of nonrespondents. Making greater use of alternate technologies (e.g., telephones) and offering people multiple ways to respond (e.g., by distributing census questionnaires at public places) may yield additional cost savings. Early research suggests that changes in the rostering method could improve within-household coverage for certain groups within the population.

Measures of gross census error will be important in evaluating the effectiveness of proposed methods for increasing census response, such as using new ways to develop household rosters, distributing unaddressed questionnaires, offering the option of telephone response, and using special "tool-kit" enumeration methods in certain small geographic areas. We believe that census methodology should strive to minimize not only omissions (that produce undercounts) but also erroneous enumerations (that produce overcounts). Aggressive research is needed to develop techniques to prevent erroneous or duplicate enumerations during a census with multiple response modes and new rostering procedures.

Other census design components—for example, continuous updating of the master address file and the use of administrative records—might also contribute to reducing the differential undercount. In spite of these actual and potential improvements, however, the panel also concludes that sampling and estimation—in particular, as part of an integrated coverage measurement program—will be needed to further reduce coverage differentials to insignificant levels.

OTHER KEY CENSUS DESIGN COMPONENTS

Address List Development

Virtually all fundamental design changes contemplated for the 2000 census depend on the existence of an accurate list of residential addresses. A geographic database that is fully integrated with a master address file is a basic requirement for the 2000 census, regardless of the final census design.

Recommendation 2.1: The Census Bureau should continue aggressive development of the TIGER (topologically integrated geographic encoding and referencing) system, the Master Address File (MAF), and integration of these two systems. MAF/TIGER updating activities for the 1995 census test sites should be completed in time to permit the use and evaluation of the MAF/TIGER system as part of the 1995 census test.

The duplication of effort, cost, and complexity involved both within the Census Bureau to compile address lists for consecutive censuses and across other federal agencies and state and local governments—including the U.S. Postal Service—suggests the value of creating and maintaining a master list of addresses over the decade. A continuously updated master address file could serve as a national utility for the federal statistical system.

Recommendation 2.4: The Statistical Policy Office of the Office of Management and Budget should develop a structure to permit the sharing of address lists among federal agencies and state and local governments— including the Census Bureau and the Postal Service—for approved uses under appropriate conditions.

We note the distinction between address information and information that identifies or characterizes individuals or households associated with addresses; the use of the latter type of information appropriately requires stronger provisions to ensure privacy and confidentiality.

Use of Administrative Records

Administrative records are already an important source of data for many statistical programs, and they can play a much greater role in the future. They can be used to provide more frequent and timely small-area data at a relatively low cost, and existing files could prove especially useful if augmented with information about race and ethnicity. Legitimate statistical uses of administrative records within the federal statistical system should be facilitated, rather than hampered, by legislation and administrative rules. In particular, legislation governing the use of health care records should permit use of basic health care enrollment data by the Census Bureau for the decennial censuses and for current population estimates and surveys.

Recommendation 5.1: Legislation that requires or authorizes the creation of individual record systems for administrative purposes should not create unnecessary barriers to legitimate statistical uses of the records, including important uses not directly related to the programs that the records were developed to serve. Preferably, such legislation should explicitly allow for such uses, subject to strong protection of the confidentiality of individual information. The panel urges Congress, in considering legislation relevant to health care reform, not to foreclose possible uses of health care enrollment records for the decennial censuses and other basic demographic statistical programs.

The Census Bureau should pursue a proactive policy to develop expanded uses of administrative records in future censuses, surveys, and population estimate programs. Effective pursuit of such a policy will require establishment of a suitable organizational structure and adequate resources for research and development activities not tied directly to ongoing census and survey programs. It will also require that the Census Bureau work closely with program agencies in the development of new administrative record systems and modification of existing ones to improve their utility for statistical uses. The panel urges Congress and the Statistical Policy Office of the U.S. Office of Management and Budget to support such interagency cooperation.

Recommendation 5.11: The panel urges the Census Bureau to adopt a proactive policy to expand its uses of administrative records, and it urges other executive branch agencies and Congress to give their support to such a policy.

Although the panel concurs with the judgment of the Census Bureau that an administrative records census—i.e., a census that relies exclusively or primarily on records from administrative data systems to produce population totals—is not a feasible option for the 2000 census, we believe the possibility should be carefully explored for the 2010 census. This program of research should begin immediately to permit, in conjunction with the 2000 census, a meaningful comparison of the administrative records census approach to the traditional approach under full census conditions.

Recommendation 5.7: During the 2000 census the Census Bureau should test one or more designs for an administrative records census in selected areas. Planning for this testing should begin immediately.

A program of sustained research and development, with the cooperation of program agencies, is needed for a thorough evaluation of the administrative records census option, taking into account the current and potential content of administrative records, the coverage of the population, and the potential for achieving significant cost reductions in censuses. It should not be assumed that a census based primarily on administrative records must duplicate all major design features of a traditional version of the census. Rather, it should be assumed that changes are possible in: (1) census content, definitions, and reference dates; (2) the census statute (Title 13, U.S. Code) and other laws and regulations governing the conduct of the decennial census; (3) laws and regulations governing access to federal and state administrative records; and (4) the content of administrative records systems.

Matching and Elimination of Duplicate Records

Record linkage is the identification of records belonging to the same unit (i.e., a person, household, or housing unit) either within a single data set or across two different data sets. In decennial census applications, records are matched either to eliminate duplication or to pool information from multiple sources.

Many census operations involve matching one list of records to another. Needs for record linkage arise when address lists and other administrative records are used, when people are given multiple opportunities to respond to the census, and when dual-system estimation is used as part of a coverage measurement program. Historically, an initial match has been performed by a computer algorithm, followed by clerical verification and resolution. Many of the innovative methods being examined in the 1995 census test would place greater demands on matching technology. Thus, improvements in the accuracy or efficiency of automated record linkage will support the 2000 census design by increasing the capability to produce reliable results within time and budget constraints.

The development and updating of an integrated MAF/TIGER system will require automated address matching and geocoding at various stages. The distribution of unaddressed questionnaires, the opportunity to respond by mail or telephone, and the application of other special methods are likely to increase the potential for duplication in the census enumeration; matching is needed to determine whether persons and housing units were enumerated more than once. The Census Bureau's recent research on rostering may lead to new approaches to ascertaining residency, which would present new complications in assigning people correctly to geographic areas. Matching may also be needed to obtain telephone numbers during follow-up of nonresponding households.

Record linkage technology will also support the development of an administrative record database for the 1995 census test sites. Procedures for integrated coverage measurement could involve the automated comparison of records from the census enumeration and independent operations. The Census Bureau will need solid capability for computer matching and elimination of duplicate records in order to perform all the above tasks in an accurate, timely, and cost-effective manner.

Recommendation 2.2: The Census Bureau should continue its research program on record linkage in support of the 1995 census test and the 2000 census. Efforts should include studies of the effectiveness of different matching keys (e.g., name, address, date of birth, and Social Security number) and the establishment of requirements for such components as address standardization, parsing, and string comparators. Existing record linkage technology should be tested and evaluated in the 1995 census test.

Limits on the ability to eliminate duplicate records may prove to be the controlling factor with regard to the feasibility of many of the innovations under consideration for the 2000 census design.

Methods for Hard-to-Enumerate Populations

The legitimacy of the census depends in part on public perception that it fairly treats all geographical areas and demographic groups in the country. Fair treatment can be defined in either of two ways: by applying the same methods and effort to every area or by attaining the same population coverage in every area so that estimates of relative populations of different areas are accurate. The objective of the census is to measure population accurately—above all, to calculate accurate population shares in order to apportion representation properly. Therefore, obtaining equal coverage clearly takes priority over using the same methods in every area. In fact, since experience shows that treating every geographical area and demographic group in the same way leads to differential coverage, the Census Bureau has a positive duty to use methods designed to close the coverage gap.

The term *tool kit* refers to the collection of special methods—for example, team enumeration, "blitz" tactics, local facilitators with community knowledge and ties, and bilingual enumerators—for hard-to-enumerate areas. The panel supports the continued research, development, and testing of methods for differential treatment of subpopulations with the goal of reducing the differentials in census outcomes across these subpopulations. The panel recognizes that experimentation with tool-kit methods in the 1995 census test will be constrained by pressures to limit operational complexity. Nevertheless, the panel believes that efforts should be made to plan variations in tool-kit application across sites or areas within sites to permit comparative assessments.

Recommendation 3.6: In the 1995 census test, the Census Bureau should include a larger repertoire of foreign-language materials than those currently available in Spanish (both written and audio). In addition, the Census Bureau should conduct more aggressive hiring of community-based enumerators (with due consideration of local concerns about the confidentiality of census responses) and should accommodate greater

flexibility in the timing of enumeration by personal visit (i.e., permitting contact during evenings and weekends).

Attention must be given to the yield from tool-kit methods—in terms of numbers of people who are accurately counted—not simply to the cost of implementing these methods. Potential problems of erroneous enumeration must be assessed during the testing and evaluation of tool-kit methods and other coverage improvement programs, and decisions about inclusion in the 2000 census should consider the relative marginal costs and benefits of these programs.

A key question concerning the ability to systematically apply differential treatments to different subpopulations relates to the effective role of the planning database being developed by the Census Bureau for use in the 1995 census test. The successful use of tool-kit methods in census operations will depend on knowing where they should be applied and on being able to apply them without creating erroneous enumerations. To the extent that the country can be stratified into easy-to-enumerate and hard-to-enumerate areas before the census, this knowledge can be incorporated into the methods used to produce a one-number census.

The general issue of prespecification versus real-time adaptation is relevant not only for application of the planning database or a formal targeting model to improve initial census response, but also for differential treatment during nonresponse follow-up and integrated coverage measurement. In these latter operations, there may be value in oversampling certain geographic areas that are known in advance to have coverage problems.

Counting hard-to-enumerate populations may also be facilitated by means other than special enumeration methods. A current legislative proposal to change the census reference date from April 1 to the first Saturday in March could alleviate problems in counting mobile households, college students, and persons with no usual residence. A greater shift toward the middle of the month could further reduce end-of-month moving problems, although the ability to complete all phases of the census mail operation within the same calendar month is also an important consideration.

Recommendation 2.3: In view of the operational advantages that are likely to result, the panel endorses the proposed change in census reference date from April 1 to the first Saturday in March. Furthermore, we recommend that changing the census reference date from early in the month to midmonth (e.g., the second Saturday in March) be reconsidered if subsequent modifications to the mailout operation would permit all census mailings to be executed within the same calendar month using a midmonth reference date.

The ethnographic research sponsored by the Census Bureau in recent years has provided knowledge about the problems of enumerating inner-city and rural low-income populations, immigrants, internal migrants, and homeless people ("persons with no usual residence"). The panel supports further comparative study of hard-to-enumerate areas and the application of existing findings to the development of cost-effective methods for counting these populations.

Recommendation 3.5: The Census Bureau should conduct further comparative studies of hard-to-enumerate areas, focusing on those parts of the country where three phenomena coincide: a shortage of affordable housing, a high proportion of undocumented immigrants, and the presence of low-income neighborhoods.

Studies of hard-to-enumerate areas may also inform census outreach and promotion efforts. The panel believes that more effective outreach and promotion efforts will require a structured research and development program and greater centralization of responsibilities for decennial census outreach and promotion.

Use of the Telephone

The telephone can and should play a much larger role in the 2000 census than it did in 1990 and in previous censuses. New technologies will allow expansion of the 800 number call-in assistance program and permit access to a wide range of automated services from any telephone in the United States. The panel supports the Census Bureau's plans to develop improved capabilities for handling incoming calls—particularly in view of the potential negative effects on public perception and response of being ill-prepared to field questions.

Recommendation 3.2: The Census Bureau should use the 1995 census test and subsequent tests to inform the design of the 800 number call-in system for the 2000 census. The Census Bureau should focus on the public's response to the menu-driven call-routing system, acceptance of the computer-administered interview, possible differential mode effects between a computer-administered interview and one administered by an interviewer, and the technical feasibility of administering interviews using voice recognition and voice recording. The Census Bureau should also develop and implement a monitoring system in these tests to collect operational and cost data on the call-in program.

The use of computer-assisted outbound calling will be possible in the 2000 census because of the availability of electronic directory services that can match telephone numbers to addresses. The Census Bureau will be able to add telephone numbers to the master address file for a significant number of address listings, and this resource can be used to make outbound telephone calls both to prompt mail nonrespondents to return their forms and to complete the enumeration by telephone. Computer-assisted telephone interviewing will also play a key role in the integrated coverage measurement program being tested as part of the 1995 census test.

Recommendation 3.3: The Census Bureau should expand the research program involving the acquisition of telephone numbers for MAF addresses by working with more companies that offer electronic directory services and developing an optimal protocol for matching addresses. If the Census Bureau is able to acquire unlisted telephone numbers for a 1995 census test site, it should carefully monitor the results obtained from calling households with unlisted numbers.

Findings in the survey research literature and in technology assessments conducted for the Census Bureau suggest that these telephone applications offer the potential for considerable cost savings and improved data quality. The panel encourages the Census Bureau to continue development of telephone-based methods for testing in 1995 and, if successful, for adoption as part of the 2000 census.

ALTERNATIVE METHODS FOR LONG-FORM DATA COLLECTION

As noted above, there is growing interest in developing capabilities to obtain information about small geographic areas and subpopulations more frequently than every 10 years. In addition, there is a perception within Congress and among other interested parties that the additional content gathered by the decennial census long form places a severe burden on respondents and negatively affects census cost, coverage, and quality.

These issues—and, in particular, the accuracy of this perception—are being addressed more thoroughly by the National Research Council's Panel on Census Requirements in the Year 2000 and Beyond. Nevertheless, we have reviewed two possible alternatives to the decennial long form, both currently being investigated by the Census Bureau, for collecting certain types of information beyond simple population counts: (1) the use of multiple sample forms in the decennial census (including the application of matrix sampling) and (2) a large, continuous, monthly survey (the so-called continuous measurement option).

The panel's consideration of these alternative methods has not been motivated by the concerns about cost and differential coverage that have been prominent in the movement for reform of the decennial census. Rather, the panel believes that the transfer of information-gathering responsibilities from the decennial long form to an alternative, such as a continuous measurement survey, should be based on judgments about the cost-effectiveness of these methods in meeting the current and future information needs of census data users. Toward that end, the panel supports continued research and development of a continuous measurement program as a potential future source of sociodemographic data for small areas and small populations, recognizing that significant issues must be addressed before such a program can be seriously considered for adoption.

Recommendation 6.1: The panel endorses further research and evaluation of a continuous measurement program. In conducting this work, the Census Bureau should establish, and continually reinforce, a commitment to simultaneous research and development of cost estimation, data collection and processing methods, estimation procedures, and user needs.

Matrix sampling refers to a technique designed to spread and reduce respondent burden by dividing a survey instrument into multiple instruments with partially overlapping contents. On the basis of its examination, the panel finds that the conditions favorable to use of matrix sampling are either unlikely to be obtained or have not been well studied in the context of the decennial census long form. The panel therefore believes that matrix sampling is unlikely to present an effective alternative to long-form data collection in 2000.

Recommendation 6.5: The panel endorses the Census Bureau's plan to investigate the impact of form length and content on mail response rates in the 1995 census test. Even if the operational feasibility of multiple sample forms is confirmed in the 1995 census test, the Census Bureau should not introduce matrix sampling without undertaking further research. Such research should be assigned low priority relative to other decennial census research projects.

1

Introduction

Census data collection involves four key steps: (1) the construction of an address frame; (2) an initial process to obtain responses that can be linked to the address frame; (3) a follow-up process to obtain responses from those not covered in the initial process; and (4) a coverage assessment process that estimates the size of the population not covered through the initial and follow-up processes.

The design of a census data collection process in essence amounts to deciding which methods of identification, enumeration, response, and coverage improvement should be applied at each of the steps; whether sampling methods (and the corresponding estimation methods) should be used at any of the four steps; and, if sampling methods are used, which methods and at which steps.

The two strongest criticisms leveled against the 1990 census are that unit costs increased significantly, continuing a trend that began with the 1970 census, and that the problem of differential undercount by race persisted and possibly worsened, despite a large investment in programs that were intended to improve coverage (see, e.g., U.S. General Accounting Office, 1992). These criticisms have contributed to the growing momentum and advocacy for fundamental change in census operations. In response to these criticisms, the Census Bureau is considering an unprecedented level of innovation for the 2000 census. As part of that effort, officials at the Department of Commerce and the Census Bureau requested a panel study by the National Research Council's Committee on National Statistics to provide independent technical evaluations of candidate methodologies.

THE ROLE OF THE PANEL

The Panel to Evaluate Alternative Census Methods studied feasible methods for the census not only for 2000, but also for 2010 and beyond. We have a mandate to make recommendations for features of census design that should be investigated and developed for censuses after the next one. Some features of these future designs could and should be tested in the near term and further developed in conjunction with the 2000 census, even though they might not be fully implemented until subsequent censuses. Our deliberations led us to consider all demographic data systems, including current estimates, sample surveys, and tabulations of administrative records.

The panel had four basic tasks: (1) identify designs to be investigated for the 2000 census; (2) evaluate proposed research on alternative census designs; (3) evaluate the results of the research and the selection of census designs for further consideration, in particular for the series of census tests that begin in 1995; and (4) recommend census designs to be explored for 2010 and succeeding years.

The determination of methods for conducting the decennial census must take into account the information requirements placed on the census in its role as a key component of the federal statistical system. Data collected by the statistical system can be classified according to one of three levels of population coverage: (1) basic information—age, race, and ethnic origin—to satisfy the requirements of the Constitution and the Voting Rights Act is collected from 100 percent of the population on the decennial census short form; (2) information that must be reliable for small geographic areas and subpopulations—e.g., education, occupation, income—is currently collected from a large sample of the national population on the decennial census long form; (3) information for which timeliness is more important than geographic detail, such as unemployment rates and statistics on participation in federal entitlement programs, is now gathered by smaller sample surveys.

Throughout our study, the panel has recognized the link between requirements and methods, although thorough examination of census requirements is beyond the scope of this panel. Our cognate panel, the Panel on Census Requirements in the Year 2000 and Beyond, is charged with assessing the needs for data currently collected in the decennial census. Both studies address issues of methodology but approach these issues from different perspectives. In considering alternative methods, the Panel on Census Requirements has been primarily concerned with implications for content and possible effects on public acceptance of results. That panel has also undertaken a more intensive review of the current census cost structure. Our primary attention has been given to technical issues of implementation and evaluation of promising methodologies.

Our evaluations of alternative census methods emphasize the implications for differential coverage and census costs, but not to the exclusion of other considerations. For example, measures of gross census error are important in evaluating the effectiveness of proposed methods for increasing census response, such as distributing unaddressed questionnaires, offering the option of telephone response, and using special "tool-kit" enumeration methods in certain small geographic areas. We believe that census methodology should strive to minimize not only omissions (that produce undercounts) but also erroneous enumerations (that produce overcounts). All undercounts and overcounts complicate the task of accurately measuring census net coverage. Undercounts and overcounts that arise from definitional problems—e.g., a person is erroneously counted in one block and omitted from the correct adjacent block—essentially balance and are not of much additional concern. But undercounts and overcounts that are nonuniformly distributed among particular areas or types of people lead to misdistribution of the estimated population, even when such errors balance at larger levels of aggregation.

The concept of total information error over a decennial period is a useful criterion against which to evaluate alternative methods for collecting small-area data that have traditionally been collected for a sample of respondents during the decennial census using a longer questionnaire. Proposals for a large, continuous survey of households and for other methods to improve intercensal estimates (e.g., expanded use of administrative records) should be evaluated by considering the needs for information with cross-sectional versus temporal accuracy. This criterion is driven by information requirements and, once established, can be used to judge alternative methods intended to address these requirements.

The panel has had regular contact with several official advisory groups that are reviewing the planning for the 2000 census. Early in 1991, the Department of Commerce established a Task Force on the Year 2000 Census to provide an organizational structure for the examination of issues regarding the 2000 census. The task force comprises a technical committee, a policy committee, and an advisory committee. The technical committee consists primarily of experienced professional staff from the Census Bureau. The policy committee includes representatives from other federal statistical agencies. The advisory committee membership includes representatives of state and local government, minority, and other interested professional organizations.

Initially, the technical committee of the task force worked with the Census Bureau to construct a set of 14 census design alternatives. Each alternative was characterized by one or more unique design components; each was also judged to have the potential to meet the current demands of the decennial census. Of the 14 designs, 6 built on the basic structure of the 1990 census, adding different provisions: multiple ways of responding to the census, varying degrees of sampling and statistical estimation, and targeted methods to overcome barriers to enumeration. Two designs relied entirely or to a very significant extent on administrative records. Four designs would have collected data on fewer topics than have been covered in recent decennial censuses. Two designs proposed collecting census data in two stages or through continuous measurement in the decade following the census year.

The panel's first report to the Census Bureau in December 1992 raised questions about the 14-design approach. Subsequently, the Census Bureau decided to remove its original set of 14 alternative census designs from further consideration. Instead, the 1995 census test will evaluate promising components of the original alternative designs. The panel's September 1993 interim report strongly supported this reorientation of the 2000 census planning process. The interim report contained 35 recommendations, many of which suggested design components for inclusion in the 1995 census test (in response to the first element of our charge). We gave particular attention to methods with potential to reduce either census costs or differentials in coverage.

Since the preparation of the panel's interim report, the Census Bureau has released two key documents (discussed below)—the 1995 Census Test Design Recommendation and the Test Design Plan—that identify census design components to be examined in 1995 and discuss plans for testing and evaluating these components. In this report, we review the progress in 2000 census research and development and, in keeping with our third task, evaluate the selection of design components for inclusion in the 1995 census test. We also study and comment on procedures being developed to implement and evaluate the 1995 census test. We continue to recognize the important considerations of cost and differential coverage, yet we also discuss issues related to other factors, such as data quality and gross census error. Finally, we comment further on the broader research program beyond the 1995 census test that will inform planning not only for the 2000 census but also for subsequent censuses and for other demographic data systems.

Many of our evaluations proceed with the assumption that the content of the census short form in 2000 will not be significantly changed from its 1990 version. We further assume that the primary instrument for collecting short-form information in the 2000 census will remain the mail questionnaire, the primary mode of data collection for the past four censuses (Goldfield, 1992).

Recent reviews of the statutory requirements for census data (Bureau of the Census, 1994a:appendix 2) indicate that legislative mandates exist for collection of most of the items currently gathered on the decennial long form, although the legislation typically does not mandate the vehicle for data collection. Later chapters of this report discuss nontraditional methods—i.e., an administrative records census, a large-scale continuous measurement survey—for collecting information that may be comparable to what is gathered on the decennial census short or long forms. We also discuss, from a technical perspective, the pros and cons of dividing the current long form into a series of intermediate-length questionnaires.

The next section of this chapter reviews work done by the Census Bureau as part of its 2000 census research and development program, and the chapter concludes with some observations about census planning for the year 2000 and beyond. Chapter 2 discusses some important issues related to the first step of the collection process, the creation of an address frame, as well as legal and operational issues. Chapter 3 considers methods with potential for improving response and coverage at various stages of the collection process. Chapter 4 addresses the possible use of sampling and estimation at each stage of the census data collection process—particularly in following up households that do not return the mail questionnaire and in measuring census coverage. Chapter 5 discusses the possible use of administrative records in the four collection steps, as well as for current estimates and other demographic programs outside the decennial census. Chapter 6 addresses issues related to alternative schemes that would spread the collection of sample information for small areas and subpopulations over a decade, rather than concentrating efforts in a single year, or would involve the use of multiple sample forms in the decennial census.

CENSUS BUREAU RESEARCH AND DEVELOPMENT

The Census Bureau has responded to the challenges of counting people in the information age by undertaking an ambitious research and development program that reflects an imaginative rethinking of census methodology. This program will lead to the large-scale field testing in 1995 of design components that represent fundamental change from current census practice. The two main areas in which innovation in census design is taking place are: (1) response and coverage improvement and (2) expanded use of sampling and estimation. Research on response and coverage improvement has led to potentially important changes in questionnaire design and implementation. Sampling and statistical estimation methods are being explored to close the remaining differentials in census coverage while controlling, or even reducing, overall cost.

The Census Bureau will test a variety of innovative design features in the 1995 census test. Collection of reliable information in the 1995 census test about the costs and effectiveness of census design components will be essential for their proper evaluation—particularly to inform decisions about allocating resources between efforts to improve primary response and efforts to use sampling and estimation methods to correct the counting operation.

Evaluation Criteria for the 2000 Census

The Census Bureau developed a set of mandatory and desirable criteria for assessing design alternatives, and it has specified that any design being considered for the 2000 census must satisfy all mandatory criteria. Any design that meets the mandatory criteria will then be assessed according to the set of desirable criteria. Six criteria are specified as mandatory by the Census Bureau for the 2000 census design:

1. not require a constitutional amendment;
2. meet data needs for reapportionment;
3. provide data defined by law and past practice for state redistricting;
4. provide age and race/ethnic data defined by law to meet the requirements of enforcing the Voting Rights Act;
5. protect the confidentiality of respondents; and
6. possess the ability to reduce the differential undercount.

Ten criteria are specified as desirable by the Census Bureau for the 2000 census design:

1. result in comparative cost-effectiveness with respect to other alternatives under consideration in real terms on a per unit basis;
2. provide small-area data that the census is uniquely capable of providing;
3. provide a single, best set of census results produced by legal deadlines for reapportionment and redistricting;
4. provide an overall high level of coverage;
5. increase the primary response rate to the census;
6. reduce the level of respondent burden;
7. minimize the degree and type of changes needed in federal or state law;
8. consider the reliance on new or unproven methods or capabilities;
9. permit full development and testing of its major design features; and
10. provide opportunities to involve the U.S. Postal Service, state and local governments, national organizations, and other private, nonprofit, and commercial enterprises.

We have already identified cost and differential coverage as important considerations in the panel's evaluations of alternative census methods. (Later, we describe some basic assumptions about the costs of census-taking that have guided the panel's deliberations.) Reduction of the differential undercount appears in the above list of mandatory criteria, along with constitutional and other legal requirements, underscoring the importance assigned by the Census Bureau and other interested parties to this objective of census reform.

The prominence of cost reduction as the first desirable criterion above is also suggestive of the significant efforts being expended to achieve a more cost-effective census design in 2000. The Census Bureau has a very detailed cost model (Bureau of the Census, 1992b) that is used for operational planning. This model has been used to estimate costs associated with several design components being considered for the 2000 census, including conducting follow-up of mail nonrespondents over a truncated period of time or on a sample basis. The cost-effectiveness of other design components, such as the use of special enumeration methods, has yet to be determined. The 1995 census test should produce better information about costs and benefits for such components. Cost estimates for the continuous measurement option should become firmer when the product is more clearly defined and a small-scale prototype survey is in operation. Similarly, further experience with the statistical use of records from administrative data systems should lead to more reliable estimates of the cost of an administrative records census.

Some relevant criteria are not explicitly identified in the above lists: in considering proposed design innovations, the Census Bureau must address potential problems with erroneous enumerations. The 1990 census had approximately 11 million erroneous enumerations (the largest number recorded to date). As noted earlier, many of these errors result from minor definitional problems and essentially balance at larger geographic areas of interest, but errors that are nonuniformly distributed across the population can reduce the accuracy of census results. Without careful implementation, such innovations as the use of multiple response modes and new rostering procedures could exacerbate the problem of gross census errors. Aggressive research will be needed to develop techniques to prevent erroneous or duplicate enumerations during a census with multiple response modes or new rostering procedures.

One-Number Census

With regard to the third desirable criterion above, the Census Bureau has developed the concept of a "one-number census" that would provide "the best possible single set of results by legal deadlines, . . . based on an appropriate combination of counting, assignment, and statistical techniques" (Miskura, 1993). In this definition, counting refers to the full array of methods used for direct contact with respondents, including mail questionnaires, personal visits, and telephone calls. Assignment refers to the use of evidence from administrative records to add people to the count for a specific geographic location without field verification. Statistical techniques for estimation include imputation procedures, sampling during follow-up of nonrespondents, and methods for measuring census coverage.

The Census Bureau has expressed its commitment to pursue a one-number census for the year 2000, based on the integration of specific counting, assignment, and estimation methods to be determined by the 2000 census research and development program. This commitment is reflected in the decision not to adopt a dual-strategy approach for the 1995 census test. The one-number approach thus represents a departure from the methodology of the 1990 census, in which two sets of population totals were produced, with and without corrections based on coverage measurement, and an ex post facto decision was made about whether to accept the corrected totals. This decision proved to be controversial because it occurred in a highly politicized environment in which interested parties perceived themselves as winners or losers, depending on which set of numbers was chosen.

Associated with the one-number census is the principle of integrated coverage measurement, the premise of which is that the three components of a one-number census are designed to complement one another in order to produce accurate results by legal deadlines. That is, the results from measurement of coverage will be fully integrated into the official census estimates (Miskura, 1993).

The definition of the one-number census does not imply a relaxation of the standards for census documentation, nor does it preclude the release or use of partial or preliminary data—that is, intermediate calculations in the process of combining information obtained from counting, assignment, and estimation methods. The fundamental change is that an appropriate methodology for integrated coverage measurement is established before the census is carried out, with the recognition that results at intermediate stages (e.g., before incorporating results from the coverage measurement program) cannot be regarded on scientific grounds as viable alternatives to the final, best set of official population totals. (Chapter 4 provides further discussion of the one-number census and includes several recommendations regarding documentation requirements for the 2000 census.)

In our interim report (Committee on National Statistics, 1993b:31), the panel expressed strong approval of the one-number census concept. We reiterate that approval by including below the text of the recommendation that appeared in the interim report:

• We endorse the Census Bureau's stated goal of achieving a one-number census in 2000 that incorporates the results from coverage measurement programs, including programs involving sampling and statistical estimation, into the official population totals. We recommend that research on alternative methodologies continue in pursuit of this goal.

The panel's position on this issue is similar to the view expressed by the National Research Council's Panel on Decennial Census Methodology convened prior to the 1990 census (Citro and Cohen, 1985:17):

Most important, the panel argues for balance between efforts to achieve a complete enumeration and efforts to improve the accuracy of census figures through adjustment procedures. The panel believes that adjustment cannot be viewed as an alternative to obtaining as complete a count as possible through cost-effective means. The United States has a long tradition of a census as a complete enumeration in which it is a civic responsibility to participate in the census process. The panel believes that it is important to continue this tradition and important that census methodology strive for a complete enumeration via counting procedures, including the use of cost-effective special coverage improvement programs. However, the panel also believes that the ultimate goal of the census should be the accuracy of the census figures. The evidence is overwhelming that no counting process, however diligent, will in fact enumerate everyone.

A key design issue in achieving a well-balanced census in 2000 will be the allocation of resources between four major steps in census data collection: construction of the address frame, the initial counting operation, nonresponse followup, and integrated coverage measurement. The allocation decision will be a critical point in development of the 2000 census design, and information obtained from the 1995 census test should provide a stronger basis for that decision.

Plans for the 1995 Census Test

The 1995 census test represents the culmination of the Census Bureau's research and development program for the 2000 census, although research activity will continue throughout the decade. Plans for the 1995 census test have been laid out with increasing specificity in a series of Census Bureau documents—including the Design Alternative Recommendations (DARs) released in May 1993, the 1995 Census Test Design Recommendation (TDR) released in August 1993, and the 1995 Census Test Design Plan released in February 1994. The Test Design Plan is a refinement of the TDR that reflects more technical work and comments offered during critical review of the August 1993 document. Further details of the 1995 census test plans are being laid out in a series of operational requirements documents (ORDs) and evaluation requirements documents (ERDs) that will eventually lead to detailed operating specifications.

The 1995 census test will be carried out at four sites: Oakland, California; Paterson, New Jersey; New Haven, Connecticut; and six rural parishes in northwestern Louisiana. The following methods are scheduled to be examined in the 1995 census test.

1. *The Use of Sampling and Statistical Estimation to Reduce the Differential Undercount and Census Costs.* Follow-up of nonrespondents to the mail questionnaire will be conducted on a sample basis. Two different sample designs will be tested: (1) a *unit* design, in which a sample of the nonresponse cases in each block is visited and (2) a *block* design, in which all nonresponse cases for a sample of blocks are visited. In addition, the Census Bureau will test a new method for integrated coverage measurement that separately estimates the number of persons missed because their housing unit was not enumerated, the number of persons missed within enumerated housing units, and the number of erroneous enumerations.

2. *Coverage Questions for Complete Listing of Household Members.* The Census Bureau is engaged in ongoing research on household roster questions and analysis of results from the Living Situation Survey and related cognitive research on residence rules. To the extent possible, findings from these studies will be incorporated into the development of questionnaires and procedures for the 1995 census test, including the reinterview for integrated coverage measurement.

3. *Making Census Questionnaires Widely Available.* The Census Bureau

proposes to place unaddressed questionnaires in accessible locations (e.g., post offices, convenience stores), particularly in areas inhabited or frequented by historically undercounted populations.

4. *Real-Time Automated Matching to Improve Census Coverage.* To support the new census design proposed for the 1995 census test, the Census Bureau will develop, to the extent possible, an automated, interactive, and real-time record linkage and matching system.

5. *Targeted Methods to Count Historically Undercounted Populations and Geographic Areas.* The Census Bureau will develop a planning database to identify small geographic areas in which there are major enumeration barriers and to support other census operations. Special enumeration (tool-kit) methods will be developed and applied during the 1995 census test.

6. *Mailout of Spanish-Language Questionnaires.* Based on results of the Spanish Forms Availability Test, the Census Bureau will mail Spanish-language forms to linguistically isolated Spanish-speaking communities. Also, census questionnaires and promotional materials will be translated into predominant Asian languages if appropriate in the 1995 census test sites.

7. *Counting Persons with No Usual Residence.* The Census Bureau will implement a new daytime enumeration method that involves visits to service providers (e.g., shelters, soup kitchens). This method is being tested as a replacement for the nighttime street enumeration procedures used on "S-Night" in the 1990 census.

8. *Respondent-Friendly Questionnaire Design and Implementation Methods.* The census forms used in the 1995 census test will have a format designed for ease of response rather than ease of processing. The Census Bureau will test a full mail implementation strategy, including a prenotice letter, an initial questionnaire, a reminder card, and a replacement questionnaire for those who have not replied by a predetermined date. The envelopes used for some questionnaire mailings may bear a message indicating that response is required by law.

9. *Automation of Data Collection.* The 1995 census test will include a telephone network to support questionnaire assistance and the use of touch-tone menu selections with voice recognition and voice recording options. Computer-assisted telephone interviewing (CATI) will be used as a primary response option and as a mode for nonresponse follow-up. Pen computers will be used during address list and map updating.

10. *Using the Postal Service to Identify Vacant and Nonexistent Housing Units.* Vacant units and nonexisting addresses will be identified earlier in census operations using information supplied by postal carriers from their experience with delivery of prenotice or questionnaire mailings. Adopting this procedure will eliminate one of the two enumerator visits conducted in past censuses by the Census Bureau, and the remaining visit can occur earlier in the process—during the check-in of mail returns and prior to nonresponse follow-up.

11. *Data Capture System for the 2000 Census Using Electronic Imaging.*

The Census Bureau plans to develop electronic imaging technology capable of scanning respondent-friendly census forms, using optical mark sensing and possibly optical character recognition software. A production prototype will be built to capture data from at least one of the questionnaire form types used in the 1995 census test.

12. *Cooperative Ventures.* The Census Bureau will explore limited joint venture options in the course of operational planning for the 1995 census test. The Census Bureau and the Postal Service are working to reach an agreement for continuous updating of the Master Address File and for identification of vacant and nonexistent housing units. There may also be opportunities to work cooperatively with local governments to improve the address list and to obtain administrative records for coverage improvement.

13. *Collecting Sample Data Using Multiple Sample Forms.* The Census Bureau plans to test a prototype matrix sampling design in the 1995 census test. Matrix sampling involves the use of two or more sample forms in which most respondents will be asked only a subset of all the sample questions that are asked.

The Census Bureau also considered experimenting with delayed sample-form follow-up in the 1995 census test. Under such a procedure, only short-form information would be gathered during nonresponse follow-up, after which sample-form data would be obtained via telephone or personal visit for a sub-sample of households that had initially received a sample long form. Because of the operational complexities involved in developing multiple CATI instruments and coordinating this effort with integrated coverage measurement, the Census Bureau has decided not to introduce delayed sample-form follow-up into the 1995 census test design, although the concept will be examined further to determine its merit for future testing.

The operational constraints on the 1995 census test underscore the importance of learning as much as possible from other research. For example, simulation studies using 1990 census data can investigate the effects of truncating nonresponse follow-up operations at different points in time, using different rates of sampling nonrespondents for follow-up, and applying different coverage measurement methods (see Chapter 4 for further discussion). Similarly, not all methods need to be tested in large-scale field settings. To ease experimental complexity, certain methods might be excluded from large-scale field testing in 1995, when such an exclusion would not disrupt the research and development program or if smaller experiments (e.g., questionnaire research, discussed in Chapter 3) conducted simultaneously with the 1995 census test will provide useful information.

Other Activities

Two activities related to 2000 census planning are being conducted independently from the 1995 census test. First, through the policy committee of the Task

Force on the Year 2000 Census, the Census Bureau has undertaken a review of the statutory requirements for census data collection. Current findings from that review (Bureau of the Census, 1994a) suggest that only 6 of 59 topics that were included in the 1990 census lack a legislative mandate for collection. Based on this review, the panel's deliberations have not assumed dramatic reductions in the content requirements currently being met by the decennial census.

The Census Bureau is also continuing its development of a prototype system for continuous data collection involving a large, monthly, national survey to produce frequent estimates based on moving averages. Such a system for continuous measurement could potentially meet many needs for timely and accurate information about small areas and small groups within the national population. Current development plans call for a prototype survey to begin in fall 1994 at several geographic sites. Chapter 6 of this report contains a thorough review of Census Bureau research on continuous measurement and considers the extent to which a continuous measurement survey might satisfy the legal requirements for the data noted above.

PLANNING FOR THE 2000 AND FUTURE CENSUSES

The Costs of Census-Taking

The panel's consideration of census costs in this report and in its interim report have been guided by a number of assumptions about the relative costs of alternative methods. First, nonresponse follow-up, particularly in its later stages, is clearly one of the most expensive parts of the census. Second, coverage improvement programs also add significantly to census costs. A previous National Research Council report (Citro and Cohen, 1985) documented the cost per case of coverage improvement programs used in the 1980 census. Eliminating inefficient coverage improvement programs and redesigning nonresponse follow-up—for example, to incorporate use of the telephone or sampling methods—should achieve cost savings.

Another general principle is that gathering information by mail is cheaper than doing so by telephone, and gathering information by telephone is cheaper than doing so by sending an enumerator to conduct a personal visit. One implication of this principle is that innovations in questionnaire design and implementation that improve mail response will save money. Similarly, the growing cost advantages of the computer over human labor suggest that further automation of census operations, such as record matching, should also produce cost savings.

Because of the panel's charge and the nature of our study, we did not attempt to conduct more precise cost-benefit analyses of current or proposed methods. We expect that the 1995 census test will provide more current and reliable information on which to base cost-benefit judgments. New cost information will be particularly useful in assessing the value of tool-kit enumeration methods, nonresponse follow-up sampling, MAF/TIGER updating, new uses of administrative records, and the continuous measurement prototype. The cost information obtained from the 1995 census test, plus improved cost modeling capabilities, should permit cost-benefit analysis as recommended by the earlier panel on census methodology (Citro and Cohen, 1985).

Goals for the 1995 Census Test

The 1995 census test is of critical importance to the goal of an improved and more efficient census in the year 2000. Because of the extensive operational planning that must occur prior to 2000, the 1995 census test represents the major opportunity to investigate fundamental reform without jeopardizing the integrity of the 2000 census. It is essential that adequate resources are invested in planning and executing this mid-decade test. Otherwise, the 2000 census will have a design very similar to that of the 1990 census, with the risk of continually rising unit costs or an inadequately tested design that risks lost demographic information and population counts of unknown or inferior quality.

The 1995 census test should be structured to provide specific information to answer a limited and well-defined set of questions about alternative census methods. To the extent feasible, controlled experiments should be carried out, although the panel recognizes that operational pressures will limit the experimental complexity of the 1995 census test. In particular, the test should include evaluation components that provide a basis for assessing cost-effectiveness.

Recommendation 1.1: In assessing the design innovations included in the 1995 census test or other research and development, the Census Bureau should place great emphasis on cost-benefit analysis as part of the overall evaluation leading to implementation decisions for the 2000 census. Requirements for evaluating new data collection methodologies in the 1995 census test should include information on such characteristics as cost, yield, and gross error that are needed to inform cost-benefit judgments.

We note that the year 2000 research and development staff became part of the decennial management division in summer 1994. It will be particularly important during this transition to ensure the continuity of the 2000 census planning process, so that the research, development, and evaluation activities proceed in an integrated, coherent, and effective manner.

We also believe it is important to maintain perspective on the role of the large-scale, mid-decade test in the decennial census research and development program. Previous panel studies by the Committee on National Statistics (Citro and Cohen 1985:21) have criticized the Census Bureau's program for placing too much emphasis on field testing over other kinds of research, including further analysis and simulation studies based on existing data. The 1995 census test, the

1990 census, and other recent Census Bureau operations are rich bodies of information that may yield answers to key research questions in the coming years if these resources are acknowledged and fully examined.

Milestones for 2000 Census Planning

The Census Bureau's current schedule calls for a final decision in December 1995 on the fundamental design of the 2000 census. Further operational development and refinement of the design will continue with a variety of small-scale special purpose tests in 1996 and 1997 and will conclude with a census dress rehearsal in 1998, the results of which will inform plans for the 2000 census operation.

As noted above, simultaneously with methodological development, the Census Bureau is engaged in a process to determine the content of the 2000 census— i.e., what information should be collected and specifically how should questions be phrased to collect this information. A test of census content is scheduled for fall 1996, and the Census Bureau will submit its proposed content for the 2000 census to Congress in spring 1997.

A third activity with implications for both census methodology and content is the Census Bureau's program to develop a prototype continuous measurement survey (see Chapter 6). The current schedule for this program calls for a decision in September 1997 about whether to retain the decennial long form for the 2000 census or replace it with a continuous measurement survey. The requirement that the Census Bureau submit in early 1997 proposed content for congressional review and approval may complicate the reaching of this decision point. At present, it is unclear whether this requirement would be met by furnishing a list of topics to be included in the 2000 census or whether the means of collecting data on these topics must also be determined by early 1997.

Longer-Term Census Research and Development

The panel's letter report (Committee on National Statistics, 1992) included the following two recommendations:

• The Census Bureau should initiate a separate program of research on administrative records, focusing primarily on the 2010 census and on current estimates programs. The research program should be funded separately from the 2000 census research and development activities, but there should be close liaison between them.

• The Census Bureau should undertake a planning study, in collaboration with other agencies and contract support as needed, that would develop one or more detailed design options for a 2010 administrative records census. The study would have two major goals: to identify the steps that would need to be taken, early in this decade, to make a 2010 administrative records census possible and to set the stage for a national debate on the desirability of an administrative records census. The study, or at least its initial phases, should be completed during the current fiscal year.

In the fiscal 1995 budget currently before Congress, the Census Bureau has included an item titled "Research for 2001 and Beyond," and the item also appears in the fiscal 1996 budget at this time. We believe these are positive steps. However, we caution that the budget for a long-term staff should be independent of the funding cycle for short-term research and development work on the next decennial census (see Bradburn, 1993). Consideration should be given to revising organizational structures to minimize the extent to which short-term and long-term research divisions would compete for personnel and other resources.

Chapter 5 includes a discussion of the long-term research that is needed to develop new, potentially cost-effective uses of administrative records for statistical purposes in the decennial census and other demographic programs. We note in Chapter 6 that the Census Bureau has established a continuous measurement development staff to pursue the research agenda for creating a system of continuous data collection. Perhaps this newly created staff will serve as a model for mobilizing resources to pursue longer-term decennial census research projects at the Census Bureau.

2

Preliminary Census Design Issues

In this chapter, we give attention to certain key activities that begin far in advance of Census Day (e.g., address list development) and that support many aspects of census operations (e.g., record linkage). We also discuss the legal and operational dimensions of some innovative methods, discussed in detail in later chapters, that are being considered for use in the 2000 census.

ADDRESS LIST DEVELOPMENT
AND RELATED ACTIVITIES

Virtually all fundamental design changes contemplated for the 2000 census depend on the existence of an accurate list of residential addresses. Historically, the address list for a decennial census has served only limited purposes after census operations are completed. For example, the address list is used for selected areas in the development of sampling frames for current sample surveys. Such uses occur during a period following the census, but the census address file has not been linked in any way to address list development in subsequent censuses. The address list for the next census has been built from scratch using combinations of commercially available lists, listings created by Census Bureau staff, and various address list coverage checks. The duplication of effort, cost, and complexity involved in address list compilation has led outside interests and internal Census Bureau experts to suggest the creation and maintenance of a master list of addresses over the decade (Leggieri, 1994).

Development of a Master Address File

The master address file (MAF) must contain the information for each residential living quarters that is necessary to support Census Bureau contact with households by mail, by telephone, or by personal visit. The content elements for the basic MAF are (Bureau of the Census, 1992a; Leggieri, 1994):

- mailing address (including nine-digit zip code and unit designators for multiunit addresses),
- location information (e.g., house number/street name address or physical description),
- census tract/block numbering area and block number,
- number of units in structure,
- telephone number of household,
- year structure built (for 1990 census units),
- type of unit (e.g., open to elements, converted to nonresidential, in multiunit structure, tenure), and
- unit status (e.g., unconfirmed delete, unverified add, duplicate address).

For group living quarters, such as college dormitories, additional information must be maintained, including name and type of group quarters and a link to a special place (e.g., a college or university).

The MAF will be linked to the Census Bureau's automated geographic database, the TIGER (topologically integrated geographic encoding and referencing) system. This linkage should provide higher-quality address list coverage and geographic accuracy, as well as improved geographic products for census data collection and local review. In addition, a linked address/geographic file can provide support for many aspects of census research and related demographic programs. (In later sections, we discuss the possible use and support of such a file by other federal agencies, states, and local governments.)

The proposed development and ongoing maintenance of a geographically linked MAF requires completion of several major steps, as outlined by Leggieri (1994):

1. Expand the TIGER geocoding capabilities and reformat the 1990 census address control file to prepare for linkage and matching.
2. Match the reformatted 1990 address file to a primary source of new address information, such as the delivery sequence file from the Postal Service.
3. Match the updated MAF to the TIGER database for assignment of geographic codes.
4. Resolve nonmatches through clerical procedures and field work.
5. Use administrative records to supplement the primary address source.

At the time of this report's preparation, address ranges in the TIGER database have been expanded, and the other steps listed above are being implemented for the three urban sites in the 1995 census test—Oakland, California, Paterson, New Jersey, and New Haven, Connecticut. This activity is not being undertaken for the rural test site—six parishes in northwestern Louisiana—because rural-style addresses cannot be geocoded into the current TIGER database. In the 1995 census test, questionnaire mailing will not be performed at the rural site. Instead, an update/leave procedure will be used; that is, census forms will be delivered to housing units by Census Bureau personnel, and the address list for this site will be updated using information collected at the time of delivery.

MAF/TIGER Benefits for the Decennial
Census and Other Programs

Lists containing address information—but without names of residents or other personal data—support several stages of decennial census operations, including distribution of mail questionnaires, follow-up of nonresponding households, and measurement of population coverage. The MAF/TIGER system would support several fundamental census design changes being considered in the 1995 census test to reduce census costs and eliminate differentials in census coverage. In particular, MAF updating with Postal Service information would facilitate the use of letter carriers to identify vacant housing units during census mailout. The MAF would also provide a frame for sampling (and subsequent estimation) during nonresponse follow-up and integrated coverage measurement. Finally, the MAF would provide a control framework for matching administrative records— compiled by other federal, state, or local agencies—as a substitute for or supplement to traditional census enumeration.

There are numerous potential uses of a continuously updated MAF/TIGER system beyond its application during a decennial census. Such a system would be required to support an administrative record census (see Chapter 5) or a continuous measurement survey of the type under current examination (see Chapter 6). In addition, the MAF could also be used for intercensal population estimates and projections, redesign of current surveys, special censuses, and quality evaluation of other lists and activities (Leggieri, 1994). A linked address/geographic file can thus provide support for many aspects of census research and related demographic programs. Indeed, its utility would be likely to extend to other federal agencies, states, and local governments.

The panel believes that a geographic database that is fully integrated with a master address file is a basic requirement for the 2000 census, regardless of the final census design.

Recommendation 2.1: The Census Bureau should continue aggressive development of the TIGER (topologically integrated geographic encoding and referencing) system, the Master Address File (MAF), and inte-

gration of these two systems. MAF/TIGER updating activities for the 1995 census test sites should be completed in time to permit the use and evaluation of the MAF/TIGER system as part of the 1995 census test.

Successful completion of MAF/TIGER updating for the test sites will enable the Census Bureau to gain valuable experience during the 1995 census test.

Frequency of MAF/TIGER Updating

In order to maintain a MAF/TIGER system that can be used throughout the decade, continuous updating would be required. Current Census Bureau plans are to conduct the full maintenance cycle several times during the decade for high-growth counties and less frequently for areas of minimal change (Leggieri, 1994). This updating is needed primarily to maintain the quality of the system— i.e., the accuracy of the listed addresses and coverage of the housing unit stock. However, the field efforts required to update the MAF/TIGER system may have other benefits for census operations by facilitating local outreach and cooperation with state and local governments. Maintenance of the system could rely heavily on local support (see the section below on cooperation with state and local governments).

High growth in new housing unit construction may not be the only criterion in determining the frequency of updating. Certain types of new housing—e.g., trailer parks, migrant worker camps—are more difficult to locate than others. Also, it is unlikely that all hard-to-find housing units could be identified by any procedure that is part of the counting phase of census operations. Integrated coverage measurement procedures will be needed to complete census coverage of housing units.

Alternatives to decennial collection of small-area information may impose more rigorous requirements on the MAF/TIGER system. If the MAF is used only once a decade, then updating might be accelerated in the years immediately preceding a decennial census. But more steady monthly updating would be needed to support the intercensal long-form survey that would be part of a continuous measurement program. A recent version of the continuous measurement prototype included a component for updating approximately 1,000 problem (i.e., nonmatched) addresses per month. Frequent updating would presumably also be needed if the MAF/TIGER system is to provide an accurate sampling frame for other current surveys.

Cooperation With the Postal Service

The logical source of national information on mailing addresses is the United States Postal Service (USPS). In 1991 the Census Bureau's Geography Division began negotiations with the USPS to develop a partnership that would build and maintain an integrated MAF/TIGER system. There was initial interest in the potential value of TIGER to further automate USPS mail delivery planning and management activities. After examining special prototype TIGER files that contained customized postal information, however, the USPS concluded that the potential value of the TIGER system was not sufficient to pursue the joint venture. The Census Bureau is exploring the possibility of collaborating with state and local governments on TIGER updating, as discussed in the next section.

The Census Bureau and the USPS are still working to develop an arrangement that would allow the Census Bureau to maintain the MAF using USPS address information. Regular updating would be accomplished by matching the MAF to the USPS delivery sequence file, which contains information about delivery addresses. The two agencies have reached an agreement in principle, but the details of a cooperative arrangement have not been settled (Leggieri, 1994).

Developmental work is proceeding under a memorandum of understanding signed by the Census Bureau and the USPS in August 1993. The memorandum of understanding authorized a pilot study to share address information for five 3-digit zip code areas. That phase of limited testing has been completed, and the project is being expanded to include exchange of address information for the four sites of the 1995 census test. A national agreement for address sharing will require amendments to federal legislation governing both agencies (see the section below on legal issues).

Developmental testing will be necessary to resolve differences between the USPS and Census Bureau conceptual definitions of an address. For example, the USPS files contain both commercial and residential addresses, but the MAF is restricted to residential addresses. Home-based businesses present a special challenge, because their addresses may be classified as commercial in the USPS file, even though one or more persons may reside there.

For USPS purposes, an address is a delivery point. This definition may cause difficulties for census coverage of some multiunit dwellings, such as high-rise apartment buildings for which the local letter carrier is responsible for only a single delivery mail drop and the building management staff sorts mail for individual residents. Multiunit dwellings also pose problems for matching, because different address sources may identify the unit designation differently or lack unit identifiers altogether.

Rural address designations (e.g., rural delivery numbers) and post office boxes are problematic for census-taking, because field enumerators cannot always locate the mailing address. Also, these addresses cannot be geocoded into the current TIGER data base. Leggieri (1994) provides further discussion of these challenges and possible steps toward solving them.

Potential USPS involvement in census-taking extends beyond address list development. One of the more promising options is to use information supplied by local letter carriers during census mailout to identify vacant and nonexistent housing units. Such a procedure could save money by eliminating one of two Census Bureau checks and would also enable address cleaning to occur earlier in census operations.

Both agencies have examined the suggestion that letter carriers be used to conduct interviews during the nonresponse follow-up stage of census operations. The USPS and Census Bureau have concluded that this is not a viable option, because of concerns about interference with mail delivery, significantly higher census costs, and erosion of public confidence in the privacy of information entrusted to the postal system. The panel accepts this conclusion. Other areas for expanded USPS-Census Bureau cooperation are described more fully in a November 1993 letter from both agencies to the House Appropriations Committee (Green and Scarr, 1993).

Cooperation With State and Local Governments

Local knowledge about living quarters can serve as an important source of information to supplement the USPS delivery sequence file. Plans for involving state and local governments in the MAF/TIGER updating process are not yet well defined. Several possible cooperative roles are under consideration for testing in the 1995 census test (see Leggieri, 1994, for further discussion). At a minimum, regional Census Bureau staff would use reference materials (e.g., maps, address lists) supplied by state and local jurisdictions to clerically resolve addresses that have not been geocoded or matched by computer.

State and local governments could be involved in an earlier and larger role if the Census Bureau accepted automated address or geographic files from local jurisdictions. Files such as tax assessment records and digital geographic files for 911 emergency response systems would be matched to the MAF/TIGER data bases, with subsequent resolution of nonmatched cases, and might prove to be valuable sources of information for updating.

Maximum involvement of state and local governments would be achieved by turning responsibility for MAF/TIGER updating over to these jurisdictions. Under this scenario, local governments would be supplied with a copy of the MAF for their jurisdiction, along with corresponding TIGER maps or files. Matching and updating would then be carried out by the local government. Implementation of this approach would require changes to Title 13 of the U.S. Code to permit sharing address information with state and local governments (see the section below on legal issues). A potential difficulty with this approach is the presumably wide variation in technological capabilities across local jurisdictions. A procedure for MAF/TIGER updating in a large, urban area may not be feasible for a small, rural area. The implications of a differential approach to MAF/TIGER updating (e.g., for coverage measurement methods) will need to be weighed in considering this option.

State and local governments can also play a role in other components of census operations (see Collins, 1994). Involvement in outreach and promotion programs and in planning and assisting the census enumeration is discussed in Chapter 3. State and local administrative records may also help to improve census coverage. The use of selected state and local administrative records for coverage improvement and other purposes have been examined in tests associated with special censuses for Godfrey, Illinois, and South Tucson, Arizona (Bureau of the Census, 1993e, 1993f) and will be explored more fully in the 1995 census test. Collins (1994) notes that experience from past censuses—e.g., the parolee-probationer program in 1990—suggests that cost-effective use of state and local records for coverage improvement will require them to be standardized, automated, and accessible, with appropriate provisions for confidential handling. Conditions for the statistical use of administrative records are discussed further in Chapter 5.

RECORD LINKAGE

Record linkage is the identification of records belonging to the same unit (i.e., a person, household, or housing unit) either within a single data set or across two different data sets. In decennial census applications, records are matched either to eliminate duplication or to pool information from multiple sources.

Many census operations involve matching one list of records to another. Needs for record linkage arise when address lists and other administrative records are used, when people are given multiple opportunities to respond to the census, and when dual-system estimation is used as part of a coverage measurement program. Historically, an initial match has been performed by a computer algorithm, followed by clerical verification and resolution. Many of the innovative methods being examined in the 1995 census test would place greater demands on matching technology. Thus, improvements in the accuracy or efficiency of automated record linkage will support the 2000 census design by increasing the capability to produce reliable results within time and budget constraints.

As discussed above, the development and updating of an integrated MAF/TIGER system will require automated address matching and geocoding at various stages. For example, the 1990 address control file will be matched to more current sources, such as the USPS delivery sequence file. Effective methods for record linkage could minimize the problems posed by duplicate address listings that occur when the same residence is listed in two different ways in different address records. Multiple listings are more likely to be found in rural areas, where they are a potential source of erroneous enumeration (Leggieri, 1994).

The distribution of unaddressed questionnaires, the opportunity to respond by mail or telephone, and the application of other special methods are likely to increase the potential for duplication in the census enumeration. These activities will result in questionnaires without housing unit control identification numbers that must be matched to census files to determine whether persons and housing units were enumerated more than once. The Census Bureau's recent research on rostering may lead to new approaches to ascertaining residency, which would present new complications in assigning people correctly to geographic areas. Matching may also be needed to obtain telephone numbers during follow-up of nonresponding households.

Record linkage technology will also support the development of an administrative records database for the 1995 census test sites (see also Chapter 5). Current plans call for the database to be used in stratification of the nonresponse follow-up and integrated coverage measurement sample designs. By incorporating information about Spanish surnames, the database may also be able to identify geographic areas in which response might be improved by distributing Spanish-language questionnaires.

The integrated coverage measurement method being tested in 1995 consists of two stages: (1) an independent housing unit listing to assess the coverage of housing units within the sampled areas and (2) a within-household reinterview to assess the coverage of persons within the housing units (see Chapter 4). Detailed procedures are still under development, but they could involve the automated comparison of records from the census enumeration and the independent operations of integrated coverage measurement. The Census Bureau will need solid capability for computer matching and elimination of duplicate records in order to perform all the above tasks in an accurate, timely, and cost-effective manner.

The Census Bureau is conducting ongoing research on methods for automated record linkage. A recent study (Bureau of the Census, 1994f) matched the 1990 census file for South Tucson, Arizona, to the file of persons enumerated in the special census of the community that was carried out in November 1992. These two independent files were used to compare the accuracy of three different computer matchers. Two of the matchers used a probabilistic algorithm to classify individual records according to the likelihood of a match. The third, and newest, matcher first attempts to match corresponding households. Persons in nonmatched households are then matched according to individual characteristics.

In this study, the "true" match status was determined through clerical operations; because of budget constraints, no field work was done to verify people's actual status. Against this measure of performance, the three matchers yielded similar results, and none emerged as uniformly superior to the others. The two individual matchers obtained results that agreed with the "true" match status 89.6 percent and 87.8 percent of the time. The agreement rate for the household matcher was somewhat lower (83.4 percent), but a slight revision to the code would have increased the agreement rate to 87.2 percent. Cross-tabulations suggest that, although the three matchers agree on many cases, there are significant numbers of cases in which the matchers made different classifications. Some combination of the household strategy and the two individual strategies might improve capabilities for matching lists in the presence of underlying household structures. The 1995 census test provides an opportunity for further comparative evaluation of automated record linkage technologies.

> **Recommendation 2.2: The Census Bureau should continue its research program on record linkage in support of the 1995 census test and the 2000 census. Efforts should include studies of the effectiveness of different matching keys (e.g., name, address, date of birth, and Social Security number) and the establishment of requirements for such components as address standardization, parsing, and string comparators. Existing record linkage technology should be tested and evaluated in the 1995 census test.**

Limits on the ability to eliminate duplicate records may prove to be the controlling factor with regard to the feasibility of many of the innovations under consideration for the 2000 census design.

LEGAL ISSUES

There are many legal issues associated with the decennial census, perhaps the most obvious being the content requirements mandated by the Constitution and other law. The Panel on Census Requirements is conducting a thorough investigation of these content requirements. However, legal issues with possible implications for census methods arise in at least five contexts: (1) census starting and reporting dates, (2) the use of sampling and statistical estimation, (3) sharing Census Bureau address lists with other government agencies, (4) accessing Postal Service address information, and (5) accessing administrative records for statistical purposes.

Census Reference Date

April 1 is mandated as the reference census date by Title 13 of the U.S. Code. Title 13 also mandates that the state population counts required for reapportionment be provided 9 months after the census date and that local-area data needed for redistricting be provided no later than 12 months after the census date. Thus, the respective deadlines for reapportionment and redistricting data are December 31 of the census year and March 31 of the subsequent year.

The 1995 census test will use March 4 as the census reference date. At the time of this report's writing, legislation has been proposed in the House of Representatives to establish the first Saturday in March as the new census reference date.

An earlier census date should alleviate problems encountered in the enumeration of households that move during census operations. Research indicates that the peak moving season in the United States begins in mid-May (Scarr, 1994). An earlier census date may also reduce difficulties in enumerating college students, who are more likely to be in residence on or near campus, and homeless people, who are more likely to use shelters and services in colder weather.

Because moves from one housing unit to another tend to occur at the end and the beginning of a month, conducting a census using one of the first days of the month as the reference date may lead to more frequent errors of misclassification. The shift from April 1 to March 4 will probably not significantly reduce end-of-month moving problems; delivery of questionnaires (and prenotice letters, if used) takes place a few days before the reference date. A greater shift toward the middle of the month—e.g., to the second Saturday in March—would probably be needed to minimize the enumeration difficulties posed by moving households. Other countries have acted on the basis of similar considerations; Canada expects gains in accuracy in future censuses by changing its census date from June 4 to May 14 (Choudhry, 1992). (See Chapter 3 for further discussion of residential mobility.)

However, adopting the first Saturday, instead of the second Saturday, as the census reference date does possess some operational advantages. Using a census reference date early in the month will enable all phases of the mail operation—from prenotice letter to second reminder after receipt of a replacement question-naire—to be completed by the end of the month, thus avoiding potentially signifi-cant problems when mail follow-up occurs in a different month than the original mailing. But if the latter stages of the mail operation (e.g., a second reminder card) do not prove cost-effective, their deletion would permit reconsideration of a midmonth census reference date.

In weighing alternative methods, concern has been expressed about the abil-ity to provide data by the legislatively mandated deadlines. The panel believes that the need for these 9-month and 12-month deadlines should be reevaluated if otherwise promising census methods would be unlikely to meet one or both dates—especially the former. This consideration could apply, for example, to any proposed methodology for integrated coverage measurement (see Chapter 4). Maintaining the December 31 and March 31 deadlines with an earlier census reference date (the current legislative proposal), such as March 4 or 11, would allow more time to implement follow-up activities and integrated coverage mea-surement to produce the official census estimates. Promising new methods that can reduce the differential undercount or substantially reduce the costs of the census should not be discarded on grounds of time constraints without further consideration of those legally imposed constraints.

Recommendation 2.3: In view of the operational advantages that are likely to result, the panel endorses the proposed change in census refer-ence date from April 1 to the first Saturday in March. Furthermore, we recommend that changing the census reference date from early in the

month to midmonth (e.g., the second Saturday in March) be reconsidered if subsequent modifications to the mailout operation would permit all census mailings to be executed within the same calendar month using a midmonth reference date.

Use of Sampling and Statistical Estimation

The legal acceptability of using sampling and statistical estimation in the decennial census is supported by rulings in every U.S. District Court case and a similarly favorable position in a recent Congressional Research Service (CRS) report (Lee, 1993). In its interim report (Committee on National Statistics, 1993a), the Panel on Census Requirements, relying on reviews by legal scholars, endorsed the CRS position that sampling and statistical estimation are acceptable provided that there has first been a bona fide attempt to count everyone (e.g., by distributing a mail questionnaire). As in our interim report, our recommendations in this report are based on this premise.

The Census Bureau is considering whether Title 13 of the U.S. Code should be amended regarding the use of sampling for appropriate purposes (Scarr, 1994). The panel has no objections in principle to enacting clarifying legislation, but we do not view passage of such legislation as necessary for implementing nonresponse follow-up sampling and integrated coverage measurement in the 2000 census.

Access to Address Information

Part of the Census Bureau's research and development program for the 2000 census has involved exploration of further possibilities for cooperative working relationships with other federal agencies and state and local governments. The ability to forge stronger cooperative relationships has sometimes been hindered by the perception that there is a one-way flow of information to the Census Bureau without reciprocal benefits to the cooperative party. This perception has been reinforced by a Supreme Court ruling that address lists—without any individually identifiable data—that are collected and recorded by the Census Bureau become confidential under Section 9 of Title 13 and therefore may only be seen by sworn employees of the Census Bureau.

The Census Bureau has stated in recent congressional testimony (Scarr, 1994) that it seeks a legislative change that would allow the agency to share its address lists with federal, state, and local officials to meet three objectives: (1) to improve the accuracy and completeness of the address lists; (2) to provide meaningful participation by governmental units in the census; and (3) to minimize the costs to the taxpayer for construction of duplicative address lists by various governmental agencies in order to implement public programs.

Title 39 of the U.S. Code restricts the USPS from disclosing lists of names or addresses, and similar restrictions on the Census Bureau appear in Title 13. Legal considerations thus impose constraints on USPS-Census Bureau cooperation. Special temporary legislation was obtained to permit the USPS to share detailed address information with the Census Bureau during the 1984 Address List Compilation Test (Bureau of the Census, 1992e). Similar permanent legislation might provide an opportunity for both agencies to realize significant gains in operational efficiency and consequent cost savings, but any joint activity will need to attend to confidentiality issues regarding the sharing of address lists.

The potential utility of a geographically linked master address file suggests the possibility that development and maintenance of such a system could be undertaken by a consortium of federal, state, and local agencies. Under such a scenario, of course, the Census Bureau would be a major customer. But this arrangement might allow the realization of efficiency gains more broadly and quickly across levels of government.

Development of a national address registry that is maintained outside the Census Bureau raises complex issues with regard to current statutes (Title 13, U.S. Code). If address information flows only into the Census Bureau, then changes to Title 13 are probably unnecessary. But, if new information about addresses is obtained by the Census Bureau in using the registry, then revision of Title 13 may be needed to permit such information to be forwarded to the custodian of the registry. Confidentiality issues will need to be resolved, particularly for data—such as occupied or residential units that do not appear on local property rolls or in building code records—that could be used for enforcement purposes. We believe that the development of an address registry for use by multiple government agencies requires the involvement of the Statistical Policy Office in the Office of Management and Budget.

Recommendation 2.4: The Statistical Policy Office of the Office of Management and Budget should develop a structure to permit the sharing of address lists among federal agencies and state and local governments— including the Census Bureau and the Postal Service—for approved uses under appropriate conditions.

Access to Administrative Records for Statistical Purposes

Chapter 5 discusses potential uses of administrative records in the decennial census and related demographic programs. The panel is concerned that research and development to expand the use of administrative records for census purposes—with potential benefits for improved accuracy and lower cost—might be impeded by unnecessary restrictions on access to some of the administrative record systems that offer the greatest promise for such use.

In its earlier letter report (Committee on National Statistics, 1992), the panel recommended:

• The Census Bureau should seek the cooperation of federal agencies that maintain key administrative record systems, particularly the Internal Revenue Service and the Social Security Administration, in undertaking a series of experimental administrative records minicensuses and related projects, starting as soon as possible and including one concurrent with the 2000 census.

We continue to support this type of cooperative research because of its potential benefits for improved census methodology.

Provisions regarding access to administrative records are the subject of current debate, mostly in connection with proposals for health care reform. A recent letter to the chairman of the House Subcommittee on Census, Statistics, and Postal Personnel from the Committee on National Statistics (Bradburn, 1994) distinguished research and statistical uses of administrative records, which are not concerned about specific individuals, from regulatory, administrative, and enforcement uses, which do affect specific individuals. A recent report by a panel of the Committee on National Statistics and the Social Science Research Council (Duncan et al., 1993) describes effective administrative and technical practices that federal statistical agencies can adopt to protect confidentiality of information on individuals while allowing access to the information for important research and statistical purposes. Chapter 5 provides further discussion of ways to improve access to administrative records and protect confidentiality.

OPERATIONAL ISSUES

Uniform Treatment

The legitimacy of the census depends in part on public perception that it fairly treats all geographical areas and demographic groups in the country. "Fair treatment" can be defined in either of two ways: by applying the same methods and effort to every area or by attaining the same degree of population coverage in every area so that estimates of relative populations of different areas are accurate. These alternatives are in some ways analogous to the competing principles of equality of opportunity and equality of outcome in the provision, for example, of education services. The proper balance of these principles is a subject of policy debate about the provision of services. In the case of the census, however, the priorities are clear: the objective of the census is to measure population accurately and above all to calculate accurate population shares in order to apportion representation properly. Therefore, obtaining equal coverage clearly takes priority over using the same methods in every area. In fact, since experience shows that treating every geographical area and demographic group in the same way leads to differential coverage, the Census Bureau has a positive duty to use methods designed to close the coverage gap, a duty recognized as a mandatory criterion for any 2000 census candidate design (see Chapter 1).

The approach of developing a tool kit of special methods and a planning database (described further in Chapter 3) is one of the Census Bureau's responses to this duty. This approach involves constructing a planning database, containing information on demographic and housing characteristics, to be used to identify areas at particular risk for low mail return rates or other enumeration problems. These are areas in which an accurate enumeration is likely to benefit most from the deployment of special techniques drawn from a tool kit of candidate methods—such as using specially trained enumerators or address locators, opening census assistance centers, distributing forms other than by mail, and distributing some forms in languages other than English. These tool-kit methods would be applied as needed in small areas of various sizes. The decision to use any particular tool-kit method would be controlled by some combination of administrative judgment, information in the planning database, and predictions from a formal targeting model.

Past censuses have also used different treatments with the goal of achieving equal outcomes. For example, in the 1970 and 1980 censuses, the Census Bureau used enumeration by personal visit in sparsely populated areas but used a mail questionnaire in other areas. In 1990, special enumeration methods were used, often at local discretion, but their cost-effectiveness has not been well documented. The targeting model would establish a more formal structure for such applications.

Beyond the tool-kit methods discussed in Chapter 3, targeting efforts might be useful for other census operations, particularly the development of address lists and administrative record databases. In the past, the Census Bureau selected commercial address list vendors using a criterion of gross coverage. A better criterion might be to equalize address list coverage in easy-to-count and hard-to-count areas. The use of administrative records, described in Chapter 5, is not part of the tool kit available to local census offices, but such use might also involve some targeting of efforts to particularly hard-to-enumerate areas or population groups. For example, a list of food stamp recipients could add more names to low-income areas. Other lists, such as state (driver's license) or local government (school registration) lists, would of necessity contribute to the count only in their areas of coverage.

Some critics worry that the use of special methods in certain areas (e.g., tool-kit methods, local administrative records) might make statistical assessments of coverage more difficult or might invalidate assumptions used to combine sample-based estimates and enumeration totals. This criticism must be taken seriously.

Plans for 2000 call for correcting differences in coverage across areas or groups by coverage measurement and estimation. These plans are described more completely in Chapter 4. The correction methodology is likely to involve multiplying counts for each poststratum (estimation cell) by a factor that is constant across the cell. For example, a poststratum might consist of all black males ages 18-29 who live in rented homes in large urbanized areas (population over 250,000) in the West, as in the calculation of estimates from the 1990 coverage measurement program. Counts for people in this group in any smaller area would then be multiplied by the same factor.

Suppose that a method designed especially to increase response among renters is applied in all large urbanized areas in the West. Furthermore, suppose that the collection of all households whose coverage is likely to be improved by this method coincides with some combination of poststrata. In other words, suppose that every poststratum containing renters in large urbanized areas in the West consists only of such people, but does not include homeowners, people outside large urbanized areas, or people outside the West. (Again, this was true of the cell definitions used for 1990 coverage estimation.) If the special method improves coverage for these poststrata, then the statistical estimation procedure used in integrated coverage measurement will find correspondingly higher levels of coverage than it otherwise would have found, and it can properly account for the effects in producing population estimates.

It is possible that the special method would be more effective in some urbanized areas than others, just as the census without special methods has better coverage in some areas than others, but there would not be a predictable bias. We therefore believe that the use of special methods, including tool-kit methods or local administrative records, would not create any new statistical problems when applied for a geographic area or population that is recognized by the estimation procedure. Any improvements that the special method causes in initial coverage through enumeration and assignment are very desirable, because with high levels of initial coverage, final estimates are less dependent on estimation and mean squared error is reduced.

More serious concerns arise if special methods are applied differentially *within* geographic areas or subpopulations that correspond to poststrata. For example, if a special method is applied to improve coverage for renters in only one western city, but people in several cities fall into the same poststrata, then the coverage measurement procedures would not recognize the differential effect on coverage of the method, and, even after estimation, the city in which the special method was used might predictably benefit at the expense of other western cities.

Several points should be considered in defense of census procedures that treat different areas differently. First, with any practical poststratification scheme (cell definition), there will be some heterogeneity within the cells, both in the underlying conditions affecting census coverage and in the conduct of the census. This has always been the case; for example, mail return rates and district office closeout dates varied substantially in the 1990 census. Second, if special enumeration methods can be targeted to areas that have relatively low coverage for their poststrata, these methods may make coverage more homogeneous within the poststratum, so population counts after estimation will be made more accurate. Thus, differences in treatment can be justified by local differences in conditions, especially if the decision to use a special method is determined by an objective decision procedure. If decisions are based on knowledge about the distribution of hard-to-count populations, such differences in treatment will tend to reduce differentials in outcome. Third, differences in treatment based on objective measures of the difficulty of enumeration or the usefulness of particular techniques in different areas are more justifiable than those that result from haphazard implementation of coverage improvement programs or the assertiveness and technical capabilities of local authorities.

However, certain practices that may arouse justified suspicion should be avoided. If special enumeration methods are targeted to certain areas but not to others with similar characteristics, their application will appear to be arbitrary. The same will be true if they are targeted toward only some ethnic or socioeconomic groups but not others with similar undercoverage problems. Systematic and complete planning for the use of these methods, based on objective criteria, can defend against the appearance of arbitrariness.

Inevitably, there will be different levels of success in operations of various district offices due to varying local conditions. By considering in advance rules for closeout of district office operations and for distribution of additional resources to district offices—rules that are designed to optimize uniformity of coverage within the constraints of varying conditions—the Census Bureau will do its best to produce uniform coverage. Of course, as in past censuses, the actual degree of uniformity attained will be limited by practical constraints.

Paradoxically, the Census Bureau's improved capabilities and success in tracking census operations, together with growing knowledge and awareness about factors that may affect differential undercount, create a climate in which even more than usual care must be given to avoid any appearance of arbitrariness or favoritism.

Residence Rules

The residence rules that define where each person should be counted in the census are crucial to census coverage for several reasons. First, it is important to have consistent rules so that each person is counted in only one place (especially when matching records or eliminating duplication from multiple information sources is done). Second, people should be assigned to the correct location, as defined by the residence rules in effect. Third, people should not be excluded solely because the residence rules do not easily apply to them.

The Census Bureau has conducted the census on the basis of de jure rather than de facto residence—that is, people are essentially asked "What was your usual residence on Census Day?" rather than "Where did you actually stay on Census Day?" De jure enumeration asks people to report themselves where the "rules" say they should be counted; a de facto approach would collect information on where people are found (see further discussion in Chapter 3). The de jure approach has the advantage of defining residency in a way that does not depend on what happened on a particular day, but it requires that the respondent understand and apply the Census Bureau's definition of "usual residence." This task can be difficult for people whose de jure residency is hard to determine or who have none at all, such as homeless people and young people who move about from place to place.

Attention must be given to defining residency consistently throughout all stages of census operations: questionnaire mailing and questionnaire return and subsequent nonresponse follow-up and coverage measurement activities. The definition of residency is particularly critical for coverage measurement programs (see Chapter 4), because they must determine Census Day residency weeks or months after the fact. The concept of residency reappears at various points in subsequent chapters. Chapter 3 contains further discussion of residence rules and reviews related research that is aimed at improving within-household coverage and handling complicated living situations. That chapter also considers ideas for collecting a "census night" roster followed by questions to assign de jure residence. Administrative records vary in how they define residency, both because of the different purposes and laws under which they are collected and because some are continuously updated while others follow set time schedules. Uses of specific administrative record systems will have to take into account the definitions used and the frequency of updating of their residence information (see Chapter 5).

Continuous Infrastructure

Common sense, complemented by anecdotal evidence, suggests several benefits associated with the Census Bureau's maintaining a continuous presence in local areas throughout the decade. Ongoing activities could contribute to more effective outreach and promotion, thus improving public response and decreasing costs associated with nonresponse follow-up. (This theme is explored more fully in Chapter 3.)

Organizational efficiencies might be realized by reducing the number of temporary staff needed in the 10-year census cycle. The potential benefits could be especially significant if a continuous measurement program is adopted. Chapter 6 assesses the pros and cons of a continuous measurement census design. The Census Bureau is planning to continue work to develop this option in parallel with the 1995 census test.

As in the evaluation of tool-kit enumeration methods, the value of maintaining a continuous presence will have to be weighed against the costs of putting in place the necessary structure, staff, training, and tools. Some benefits can be readily quantified; others are more qualitative and may require subjective assessment.

3

Response and Coverage

One of the most important findings of the 1990 census—the increasing diversity of the United States—also identifies one source of its challenges. Diverse housing, living arrangements, and language proficiencies all complicate the task of counting a population that is also increasingly mobile. Many people continue to be persuaded by appeals based on citizenship and a common national duty, and many have the skills and motivation needed to respond to the census mail questionnaire. But sizable and perhaps increasing proportions appear to be motivated primarily by local interests and appeals, demand control over portions of the census process or outcomes, or require specialized help or media in order to participate. Others seem simply unmotivated or distrustful of government efforts to collect information. If the trends documented by the 1990 census continue, as expected, the 2000 census will face even larger obstacles. Measuring the effectiveness of census reform may therefore be complicated, because even greatly improved procedures may not yield greatly improved outcomes (e.g., in terms of public response to the mailed census questionnaire). A recognition that the population of the United States is simply and fundamentally becoming ever more difficult to count must be incorporated into planning for 2000 in order to develop viable strategies and the organizational and political consensus to implement them.

Much of the Census Bureau's research on response and coverage for the 2000 census addresses two main criticisms raised about the 1990 census: the high unit cost of the census and the persistent differential undercount by race. Increasing the primary mail response rate is vital both to improving data quality and to reducing follow-up costs, thereby conserving resources for the task of reducing the differential undercount.

Problems of differential coverage can and should be addressed at the counting stage of census operations, using methods to improve response and coverage, as well as at other stages.[1] Reducing the differential undercount through improving the initial count necessarily requires a large investment to reach a small proportion of the population that is relatively inaccessible to routine standardized procedures. Under such circumstances, controlling costs and the differential undercount in 2000 may require a massive reorientation—both conceptually and organizationally. The 1990 census attempted to apply a standard, and standardized, approach everywhere, but the outcome was still a differential undercount. Furthermore, standardization necessarily broke down in many geographical areas, particularly those in which response to the mail questionnaire was low, as enumerators with only brief training were sent out and ultimately empowered to make last-ditch enumerations, using procedures known as *last resort* and *closeout* that permitted contacting persons who were not residents of the household. As discussed in Chapter 2, we recommend pursuing uniform outcomes, tailoring operational methods in controlled ways.

The 1990 experience with coverage improvement programs suggests that the real alternative to recognizing the increasing diversity of the country and planning for it may be using different approaches in a haphazard or ill-designed manner. The second phase of the 1990 parolee-probationer check, in which information about parolees and probationers was gathered from administrative lists, was not planned in advance of census operations. The vacant/delete check of housing units that were identified as vacant or nonexistent during nonresponse follow-up required enumerators to determine, months after Census Day, housing unit status on Census Day. Both programs apparently introduced large numbers of erroneous enumerations (Ericksen et al., 1991). Uncontrolled variation in operational procedures becomes even more problematic under integrated coverage measurement (see the section on uniformity of treatment in Chapter 2). We believe that a system could be designed that is flexible enough to control or reduce the differential undercount yet maintain important aspects of standardization (such as definitions of household membership).

It is unlikely that the methods discussed in this chapter for improving census response and coverage will completely eliminate differentials in coverage. However, their use will contribute to two key goals: preserving the credibility of the census and addressing social changes that would otherwise tend to exacerbate differential coverage problems. Also, efforts to improve response and coverage—and, in particular, to reduce differential coverage—during initial census operations will improve accuracy at intermediate stages and therefore reduce the

---

[1] New approaches to address list development, discussed in Chapter 2, could improve coverage of hard-to-locate housing units, and sampling and statistical estimation can be used to measure and correct for differentials in census coverage, as discussed in Chapter 4.

burden on sampling and statistical estimation in producing results from the one-number census (see Chapter 4).

Conversely, response and coverage improvement methods that are too expensive to be implemented on a large scale during the counting stage might be valuable tools in the field operation for integrated coverage measurement. Thus, sampling and statistical estimation can reduce the burden on coverage improvement efforts and improve the cost-effectiveness of the counting operation. As noted in Chapter 1, the allocation of resources among the major stages of census data collection will be a critical point in the development of the 2000 census design.

RESEARCH ON RESPONSE AND COVERAGE ISSUES TO DATE

The various research programs for the 2000 census have approached the two broad goals described above along several fronts. This chapter considers components of the research program that are concerned primarily with updating, expanding, and improving data collection methodologies—ways people participate in the census—to achieve better initial response and coverage and to control or reduce the differential undercount. The topics and research programs we review address the following issues: improving the implementation of the residence rules to increase the accuracy of coverage within households (referred to here as roster improvement research); increasing the response rate to the paper questionnaire (response improvement research); using the telephone to answer questions and to accept interviews from citizens who call in during the initial (mailout) phase of the census, to conduct interviews during nonresponse follow-up, and to conduct reinterviews as part of integrated coverage measurement (use of the telephone); expanding traditional data collection methods to include other automated technologies (using other technologies); developing methods tailored for groups that may be difficult to enumerate (hard-to-enumerate populations, tool kit and planning database); encouraging participation in ways that will be effective in addressing the differential undercount (outreach and promotion); and attempting to further develop links with lower governmental units (state and local cooperative ventures).

The various research programs aimed at response and coverage issues necessarily developed at different rates. The response improvement research, which developed methods for improving the initial response rate, was yielding results before this panel was constituted. It has already contributed very promising techniques for further evaluation in the 1995 census test. The procedures tested in the experiments reviewed below do require some further refinement. But the principal challenges for this research program now are ensuring that the methods can be made fully operational in a census. Reaping the benefits of respondent-friendly census forms, for example, requires continued progress in the development of methods for scanning forms and capturing data. The continued research on new methods of rostering should result in a final census form that is substantially different from those already tested in the response improvement research. Close and continuing communication among those developing new methods of rostering, those designing ways of presenting census forms, and those familiar with the technical and operational details of producing and processing census forms is needed to ensure that the response improvement research yields the gains it promises.

Other portions of the research program on response and coverage issues have developed more slowly but are very promising. Research aimed at improving rostering and targeting barriers to enumeration have the potential to produce important innovations and possibly reduce the differential undercount. The roster improvement research is beginning to produce findings that may lead to redesigned instruments that elicit more accurate responses, particularly from those living in complex households. But this program requires sustained efforts and funding beyond the 1995 census test if its important potential is to be realized by 2000, and the same is true for research that examines application of the tool kit to reach hard-to-enumerate populations. Research about outreach and promotion has barely begun—despite evidence that continuous outreach is important, at least in some geographic areas or with some groups (Bentley and Furrie, 1993).

The very successful research on improving the initial mail response rate has developed strategies that promise to help control costs in 2000. Although increasing the initial response rate may leave the differential undercount unchanged—or even exacerbate it somewhat—a higher initial response rate means better-quality data, fewer nonrespondents to follow up, and better control over cost. Techniques that control costs also potentially make resources available for reducing the differential undercount. Research should now focus on techniques that have potential to improve coverage within households or to reduce the differential undercount. The current state of promising research on improving rostering, incorporating the telephone and other technologies into the design of the census, evaluating the tool kit, and developing and evaluating outreach and promotion activities makes it clear that research and development in these areas must continue beyond the 1995 census test. Although this development is likely to continue in the normal transition after the mid-decade census test for topics with an obvious operational component (such as use of the telephone, data capture, and design of census forms), sustained research on other basic topics, such as improvements in rostering, may require that the Census Bureau give more attention to research and development in the latter half of this decade than has been given in the latter half of past decades.

The remainder of this chapter discusses and makes specific recommendations on a range of topics related to response and coverage issues. We consider research completed and currently under way and propose directions for future investigations. Four major themes emerge from our discussion.

1. *Focus on reducing the differential undercount.* We recommend planning and limited experimentation now so that the most promising methods for reducing the differential undercount can, where feasible, be given operational trials and experimental and cost evaluation in the 1995 census test. It is important that the proposals embodied in the tool kit be evaluated or tested in 1995. Focusing research on methods that may reduce the differential undercount is important given the limitations of resources and time, and it can be justified by the more advanced state of research on improving mail response rates. Analyses of 1980 and 1990 census data that include operational variables, such as the date on which a case was received and how the form was completed (household informant or enumerator), could supplement ongoing experiments by characterizing past response patterns. We urge the Census Bureau to devote resources to analyses of existing data and smaller studies whenever potentially valuable information can be obtained through such alternatives to large, expensive experiments.

2. *Examine the implications of structured reliance on multiple instruments and response modes.* Past censuses have largely relied on a single instrument, the paper questionnaire, which was usually self-administered but was sometimes administered by an enumerator. The 2000 census is likely to use a paper instrument and a computer-assisted instrument for nonresponse follow-up. (A different computer-assisted instrument would be used for the integrated coverage measurement reinterview.) These instruments will also be used in different modes: the paper instrument used in the mailout will usually be self-administered but will sometimes be completed by enumerators (either in an interview or, possibly, with neighbors or by observation in last-ditch operations). The computer-assisted instrument developed for integrated coverage measurement is likely to be used in two modes—telephone and face-to-face. The different instruments and response modes can affect results in two important ways: they can affect the likelihood that a household will be enumerated (coverage of households), and they can affect the responses obtained during enumeration (coverage within households). Proposals to make census forms widely available and accessible raise similar substantive issues—such procedures may contribute different amounts to overall response in different areas and create operational problems, such as how to match records and eliminate duplicates.

3. *Go local.* The targeting model and tool kit proposed in the Census Bureau's research program provide for localized, decentralized outreach and enumeration activities. But more may be needed. Because undercounted groups are clustered and because their reasons for not participating may vary greatly by locality, reducing the differential undercount will probably require a major reorientation in the Census Bureau's practice. Outreach and enumeration activities may need to be more decentralized. Even when they know where to find undercounted groups, staff in national and large regional offices may not have the credibility or contacts needed to motivate members of these groups to participate. Gaining access to local media markets and learning how to localize outreach,

promotion, and enumeration should be central to planning for the 1995 census test, as should the development of designs to evaluate the success and to estimate the costs of such efforts. Good procedures for eliminating duplicate records (see Chapter 2) are also needed if the Census Bureau is to be able to manage more flexible enumeration procedures that respond to local needs (e.g., filling out a form in the shopping mall) without losing accuracy.

4. *Evaluate alternatives, considering their cost and contributions to reducing the differential undercount.* Evaluating and comparing alternative strategies requires both solid research design and attention to costs. Controlled experimental designs could be augmented by studies that use planned variation in methods to provide a comparative basis for assessing the usefulness of operational procedures. The environment within which costs are evaluated will be very different in 2000 than it was in 1990. If new design and implementation techniques yield a higher initial mail response, households that are followed up by other means may be less cooperative on average than nonresponding households in 1990. And as the primary response improves, it becomes more difficult to estimate the impact of follow-up techniques in experimental studies, because the exact characteristics of mail nonrespondents are likely to be affected by the census climate and because even optimal follow-up techniques will affect only a small percentage of cases. Nevertheless, efforts to determine the relative costs of alternatives should be an integral part of their evaluation.

ROSTER IMPROVEMENT RESEARCH

Promotion, outreach, and increasing the number of ways households can be counted (described in later sections) will probably have their greatest effect on coverage of households, not on coverage of people within households. Approximately 32 percent of people who were not enumerated in the 1990 census were in households that were enumerated (Childers, 1993), so improving the quality of coverage within households—households that are increasingly complex and diverse—is crucial. Within households, coverage errors are response errors. Improving coverage of persons within households—and reducing the contribution of within-household coverage errors to the differential undercount—requires reducing response error, because it is household respondents who implement the residence rules as they fill out the census form or talk with a Census Bureau enumerator. Improving the quality of the initial count obtained by household rosters—that is, reducing omissions and erroneous enumerations—has the important general benefit of reducing the variance of coverage measurement. As with other methods for improving coverage, enhancing the quality of coverage in the initial count should help control costs and develop support for the credibility of subsequent estimation. But in addition to these general benefits, methods of rostering that respond to changes in the structure of households in the United States promise to help reduce the differential undercount, and at a relatively low cost.

Attention to methods of rostering assumes greater importance for 2000 for another reason: the 2000 census will use several different instruments administered in different modes, and it is important that the different instruments (and modes) used in obtaining the count provide comparable results. Past censuses relied on a single instrument, the paper questionnaire. This instrument was usually completed by a household informant. But during follow-up operations, enumerators might administer the form in an interview or, in extreme cases, complete it by observation. The 1990 census form used an "include-exclude" list of 13 items to instruct the household informant whom to include or exclude from the roster of household members. As implemented in 1990, the include-exclude list was designed to be used in a self-administered instrument, that is, the list was to be read by the respondent who was completing the form. This approach relies on a motivated respondent to review and implement the Census Bureau's definition of who is a member of the household. The include-exclude list thus presents problems even on a self-administered form, because many respondents will not read the list.

In addition, it is not clear how one might effectively translate the include-exclude list to another data collection mode. Like respondents who completed the paper instrument themselves, enumerators who administered the 1990 form as an interview probably varied in whether they read the include-exclude list. The problems of formally adapting the include-exclude list for an interview are suggested by the procedures adopted in the Mail and Telephone Mode Test (described in more detail in the next section), in which the include-exclude list was available to the interviewer on a help screen; the rules were not integrated into the structure of the questions that respondents were asked. Although such an implementation may make the results of the self-administered and telephone versions more comparable—if neither respondents nor interviewers read the include-exclude list—this comparability probably has a cost in validity.

Developing improved methods for rostering household members that provide comparable results with different instruments (paper and computer-assisted) and across modes (mail, telephone, and field enumerator) assumes critical importance for the 2000 census. The 2000 census will incorporate a structured reliance on different instruments and modes of data collection: self-administered instruments, paper or computer-assisted personal interviewing instruments administered by enumerators in the field (e.g., as part of a "blitz" enumeration or nonresponse follow-up), and paper or computer-assisted instruments administered by telephone as part of nonresponse follow-up. (Computer-assisted telephone interviewing and computer-assisted personal interviews will also be used as part of integrated coverage measurement, and we turn to this issue in the discussion.) Without careful instrument design, there are likely to be substantively important differences in the results obtained by the different instruments and, in some cases, by the same instrument used in different modes (e.g., paper instruments may be self-administered or used by an enumerator).

Planning for the use of different instruments and modes permits better solutions than simply accepting ad hoc adaptations of the self-administered form by individual enumerators, as necessarily happened in the past. In producing a final estimate from integrated coverage measurement, it is important to be able to treat counts for different blocks as comparable, even though the proportion of a block that is enumerated by self-administered form, by face-to-face enumeration, or by computer-assisted telephone interview during nonresponse follow-up will vary. Obtaining counts that are comparable across instruments and interview modes requires developing rostering questions that can be implemented similarly on paper and computer-assisted instruments and for which the instrument and mode differences that do remain are tested and understood.

Several research projects that are under way address questions that must be answered in order to increase the accuracy of coverage within households, and these projects can also provide insights that will be needed to develop rostering techniques that can be implemented in comparable ways across modes. The Living Situation Survey, cognitive research on residence rules, and the National Coverage Test (the 1994 census test) are essential first steps in this research. But a sustained effort will be needed to develop the instruments that the 2000 census will require. This is particularly true because the results from the Living Situation Survey and the National Coverage Test will not be fully analyzed by the time the instrument for the 1995 census test must be made final. The priorities for future research and other recommendations are discussed at the end of this section.

Living Situation Survey and Cognitive Research on Residence Rules

Various complex living household situations—unrelated people sharing the same living quarters, children in shared custody arrangements, people with no stable place of residence, and others—pose special problems for respondents attempting to apply the Census Bureau's residence rules accurately. The Census Bureau initiated research on these problems by considering the roster questions used in the Survey of Income and Program Participation (SIPP). This research found that, on average, more black males were listed as usual residents when respondents were not required to give names of those added to the roster (Kearney et al., 1993). This research also suggested that several characteristics increased the likelihood that someone listed on a roster would be described as a usual resident: contributing money to the household, considering themselves a member of the household, not staying other places often, and staying in the household many nights in the past month.

Many of the issues raised in the SIPP roster research are examined further in the Living Situation Survey (LSS), a national sample of approximately 1,000 households with an oversample of households with minority populations and renters. The LSS interview uses 13 questions to list people with many different kinds of attachments to a household. Subsequent questions then attempt to determine which people on the list are usual residents of the household. Data from the LSS should provide a systematic description of a wide range of complex household arrangements and an evaluation of the effectiveness of different strategies for determining who resides in a household.

Although these data are only recently available, initial analyses address questions important both to improving coverage and to reducing the differential undercount. For example, asking "Who slept here last night?" and then "Who lives here but wasn't here last night?" identifies approximately 99 percent of those later named as usual residents (Sweet, 1994:10). These questions appear, however, to capture males, blacks, Hispanics, and those ages 18-29 at a lower rate than others (Sweet, 1994:13).

This research also examines how people understand terms commonly used in rostering household members. Meaning is often flexible and contextual, and this poses potential problems in wording questions for a census. The LSS interview asked respondents about the meaning of *live* and *stay*. The cognitive research on residence rules extended this line of inquiry using cognitive interviews with about 30 people to explore how they understood residence concepts. There appears to be some regional variation in the meaning of *live* and *stay*: respondents in the Northeast and the West judge the words as different more frequently than do respondents in the South and the Midwest. It seems that the words *live* and *stay* alone cannot be used to distinguish between permanent and temporary residents. Not surprisingly, technical vocabulary such as *usual residence* is not used spontaneously by respondents; respondents are likely to interpret technical words as referring to more familiar concepts (Gerber and Bates, 1994).

Full results from the LSS will probably not be complete before the instrument for the 1995 census test is final, but combining results that are available with those of the National Coverage Test (see below) could lead to major innovations with considerable promise for improving coverage within households and reducing the differential undercount. By building on this research for the 1995 census test, effects on coverage (including erroneous enumerations) can be assessed. For example, approximately 5 percent of the people listed in response to each of the two initial roster questions discussed above are not usual residents (Sweet, 1994), so extending these methods to the census requires efficient ways of identifying people who might be listed at more than one housing unit. The results from this research are very promising, but the complexity of rostering will require that research both on instrument design and on how to allocate those listed on a census form to households continues beyond the 1995 census test.

National Coverage Test

The National Coverage Test compares two different approaches to counting people within households. One instrument is a respondent-friendly form with content similar to that used in 1990 (and the Simplified Questionnaire Test, see below). The other instrument collects an extended roster (e.g., by asking respondents to list ". . . everyone living or staying at this address on Saturday January 29" and ". . . anyone else who you consider to be a member of this household") and then asks questions to identify which of the people listed should not be counted as usual residents (e.g., "Is there another place where this person lives or stays?"). The first form corresponds to the traditional practice of requiring respondents to implement the Census Bureau's residence rules (via the include-exclude list) in deciding who to list. This approach asks people to report themselves where the rules say they should be counted; that is, it is a de jure enumeration. The second form does not use an include-exclude list and instead requests information about people who lived or stayed at the address on Census Day or who are considered by respondents to be members of the household. The form also requests information that enables determination of whether those on the extended roster satisfy the residence rules (de jure).

In the National Coverage Test, a reinterview will be used to estimate the impact of the extended roster form on gross coverage error, which includes erroneous enumerations and missed persons. The effect of the form difference on mail response rates will also be estimated. This innovative and important experiment provides the first trial of the "collect de facto, tabulate de jure" method— perhaps more precisely described as "collect de facto *and* de jure, tabulate de jure"—that was discussed as a possibility but not implemented for the 1990 census (Schwede, 1993; CEC Associates, 1987:26).

Discussion and Recommendations

Better instrument design is needed to help respondents provide more accurate answers. Improving the operational form of residence rules in the various instruments is especially attractive because it could both improve the quality of the initial count and reduce the differential undercount among responding households—both at relatively low cost. In addition, the new approach to rostering should be designed to give comparable results whether a household informant completes a paper instrument or an enumerator interviews the informant with a computer-assisted instrument.

The results from the LSS and the cognitive research on residence rules, together with the ethnographic evaluations conducted for the 1990 census (see discussion below), can contribute to improving the conceptualizations incorporated in the Census Bureau's residence rules (see, for example, Bureau of the Census, 1987), as well as their application in rostering questions. Because of the timing of these different streams of research, the instrument designed for the National Coverage Test was able to build on the Census Bureau's experience in designing the LSS and the cognitive research on residence rules but was not able to incorporate fully the results of that research, which is still being analyzed. If the results of the National Coverage Test are promising, the development of the extended roster form will require research continuing after the 1995 census test. Improvements in coverage from changes in rostering are likely to be bought at a relatively low cost. In addition to bringing together the results of these parallel lines of research, this extended research program must take on the important task of designing a version of the instrument to be used with computer-assisted telephone and personal interviews during nonresponse follow-up and estimating effects of various instruments and modes of administration.

For example, if the telephone will be used for nonresponse follow-up in 2000, the comparability of self-administered paper instruments and computer-assisted instruments administered by telephone must be evaluated and measured before the census. This evaluation would not necessarily require a study of the magnitude of the response improvement studies discussed below or the National Coverage Test. Similar tests should determine the effects of having the census form administered by an enumerator, as would happen in a blitz enumeration. After instrument and mode effects are first estimated, it is likely that all instruments will require modification and small-scale testing (such as cognitive interviews), and that mode effects will need to be estimated again. Thus, the schedule for this research must allow time for several cycles.

Although the Census Bureau did not develop an instrument simultaneously for a paper self-administered form and computer-assisted interview (as recommended in our interim report), it seems likely that the extended roster approach used in the National Coverage Test will be less susceptible to differences in the mode of the instrument than the 1990 form probably was. This is because the instrument does not rely on the respondents' reading of an include-exclude list, but instead asks direct questions about the relevant criteria. Continued development of the census form should consider that the 2000 census will rely on several instruments and modes of data collection. Because of the way instruments will be used, what might be, strictly speaking, instrument effects and mode effects will be somewhat confounded; of the two, instrument effects are likely to be greater and to have a more profound impact on within-household coverage than pure mode effects that occur when completely identical questions are administered via different modes. Information on the presence and size of instrument and mode effects on within-household coverage will be important in specifying the models used in mixed-mode coverage measurement methods.

The challenge of these new methods of rostering extends beyond that of designing new instruments. Processing programs must be developed to allocate those listed on the rosters for a final count. Tabulating de jure using a roster of persons who "reside" at the address or are otherwise associated with the household and additional information collected at the time of rostering is a substantial task in itself. A roster that increases the likelihood that everyone will be counted almost certainly increases the chance that some will be counted more than once. The extended roster used in the National Coverage Test requests the alternate address of anyone listed who also has another residence. Assuming similar techniques are used in the 1995 census test and then in the census, the computer programs must be developed and tested to make these matches, reconcile ambiguities, and allocate the count. Continued experimentation with forms that gather additional information (e.g., on number of different residences, frequency of travel) about people listed on an extended roster might lead to improvements in the ability to eliminate duplicate census records.

The Living Situation Survey and the cognitive research on residence rules are likely to yield some complex methods that may be more suitable for use in the reinterview for integrated coverage measurement than in the instruments developed for the initial count. The results of this research and the National Coverage Test should be evaluated together, keeping in mind the complementary goals of improving the initial count and developing more intensive methods for integrated coverage measurement. (If the rostering procedure proves feasible but too costly for the counting phase of the census, it might be used as part of the integrated coverage measurement phase.)

In summary, when developing and applying residence rules, the Census Bureau should consider both the need to accurately enumerate diverse household structures and the demands of a design that uses multiple instruments and multiple modes. In the 2000 census, it seems likely that households could be enumerated by a household respondent completing a form, providing an interview by telephone to an interviewer in a centralized facility, or being interviewed in person by an enumerator.

Recommendation 3.1: A program of research extending beyond the 1995 census test should aim to reduce coverage errors within households by reducing response errors (e.g., by using an extended roster form). This research should also evaluate the impact of these new approaches on gross and net coverage errors, as well as assess the effects on coverage of obtaining enumerations using different instrument modalities (e.g., paper and computer-assisted) and different interview modes (e.g., paper instrument completed by household respondent and by enumerator).

RESPONSE IMPROVEMENT RESEARCH

The most developed component of the Census Bureau's research on response issues addresses the problem of reducing the unit cost of each response by increasing the number of people who return the mail questionnaire. As we said, although increasing the initial response rate may leave the differential undercount unchanged—or even exacerbate it somewhat—a higher initial response rate means better-quality data, fewer nonrespondents to follow up, and better control over cost. For these reasons, an important role has been played by the experiments demonstrating that response rates can be improved by better design of the questionnaires; sending advance letters, reminder cards, and replacement questionnaires; and stamping "mandatory" on the envelope.

Taken as a whole, the Census Bureau's response improvement research program attempts a coordinated approach to a wide range of issues, and the program clearly has the potential to mitigate the decline in mail return rates or even to increase the rates. The use of a respondent-friendly questionnaire, an advance notification letter, a reminder postcard, and a replacement questionnaire are all methods that have been widely adopted in surveys, and their extension to the census is both overdue and promising.

Simplified Questionnaire Test and Implementation Test

The Census Bureau conducted the Simplified Questionnaire Test (SQT) in April 1992. Its primary purpose was to compare the final mail completion rates for four alternative short-form questionnaire designs (booklet, micro, micro with Social Security number, and roster) with the 1990 census short-form questionnaire in a survey environment (Bryant, 1992). The SQT also included a replacement questionnaire for those addresses that had not returned a form. The overall SQT completion rates were 63.4 percent for the 1990 short form and 66.8 percent for the respondent-friendly version of the 1990 short form. Thus, the test yielded an increase of 3.4 percentage points in response rate using the latter.

The Implementation Test (IT) was designed to test the benefits of three components in the mail implementation plan for the short-form sample—a prenotice letter, a stamped return envelope, and a reminder postcard (Bureau of the Census, 1992d). The IT was carried out by the Census Bureau in October 1992. The test yielded a completion rate of 50 percent for the shorter respondent-friendly version and 62.7 percent for the treatment that included a prenotice letter and reminder card. Thus, the IT experience was that use of a prenotice letter and reminder card together produced a gain of 12.7 percentage points in the response rate. On the basis of the SQT and IT results, Census Bureau statisticians estimated that the use of a replacement questionnaire increased response by approximately 10 percentage points (Dillman et al., 1994). Although it is less clear exactly how effective these techniques will be in a census or whether they will reduce the differential undercount, any increase in routine mail responses improves data quality and helps to control costs.

Mail and Telephone Mode Test

The Mail and Telephone Mode Test was designed to examine whether offering respondents the option of calling in a response or receiving a replacement questionnaire increases the response rate. The treatments varied in when the offer was made, and one treatment (the "preference" treatment) allowed respondents to call when they first received the form. The experiment was conducted in April 1992, and results suggest that offering people the opportunity to call in to be enumerated does not increase the total response rate (Clark et al., 1993) and that a small percentage who would otherwise mail back their form use the telephone when it is offered. This finding suggests that offering people more high-tech response modes (e.g., fax, personal computer), which are similar to the telephone in requiring citizens to take the initiative in responding, are similarly unlikely to increase the total response rate. The telephone is more likely to be a useful tool in nonresponse follow-up and integrated coverage measurement; we discuss these applications at length later in this chapter.

Appeals and Long Form Experiment

The key substantive issue explored by the Appeals and Long Form Experiment (ALFE), conducted in July 1993, is how to better motivate participation. This is a question that also affects other components of the census (see discussion below of outreach and promotion). One component of this experiment tested the effects on short-form response rates of two different motivational appeals, one emphasizing the mandatory nature of the census, the other stressing the benefits of census participation. A second component compared strong and standard assurances of confidentiality. The results obtained with the short form suggest that simply noting on the envelope that participation in the census is required by law could significantly increase response. Results appear similar in both high-response and low-response areas, so that the difference between these strata is not decreased. Debriefings with respondents indicated that the message that the census was mandatory was not perceived more unfavorably than a message about the benefits of participation (Treat, 1993; Singer, 1994). Of the respondents who were debriefed and who said they remembered seeing the message on the envelope, most gave the message a positive rating regardless of experimental treatment (mean ratings ranged from 4.42 to 2.78 on a scale from 1 to 10, with 1 being most favorable) (Singer, 1994:9). These results suggest a very cheap, simple, and effective method for increasing initial mail response. Further testing might consider whether the use of the "mandatory" message has a negative, backfire effect on mail response among some groups—who were nonrespondents in ALFE and so were not included in the debriefing study. It is conceivable, for example, that the message would be as effective when used only on the replacement questionnaire envelope as when used during the initial mailing, while inviting fewer negative reactions. Such issues could be investigated by incorporating simple treatment variations in the 1995 census test or other experiments in which participation is mandatory.

In the long-form component of the experiment, a long form that provided a space for each person in the household obtained a better response rate than the 1990 long form, but also had greater nonresponse to the housing questions (Treat, 1993). A form that used a row-column matrix format did not obtain a better response rate than the 1990 long form. A program that combined design work with cognitive testing of alternative forms could attempt to build on the advantages of the individual-person form and avoid its weaknesses.

Spanish Forms Availability Test

The Spanish Forms Availability Test (SFAT), conducted in 1993, was the Census Bureau's first attempt to provide forms in a language other than English as an initial response option. Because research on the 1990 census suggested that language barriers may have had a large negative effect on the initial mail response rate in some areas, the SFAT examined whether providing either bilingual forms or both English and Spanish forms could increase response to the initial mailing. The sample included a stratum in which 15-30 percent of the households were linguistically isolated and a stratum in which more than 30 percent of households were linguistically isolated. Households were defined as linguistically isolated if no one over age 14 spoke English or if no one in the household spoke English very well (Bureau of the Census, 1993a:August). The preliminary results suggest that response to the initial mailing was positively affected by the treatment in the stratum with a higher proportion of linguistically isolated households.

This kind of tailoring of response options is discussed further in several sections below. But the results of the SFAT suggest that the targeting of methods that could increase initial mail response in areas with specific barriers should continue to be considered. Another potential benefit of Spanish or other foreign-language questionnaires is that better information about within-unit residents and their characteristics might be obtained from respondents who answer in their language of choice.

Discussion

The program of research on improving initial mail response rates could lead to an impressive series of innovations in the census. Although exactly how these methods will be received in a census climate remains to be seen, these experiments suggest that the mail form to be used in 2000 will be more widely accepted than that used in 1990. Because these treatments were not all tested in combination with one another, we cannot confidently assess their joint result. But the effects of many of the factors that increase response—the prenotice letter, the reminder postcard, the replacement questionnaire, a respondent-friendly design with a space for each person, and the mandatory appeal—appear to be largely additive (Dillman et al., 1994). The magnitude of these treatment effects in the environment of an actual census year is unknown. Nevertheless, the strength of the experimental findings suggests that these features are likely to have a significant positive effect on response rates in the next decennial census.

We do not recommend abandoning research on improving initial mail response, given its critical role in controlling costs and in the overall success of the census. It is also necessary to develop the implications of these experiments for a full census, to integrate these results with those of other experiments (for example, the roster improvement research), and to understand better the effects of the length of the questionnaire on response. But efforts to improve initial mail response should focus on planning for key instrument and implementation evaluations in the 1995 census test and later tests. As the content of the instrument is made final, the respondent-friendly design of the final form will necessarily change and therefore need some further testing. The effects of a modified extended roster form, for example, on both the initial response rate and the differential undercount could differ from estimates obtained in the SQT or the National Coverage Test; the 1995 census test could augment the results of the earlier tests to include information on the effects of incorporating these innovations in the instrument. The respondent-friendly instrument design also assumes that the needed technologies for capturing data—i.e., extracting relevant information from individual census forms—will be available, and this work must also be pursued.

In addition, the methods to be used for data capture constrain how respondent-friendly an instrument can be. Because the technology for data capture to be used in 2000 is still in development, the overall design of the instrument cannot be finalized. The breakthroughs needed for automated data capture of the respondent-friendly instruments tested in this research program may not materialize for the 1995 census test or by the year 2000. In that case, the initial response rate improvements projected for the respondent-friendly instruments may prove optimistic.

Planning for operational implementation in the 1995 census test should draw on both research already conducted at the Census Bureau and other findings reported in the literature—for example, on the use of telephone for reminder calls and follow-up—to test the best feasible implementation methods.

USE OF THE TELEPHONE

It is clear that the telephone will play a much larger role in the 2000 census than it did in 1990 or in previous censuses. New technologies will allow the Census Bureau to greatly expand and automate the 800 number call-in assistance program and to use computer-assisted outbound calling for the first time. Callers to the 800 number will be able to access a wide range of automated services from any telephone in the United States, and the Census Bureau will be able to place outbound calls to mail nonrespondents to prompt them to return the census form or to complete it over the telephone. Telephone interviewing will also play a key role in the integrated coverage measurement program.

First offered in 1990, the Census Bureau's 800 number questionnaire assistance call-in program fell far short of providing prompt and efficient assistance to callers. According to a technology assessment commissioned by the Census

Bureau, 4 million call attempts were recorded during the first week after Census Day, but less than 50 percent were answered due to high peak volumes (Ogden Government Services, 1993b). In total, the Census Bureau estimates that about 7 percent of all households tried to call the 800 number in 1990, with most of the calls concentrated in a short time frame. The shortcomings of the 800 number call-in system quite possibly contributed to the drop in the mail response rate in 1990.

Telephone technology has made great strides since 1990, and there is little doubt that the telephone infrastructure will be able to meet the operational requirements of the 2000 census design both reliably and efficiently. The one caveat is that the Census Bureau must be able to provide precise estimates of the calling volume and its distribution by time of day and day of week (Ogden Government Services, 1993a). Fortunately, emerging related technologies such as touch-tone data entry, voice recognition, and automated voice recording will make it possible to provide a wide range of services to callers without human intervention, up to and including the conduct of a computer-administered interview without assistance from a live operator.

A major innovation for the 2000 census will be the use of computer-assisted outbound calling. Outbound calling is possible because of the availability of electronic directory services that can match telephone numbers to addresses. Thus, it will be possible to add telephone numbers to the Master Address File (MAF) for a significant percentage of MAF address listings and to use this resource to make outbound telephone calls both to prompt mail nonrespondents to return their forms and to complete the enumeration by telephone.

The use of computer-assisted telephone interviewing (CATI) to complete enumeration with mail nonrespondents in the nonresponse follow-up component of the census offers several advantages over the alternative of follow-up by field enumerators. The cost of a census telephone interview is estimated at $3.55 compared with $10 for an interview completed by a field enumerator (Ogden Government Services, 1993a). These estimates are compatible with the survey research literature, which has consistently found telephone interviews to be less expensive than comparable face-to-face interviews (see, for example, Weeks et al., 1983). Also, the literature clearly indicates that CATI provides enhanced data quality when judged against comparable paper-and-pencil surveys (see, for example, Weeks, 1992). In the context of the census, using telephone follow-up when possible would also reduce the number of enumerators required and could potentially improve the quality of their work by enabling the Census Bureau to be more selective in its recruiting process.

The integrated coverage measurement program that will be tested in 1995 will also use CATI whenever possible to conduct reinterviews with census respondents for purposes of measuring within-household coverage. Households without telephones in the integrated coverage measurement sample will be contacted by a field enumerator, who will use a laptop computer to conduct the reinterview. The computer assistance will enhance data quality under either mode, although the use of CATI from a centralized telephone facility will offer significant cost savings over field visits by enumerators.

These telephone applications offer the potential for considerable cost savings and data quality improvements, but they also raise a number of operational and methodological issues. We comment on these issues as we describe the new telephone applications in more detail.

Inbound Calls

We understand that the Census Bureau's goal for the 2000 census is to offer the public a questionnaire assistance call-in program through a single integrated telephone network so that anyone can access the system from any telephone in the United States by calling a single 800 number. Services will be accessed through a menu system, either by touch tone or voice recognition; for example, the caller will be instructed by the system to either press the "1" key or else to say the word "one." The Census Bureau seeks to offer as many services as possible without human intervention. However, there will always be an option for the caller to exit the menu system to speak to an operator.

The 800 number will be printed on every census document and widely advertised through the media campaign. The services offered will include prerecorded messages that address a long list of general questions, as well as operator assistance in completing the census forms. The promotion surrounding the 800 number, however, will focus on questionnaire assistance rather than on calling to complete the form over the telephone. While telephone interviews are less expensive than face-to-face field interviews, the mailback response mode is by far the least expensive of the three modes, and the Census Bureau learned in the Mail and Telephone Mode Test that there is nothing to be gained from offering a telephone response as an alternative to a mail response.

Although the Census Bureau will not encourage a telephone interview with an 800 number caller, the interview may be conducted by telephone as a last resort—that is, if the caller indicates that he or she will not, or cannot, respond by mail. In this circumstance, the Census Bureau operator will ask the caller if he or she will consent to a computer-administered interview. If the caller agrees, the interview will be conducted using voice recognition, with support from automated voice recording if necessary. If the caller declines the computer-administered interview, the operator will proceed to administer a CATI interview. Computer-administered interviewing with voice recognition technology will probably not be ready for testing in 1995 and therefore should be included in subsequent tests conducted by the Census Bureau.

The Census Bureau has commissioned the Spoken Language Research Laboratory at Oregon Graduate Institute to undertake research on the use of voice recognition and voice recording to conduct a census interview. Although the results are not yet in, this approach was recommended for development in the Census Bureau's technology assessment (Ogden Government Services, 1993a), and it seems reasonable to assume that the combination of voice recognition and voice recording will be technologically feasible in time for possible use in the 2000 census.

When conducting the interview with the 800 caller, the voice recognizer will assess whether it can recognize the caller's speech. If not, it will automatically refer the respondent to a live operator. As a further safeguard, callers will be told at the beginning of the interview that they can switch to a live operator if they encounter problems interacting with the automated system.

The voice recording utility is involved when the caller provides long or complicated answers. In this circumstance, the voice recognizer will automatically turn on a recorder to capture the respondent's response. This action will not be apparent to the respondent. Later, after the interview has been completed, the recorded responses will be keyed by data entry operators and matched with the respondent's interview record.

The Census Bureau is working with the current Federal Telecommunications System (FTS) contractor, AT&T, to develop the 800 number call-in system. FTS is a government network of leased long-distance telephone circuits that are paid for on a monthly contract basis rather than by the minute. A specific FTS contract was awarded to AT&T by the General Services Administration. In the 2000 census, the long-distance carrier will handle the initial receipt of calls, the presentation of the menu system, and the playing of prerecorded messages. The only calls that will be forwarded to the Census Bureau (or its contractors) will be those requiring a live operator or a voice recognition interview.

The Census Bureau anticipates using multiple contractors in the 2000 census to provide live operators and computer-administered interviews. In the 1995 census test, plans are to use two telephone centers—one operated by the Census Bureau and one provided by a contractor.

For all 800 calls referred to an operator, the callers will be asked for their name, address, and phone number. With this information, the Census Bureau can contact people again by telephone if they do not return the mail questionnaire. For 800 callers who say that they did not receive a form, the operator will check their addresses against the MAF to verify that they can be geocoded. In 2000, this check will be done on-line; in the 1995 census test, it will be done manually after the call is completed. If an address cannot be geocoded, the operator will call the person back to try to get better address information. In 2000, the goal is to be able to verify addresses against the MAF and to geocode the address while the caller is on the phone. With this capability, the operator can probe for a codable address during the initial telephone conversation.

We are impressed with the scope of the research program to design and test the optimal 800 number call-in system. Census Bureau staff appear to have explored the relevant issues in depth, and they have sought and received expert advice from knowledgeable sources both from within and from outside the Census Bureau. We commend the Census Bureau for recognizing the importance of developing a state-of-the-art 800 number call-in system for the 2000 census and for launching a thorough research and development program to achieve this goal.

In implementing such a system, however, there are issues that we believe will deserve further consideration. One obvious concern is the public's reaction to yet another menu-driven call-routing system. We understand that AT&T has conducted research on the public's tolerance of menu systems and has developed guidelines on the number and length of menus. However, the technology is still very new, and we suspect that a caller's patience when interacting with call-routing menus is highly correlated with the importance he or she attaches to the purpose of the call. Consequently, the limited research in this area may reflect the idiosyncratic features of the specific applications investigated, and the findings may lack generalizability to other applications. Therefore, we encourage the Census Bureau to undertake research designed to test and evaluate the public's reaction to alternative menu configurations. If possible, experiments addressing this issue should be included in the 1995 census test.

Another concern is the public's willingness to participate in an interview administered by a computer instead of a live interviewer. Although callers may initially agree to the interview, they may get frustrated or upset as the interview progresses and simply hang up, even if they are given the option of summoning a live interviewer. A related concern is the possibility of differential mode effects between computer-administered and interviewer-administered interviews. For example, respondents cannot easily ask questions when they do not understand an item on the census form if they are interacting with a computer instead of with an interviewer. These issues need to be resolved through the Census Bureau's research program.

The 1995 census test will provide a unique opportunity to collect data on the operational and cost aspects of the call-in system. To gain maximum benefit from the test, the Census Bureau will need to develop and implement a comprehensive monitoring plan that will capture relevant data on all aspects of the system. Some examples of items that will require monitoring include the number and timing of call attempts, network processing of the calls, disposition of each attempt, frequency of use of menus and menu options, reaction to the offer of a computer-administered interview, results of the computer-administered interview, comparison of the computer-administered interview and the operator-administered interview, reaction to the request for the caller's name, address, and phone number, and timing and cost data on all facets of the system. The Census Bureau should also consider conducting a follow-up survey of caller satisfaction for a sample of 800 number calls.

In all likelihood, the Census Bureau will have to contract with several vendors in the 2000 census to create a network of regional telephone centers capable of handling the anticipated telephone workload. The 1995 census test will provide experience in working with an external telephone center and will inform the development of appropriate oversight and quality control procedures. The 1995 census test will also provide operational and cost data that can be used to estimate the number of telephone centers required for 2000 and the approximate cost involved in building a system to serve the entire nation.

Recommendation 3.2: The Census Bureau should use the 1995 census test and subsequent tests to inform the design of the 800 number call-in system for the 2000 census. The Census Bureau should focus on the public's response to the menu-driven call-routing system, acceptance of the computer-administered interview, possible differential mode effects between a computer-administered interview and one administered by an interviewer, and the technical feasibility of administering interviews using voice recognition and voice recording. The Census Bureau should also develop and implement a monitoring system in these tests to collect operational and cost data on the call-in program.

Availability of Telephone Numbers for Outbound Calling

The Census Bureau is conducting research on the availability of telephone numbers for use in making outbound calls. This is important because the use of outbound calling to prompt people either to return their census forms by mail or to provide information over the telephone hinges on the availability of telephone numbers for MAF addresses.

Commercial companies offer electronic directory services that could be used to match addresses on the MAF and provide associated telephone numbers. These companies buy files of telephone numbers from the regional Bell telephone companies. However, the telephone companies can release only listed numbers; state regulations prohibit the release of unlisted telephone numbers. To expand their coverage, the commercial companies supplement the Bell directory files with address and telephone number lists purchased from third parties (such as credit card companies).

The first phase of the Census Bureau's research program in this area was designed to measure the ability of the commercial companies to match addresses and provide accurate telephone numbers. The Census Bureau selected one such company, MetroMail, and sent the company a sample of addresses drawn from the addresses used in the Census Bureau's response improvement research. MetroMail succeeded in matching 35 to 40 percent of the addresses and provided the telephone numbers for 25 percent of the sample addresses.

In the next phase of this research, the Census Bureau will select about 20,000 addresses from households that did not respond to the National Coverage Test and will send the selected addresses to MetroMail, which will attempt to match the addresses and provide the telephone numbers. The Census Bureau will then select a sample of about 1,500 matched cases with telephone numbers, call the numbers, and try to complete the interview. This research will measure the accuracy of the address matches and telephone numbers. Interestingly, the study will also measure the willingness of nonrespondents to a census-type mail survey to participate in a nonrespondent telephone follow-up survey; the results will be of interest to those involved in designing the telephone nonresponse follow-up survey for the 1995 census test.

The third phase of this research will involve an evaluation of various address-matching algorithms. The Census Bureau plans to purchase the directory files from the four regional Bell telephone companies that serve the four 1995 census test sites and then apply various address-matching algorithms to determine whether the results achieved by the commercial companies can be improved.

The fourth phase of this research program will involve legal research on the right to privacy of telephone subscribers. We understand that there are no federal regulations concerning the release of unlisted telephone numbers. Rather, the privacy guarantees that telephone companies give their subscribers who request an unlisted number are based on agreements between the local companies and the state regulatory agencies. In certain circumstances, it may be possible for the federal government to obtain an exemption from the state regulations. The Census Bureau is considering asking one of the states involved in the 1995 census test for a one-time exemption so that unlisted numbers could be provided for use in conducting nonresponse follow-up by telephone.

The research program outlined above addresses the major issues in this important area. Some suggestions follow that we believe would enhance this program. First, we suggest that the Census Bureau gain more experience with the companies providing electronic directory services. The matching services are relatively inexpensive and could prove to be very cost-effective when compared with the cost of field follow-ups by enumerators. At a minimum, the MAFs for the 1995 census test sites should be sent to several companies for processing. The Census Bureau could then compare the results achieved by the individual companies and could add as many telephone numbers to the MAF as possible for use in the 1995 census test.

The investigation of address-matching algorithms is interesting. If the companies providing electronic directory services will supply the Census Bureau with the algorithms they use, these algorithms could be evaluated as well. The product of this research could be the development of an optimal matching protocol that could then be given to the commercial companies for their use in processing the MAFs.

The legal research is probably worthwhile; however, it raises a concern about the potential effect on public relations of calling people with unlisted telephone numbers to prompt them to return the census form or to complete a telephone interview. Some people may consider such a call an unwarranted invasion of their privacy and may refuse to participate in the census. If the Census Bureau is successful in acquiring unlisted telephone numbers from the regional Bell telephone companies, the results obtained from calling these households should be carefully monitored and compared with results of calls to households with listed numbers.

Recommendation 3.3: The Census Bureau should expand the research program involving the acquisition of telephone numbers for MAF addresses by working with more companies that offer electronic directory services and developing an optimal protocol for matching addresses. If the Census Bureau is able to acquire unlisted telephone numbers for a 1995 census test site, it should carefully monitor the results obtained from calling households with unlisted numbers.

Outbound Reminder Calls

New technology now exists that makes it possible to conduct computerized outbound calling. Using what is called *predictive dialing* technology, the computer dials numbers automatically and senses when a person answers. At that point, the system can either play a prerecorded message or else route the call to a waiting operator. Predictive dialing improves the efficiency of large-volume calling efforts by automating both the dialing process and eliminating nonworking and no-answer numbers. Predictive dialing can also eliminate human intervention altogether if prerecorded messages are used.

The Census Bureau has considered using predictive dialing for making prompting calls in lieu of sending a reminder postcard. Given the anticipated volume of calls, the Census Bureau would have to use prerecorded messages instead of live operators, although the people who are called would be given the option of requesting a live operator.

There are several problems, however, with using predictive dialing for outbound reminder calls. The Census Bureau would like to reach an adult household member with the prerecorded message, but the current systems have trouble distinguishing when a child answers instead of an adult. This objective suggests the need for some type of automated screening procedure, which could be problematic. Another problem is that some states prohibit calls with recorded messages, and 12 states require the caller to ask permission before playing a recorded message.

The MAF is likely to contain telephone numbers for only a small percentage of the addresses. Consequently, the use of random-digit dialing may be required to increase the coverage of households with telephones. However, random-digit dialing will also increase costs and reduce efficiency because most samples of random telephone numbers contain a large proportion of nonworking or nonresidential numbers. Even with a computerized system, there is some cost associated with calling out-of-scope numbers.

Finally, there is concern about the relative effectiveness of a computerized phone message versus a reminder postcard. The latter is a well-established mail survey procedure that has been proved effective in the Census Bureau's own research as well as in the wider survey community. We know of no research indicating that a computerized phone message is more effective. The Census Bureau would need to undertake such research before deciding to use the phone message in lieu of the postcard.

We understand that computerized outbound calling will not be included in the 1995 census test but will remain on the Census Bureau's long-range research agenda. In view of the problems associated with this procedure, we concur with this position.

Use of CATI for Nonresponse Follow-up

The Census Bureau plans to use computer-assisted telephone interviewing for nonresponse follow-up in the 1995 census test. Nonresponse follow-up will occur after the full set of mail survey procedures (advance letter, initial questionnaire mailing, reminder postcard mailing, and replacement questionnaire mailing to nonrespondents). After the mail operations have been completed, the frame for nonresponse follow-up will be constructed (all mail nonrespondents as of the mail survey cutoff date), and a sample of nonrespondent households will be selected. The sample is expected to be about 33 percent of the total nonrespondent universe. Sample cases that have telephone numbers will be sent to the two telephone centers for follow-up calling. Cases without telephone numbers will be sent directly to the field offices for assignment to field enumerators. The field enumerators will also be assigned the residual of the telephone cases that could not be completed by telephone for other reasons (e.g., refusal, inability to contact).

The 1995 census test offers a unique opportunity to examine a number of methodological, operational, and cost issues related to the use of CATI for nonresponse follow-up. A key task is to determine which calling protocols are most successful in obtaining the census data from the mail nonrespondents in the follow-up sample. There are several options when implementing telephone follow-up. For example, the interviewer could either prompt the contacted person to return the census form by mail or attempt to obtain the data over the telephone in a CATI interview. If a prompting approach is used, the interviewer would presumably enter a follow-up date into the case management system, and the system would then schedule another follow-up call if the contacted person's form is not returned by that date. If the person no longer has the census form, the interviewer could either attempt to complete the interview or enter an order into the system to have a replacement form sent to the person. In this case, the system would schedule the case for a follow-up call if the form is not received by a specified date. There are other possible permutations for various types of cases. The point is that the Census Bureau will need to develop, implement, and evaluate calling protocols in the 1995 census test in order to develop the optimal set for use in the 2000 census.

The optimal timing of calls to nonresponding households also warrants investigation. There is a considerable body of literature on this topic (see, for example, Weeks, 1988; Kulka and Weeks, 1988; Weeks et al., 1987); however, every survey application has its idiosyncrasies, and the Census Bureau would be well advised to build into the design of the 1995 census test some controlled experiments in this area.

Another question is when to send cases to field enumerators for follow-up by a personal visit. That is, at what point does it become more efficient to send the cases to the field instead of continuing to work the case by telephone? A related issue is whether to try to work the telephone cases in geographic clusters so that the residual can be sent to the field in clusters, thus saving on field travel costs.

The use of both CATI interviews and paper-and-pencil field interviews in the nonresponse follow-up component of the 1995 census test raises concern about the potential for mode effects. The two interview modes are radically different in two respects: the use of the telephone versus a face-to-face interview, and the use of computer assistance versus an unassisted interviewer-administered questionnaire.

An important operational issue is the design of the automated case management system. This system must be able to initialize cases, schedule them for calling using preprogrammed protocols, prioritize cases across and within calling queues, assign cases to appropriate interviewers, close out completed cases, identify cases that are ready to be assigned to the field, and produce a variety of monitoring reports. CATI case management systems vary considerably in their design and capabilities (see Weeks, 1988, for a discussion of various systems). The Census Bureau should consider investigating a variety of extant systems, including those currently used in its own telephone centers, to determine the optimal design for use in the 1995 census test.

As noted above, the 1995 census test will give the Census Bureau an opportunity to gain experience in working with an outside telephone center. The test will also provide data that can be used to develop workload and cost estimates in planning the 2000 census. The Census Bureau should take care to design and implement a comprehensive monitoring system that will collect these operational and cost data.

Using CATI in the Integrated Coverage Measurement Program

The Census Bureau is developing an integrated coverage measurement (ICM) design that involves an independent reinterview with a sample of census respondents followed immediately by a comparison with the original census data and a reconciliation of differences. For several reasons, such a design suggests an ideal application for CATI. First, the telephone number for sample cases is likely to be available from the initial census form. Second, the data from the first interview can be preloaded into the computer, and the comparison of the first and second interviews can be done by computer. Finally, the computer program can be written to script customized questions and probes for use by the interviewer in reconciling the two interviews.

In current plans for the 1995 census test, ICM interviews with no-phone households will be conducted via computer-assisted personal interviewing (CAPI), which involves equipping enumerators with laptop computers. Both CATI and CAPI will presumably be conducted using the same interview program. However, because CATI will be conducted by telephone and CAPI will be conducted by personal visit, the possibility for mode effects will also exist in this phase of census operations.

The use of CATI in the ICM program offers the potential for significant cost savings in comparison to CAPI. However, the Census Bureau will need to design and implement a monitoring system that is capable of collecting the data necessary to quantify the relative cost of the two modes and to inform cost modeling for the 2000 census.

OTHER AUTOMATED RESPONSE TECHNOLOGIES

The Census Bureau is also evaluating a number of other automated response technologies. These are briefly reviewed below.

As noted above, the Census Bureau plans to use CAPI (as well as CATI) in the ICM component of the 1995 census test. However, CAPI will not be used to conduct field follow-up interviews in the nonresponse follow-up component. There are several reasons for this decision. First, it would probably be prohibitively expensive to equip an army of field enumerators with laptop computers for the very short time the equipment would be used. Second, the use of CAPI would make it more difficult to recruit qualified enumerators, and those who were selected would have to receive an expanded training program. Finally, Census Bureau staff expect that they will continue to learn about CAPI through the Census Bureau's ongoing demographic surveys that are converting to CAPI (e.g., the Current Population Survey) and through the limited use of CAPI in the ICM program.

The Census Bureau does plan to equip field staff with pen-based computers in the 1995 census test to update address lists and maps and to compile the independent listing of addresses in the ICM blocks that will be matched to the census address list (see Chapter 4). The computers will be preloaded with geocode information so that addresses will be automatically geocoded as they are listed.

The multimedia kiosk is another response technology under consideration. A prototype is currently under development, and the Census Bureau may test this technology in one of the 1995 census test sites. The Census Bureau is part of a consortium with several other federal agencies (the Social Security Administration, the Internal Revenue Service, the Postal Service, and the Department of Veterans Affairs) considering a potential joint investment in a network of kiosks. Kiosks would be located in federal buildings, post offices, Social Security offices, etc., to provide information about government services. The Census Bureau could use this network to provide information to the public during the decennial census.

The technology assessment of interactive cable television commissioned by the Census Bureau concluded that this technology will not be mature enough by 2000 to warrant consideration as a data collection method (Ogden Government Services, 1993a). However, interactive cable television is changing rapidly, and the Census Bureau plans to continue to monitor the progress of this technology.

The technology assessment of personal computers (PCs) is also not encouraging. It is estimated that less than 40 percent of households will have PCs by the year 2000, and only 12 percent will have modems (Ogden Government Services, 1993a). Consequently, the Census Bureau does not plan to experiment with PCs as a response option in the 1995 census test. However, this response mode remains on the long-range research agenda. One possible project would be to establish a computer bulletin board through an existing on-line service.

The technology assessment of reporting from businesses recommended that the Census Bureau conduct a national survey of businesses to assess their willingness to promote the census and to allow their employees to use business telephones, fax machines, and modem-equipped PCs as response modes. The Census Bureau will not pursue this activity in 1995, but the option remains on the long-range research agenda.

In our opinion, the Census Bureau has made a commendable effort to identify and evaluate alternative response modes. The technology assessments have been comprehensive and thorough, and the Census Bureau's responses have been appropriate. We encourage the continuation of this line of forward-looking research.

HARD-TO-ENUMERATE POPULATIONS

As noted above, neither improvements in questionnaire design and implementation nor the development of automated response technologies is likely to address particular difficulties that historically have hampered attempts to count certain subpopulations. In this section, we review what the Census Bureau has learned in recent years about the problems of enumerating inner-city and rural low-income populations, immigrants, internal migrants, and homeless people ("persons with no usual residence"). We then discuss some of the remedies the

Census Bureau is considering for evaluation during the 1995 census test, with a view toward reduction of the differential undercount in the year 2000.

Challenges in Counting Poor and Migrant Populations

In the course of the 1990 census, the Census Bureau conducted an alternative enumeration in 29 sample areas of the United States and Puerto Rico called the Ethnographic Evaluation Project. The areas were chosen for their high concentration of particular minority subpopulations, both urban and rural, as well as the presence of a large number of undocumented immigrants who are known to fear participating in the census. Experienced ethnographers familiar with the target populations conducted the alternative enumeration. They were able to improve the count by using their existing relationships with members of these communities, familiarity with the native languages of the immigrants, and their knowledge of the particular housing practices of poor populations—both native and immigrant. Results of these special census projects were compared with the enumerations of the same areas in the 1990 census.

From this comparison the Census Bureau learned a great deal about the sources of undercount and overcount. Substantial numbers of erroneous enumerations and omissions occurred at the sites, and the net undercount rates varied considerably (Brownrigg and de la Puente, 1993). The two extreme cases reported a net undercount of 47 percent and a net overcount of 53 percent; the median net coverage was a small undercount of approximately 1 percent. Clearly, the sites present very difficult counting conditions that create both types of census error. These errors occasionally cancel out within a geographic area, but they are more likely to result in surpluses of omissions or erroneous enumerations that produce the large variations in net undercount that were observed in 1990. For the affected communities, undercounting is a source of great policy concern because of implications for political representation and allocation of federal and state program funds. The primary task now should be to capitalize on this research and to implement the valuable policy suggestions that emerged from this study in designing the 1995 census test and developing the tool kit of methods for the 2000 census field offices.

An excellent summary of the 29 ethnographic coverage reports (de la Puente, 1993) identifies five sources of undercount or overcount: (1) irregular and complex living arrangements, (2) irregular housing, (3) residential mobility, (4) distrust of government, and (5) limited English proficiency. Almost all of these point to the difference between the underlying norms expressed in the census (nuclear families, discrete households, long-term or permanent residences) and the living arrangements of poor people in this country, whether foreign-born or native. Some of these problems are related to the difficulty of enumerating the population in question: gaining trust, counting all the people in a household, and the like. Others are related to locating dwellings in poor areas of the nation's cities and rural communities and are of great importance in updating the Master Address File. The Census Bureau will need to give serious consideration to the policy options suggested by the ethnographic studies for both of these domains.

Irregular and Complex Household Arrangements

The first source of enumeration difficulties involves the irregular and complex household arrangements that typify poor minority and immigrant communities. Households defined as irregular or complex contain unrelated individuals, people who are mobile or present for no other reason than to share the burden of the rent, and multiple nuclear families. Households structured in this fashion become extremely difficult to enumerate accurately. Census rules of residence, which ask the respondent to identify members of their household in relation to "person 1," cannot easily accommodate the composition of these living groups and often contradict the respondent's definitions of family or household. In such cases, residence rules are hard to apply; the individuals who "should" be counted may be absent and thus excluded. As an ethnographer working in rural Marion County, Oregon, noted (cited in de la Puente, 1993:4):

> If all members are not present, . . . obtaining the data pertaining to persons outside, asleep, at work, or temporarily absent is virtually impossible. It is as if those persons do not exist.

These households may also contain unrelated males who have assembled solely to cut the cost of the rent, who work long hours, and share living space in very dense fashion—with beds lining the rooms and individuals sleeping in shifts.[2] Nothing, other than expediency and common ethnicity, binds these individuals into anything they would define as a *household* of people related to person 1, with emphasis on the term *related*. As Rodriguez and Hagan put the matter (cited in de la Puente, 1993:7):

> For recent immigrants from Central America and Mexico, household and family are viewed as the same. Boarders and unrelated individuals are not part of the family and thus not part of the household.

At some sites, ethnographers discovered that up to half of the individuals living in complex households of this kind were left out of the census (see, e.g., Romero, 1992). The same pattern of undercount was likely to develop in Haitian households, which were composed of a "core" family and a series of peripheral individuals who are "just passing through" but sometimes stay for years. Chinese families in New York may be equally perplexed by the census definitions of household and may augment those present in a household with relatives who are

---

[2] In some immigrant communities, this kind of dense subleasing is an important source of income for older immigrants, who build a housing pyramid on the basis of holding a lease and exploiting recent arrivals who have no other options (see Mahler, 1993).

family (e.g., adult children) but no longer living in the house. Again, the residence rules on the census forms confuse even the willing participant—resulting in undercounts (the Haitian example) and overcounts (the Chinese example).

Irregular and complex household structures are generally to be found wherever there are high housing prices and a concentrated poor population (native or immigrant). This is an important finding in and of itself, for researchers (perhaps including the ethnographers working on this project) are prone to believe that these patterns are expressions of cultural differences. The regularity of the ethnographic findings across ethnic subpopulations and in disparate parts of the United States suggest there may be little that is culturally specific about the formation of irregular households. Rather, irregular households form in response to structural conditions that bring poor people into areas of expensive housing, resulting in these fairly uniform "irregular" practices. If this is true, then it should be possible for the Census Bureau to identify many of these areas in advance and target special resources for enumeration within them.

Irregular Housing

Irregular housing is the second major source of the undercount, one that presents difficulties in locating housing units, rather than in enumerating the individuals living in them. Brownrigg (1991) estimates that across the 29 sample areas subjected to ethnographic evaluation, perhaps as many as 40 percent of the people who should have been included in the count, but were missed, were missed because the housing unit itself was overlooked or misidentified. Typically, these dwellings were hidden from public view (in backyards or down rural roads) or were illegally built (and often concealed in single-family homes or garages). Irregular housing also causes overcounts because buildings have multiple addresses or multiple entrances or are temporary dwellings that move around but have already been counted elsewhere—e.g., trailers in the neighborhood just for the weekend (see de la Puente, 1993:12). Irregular housing goes hand in hand with irregular and complex households, thus compounding the enumeration problems discussed above. Families are likely to double up in areas where affordable housing is in short supply, stimulating the construction of illegally converted housing.[3]

The success of the ethnographic teams in locating irregular housing was impressive, particularly when compared with the 1990 census. One case study reported a census undercount of nearly 50 percent, much of which could be attributed to missed housing units. The alternative enumeration was often able to identify these irregular dwellings, drawing on the detailed knowledge of locally based ethnographers and their skill in cultivating informants who could guide

---

[3] Descriptions of these areas leave little doubt that they can be forbidding places for enumerators to survey. Ethnographers were sometimes exposed to threats to their physical safety.

them into the nether world of warehouses, back alleys, unscrupulous landlords, crack dens, and other unlikely places for private housing.

Residential Mobility

Residential mobility was the third reason given for enumeration difficulties in the 29 sample areas. Some populations that the census generally undercounts tend to move often, to reside in one place for a shorter period of time than middle-class citizens think of as the norm, and so to be difficult to enumerate. High residential mobility goes hand in hand with seasonal and low-wage labor markets, patterns of return migration, and the pressures of accommodating large numbers of "peripheral" members in a household (who are likely to move when the strain becomes too great). Difficulties with landlords give rise to eviction, resulting in greater mobility for poor people than others. Mahler (1993:8, quoted in de la Puente, 1993:22) notes that Salvadoran immigrants move as often as three times a year in search of cheaper housing or jobs or because they are reunited with family members.

These circumstances not only make it difficult to count individuals but also exacerbate the difficulties that many native-born and immigrant poor people face in applying the residence rules. Are temporary household residents "members"? They may be deemed such if they are also relatives, but otherwise they may be excluded because they are both highly mobile and unrelated. As noted above, experimentation with questions that ask "Who stayed here last night?" has already yielded some interesting results.[4] New formulations of the roster questions might identify a significant percentage of individuals who have traditionally been missed in the census. Research from the Living Situation Survey (Sweet, 1994) should inform the development of roster questions for the 1995 census test and the 2000 census.

Distrust of Government

Distrust of, or ambivalence toward, the government is another cause of undercounts. In the 29 communities surveyed, many members of the target populations believe they have little to gain in cooperating with the census and fear the possible consequences of yielding information—particularly if they are among the large number of undocumented immigrants or participants in the underground economy. Contending with this problem proved difficult for the ethnographers who worked on this special project, for they were rarely equipped

---

[4] Cognitive research aimed at uncovering the connotation of phrases such as *lived here* or *stayed here* has been helpful in illuminating possible causes of within-household omissions. Regional differences may play a role in divergent personal interpretations of census roster questions, with potential implications for differential response and coverage (see Gerber and Bates, 1994).

to survey drug enclaves, shanty towns, and the like. They had to contend with the dangers of the street and, perhaps more important, the hesitance of ordinary (law-abiding) individuals living under these conditions to open their doors to strangers.

It is clear that many people in immigrant and native-born minority groups do not believe that the census is confidential. Those who harbor an undocumented individual in the household are especially fearful of discovery through participation in the census; others who are receiving public assistance are concerned about the government finding undeclared partners. It also seems likely that some immigrants would be wary of government initiatives to count individuals and skeptical about confidentiality claims because of their negative experiences with government activities in their native countries.

Limited English Proficiency

Finally, the ethnographic studies found that lack of English proficiency was a major source of undercounts in some communities. The studies made use of native-speaker enumerators who could conduct the census in Haitian creole, Spanish, Chinese, and a variety of other languages. Multilingualism proved to be enormously important, both enabling effective communication and inducing the respondent to trust the enumerator. In addition, immigrant populations are often characterized by a high incidence of illiteracy in the native tongue. Ethnographers sometimes found that members of their target population were unable to read or write in any language. Illiteracy necessitates even more intervention or interpretation in the enumeration process and undoubtedly introduces standardization problems. Coverage was undoubtedly improved in these case studies; consistency may be another matter.

Persons With No Usual Residence

In recent years, research attention has focused on the problems of enumerating the homeless population, a subset of persistently poor people who have no regular domicile. This population is of particular concern to city agencies who have to provide services and who, in turn, depend on an accurate count in order to budget for their needs. Advocacy groups have also played an important role in drawing attention to homeless people.

The Census Bureau adopted new measures for enumerating persons without a usual residence in the 1990 census. Based on prior research, the Census Bureau assumed that these people would be found in one of four situations: (1) living temporarily in someone else's household (often referred to as "doubling up"); (2) living in facilities such as commercial campgrounds, hotels, and boarding houses or noninstitutional group quarters; (3) staying temporarily in shelters or other emergency facilities (or cheap hotels); or (4) spending the night "in the street" (on sidewalks, in vehicles, in abandoned buildings, etc.). The 1990 census counted people in the first situation via the regular household enumeration process, depending on the wording of the residence rules to "capture" those who were temporarily located in a given household. For the second situation, census procedures for enumerating individuals living in group quarters were invoked. In the third and fourth categories, a special census was conducted in March of 1990 that has come to be known as S-Night, short for Shelter and Street Night (Kalton et al., 1994: 2-2).

S-Night convinced the Census Bureau that major methodological problems attend the attempt to enumerate the street population. Using various controls, the Census Bureau determined that enumerators often failed to locate many of the preidentified sites where the homeless congregate, that departures from standard procedures were common, and that enumerators were selective in approaching individuals because of safety concerns.

Policy Initiatives for 2000 and Future Censuses

It is important to remember that the Ethnographic Evaluation Project was conducted in particularly hard-to-enumerate neighborhoods. Nonetheless, the project sheds light on the causes of undercounts and overcounts and suggests valuable policy initiatives for improving census coverage of such neighborhoods. Similarly, the Census Bureau's efforts to improve methods of counting the nation's homeless population have yielded some important insights that will make the 2000 census more complete, even for those who are the hardest to enumerate.

We emphasize that the insights developed thus far should evolve into (a) further research programs, if needed, and (b) experiments to be undertaken during and after the 1995 census test to evaluate the cost-effectiveness of special methods designed to reduce the differential undercount. Strategies suggested for possible use by headquarters and by regional offices make insightful use of the lessons contained in the studies of hard-to-enumerate populations. At present, Census Bureau staff are in the process of evaluating these strategies in order to determine which ones might be incorporated into the 1995 census test.

Our discussion and recommendations focus on the following areas of concern: (1) creating ongoing local ties, (2) further comparative studies of hard-to-enumerate populations, (3) strategies for reducing differential undercount, (4) counting persons with no usual residence, and (5) cognitive research on race/ethnic classification.

Creating Ongoing Local Ties

The ethnographic research suggests that individuals familiar with the native languages, the customs, and the physical layout of the communities in question were far more successful than traditional enumerators in locating and surveying hard-to-count populations. The project directors concluded, and this panel concurs, that the Census Bureau should create a more effective partnership with locally based, grass-roots organizations in order to address the coverage problem. Some of these organizations have regional and even national representation (e.g., the Urban League, the Mexican American Legal Defense Fund); others are entirely local in orientation. These two kinds of ethnic organizations appeal to different groups and would require different partnership strategies with the Census Bureau, but both must be approached and integrated into the 2000 census.

Effective partnerships between the Census Bureau and local leadership will have to be inaugurated well before Census Day. A well-designed continuous outreach, promotion, and enumeration operation in targeted areas may prove cost-effective in comparison with the start-and-stop approach that has been used in past censuses. Developing local ties that work—that is, that help to reduce the differential undercount by creating a participatory spirit or simply by using the superior knowledge of local ethnographers—is not an overnight operation. If such efforts prove effective—as they have, to some extent, for Statistics Canada with regard to the Canadian aboriginal population—they should pay off in terms of reduced undercount and more effective targeting of Census Bureau resources.

Implementing an in-depth, localized, network approach will demand an enormous change in the culture of the Census Bureau, for which, for perfectly understandable reasons, centralized control and standardized methods have been paramount. Involvement of community organizations at the level suggested by the ethnographic studies will mean yielding a degree of control and fostering a sense of trust that would probably be unparalleled in the agency's history. Community leaders speak of the importance of defining the census as "theirs," the critical need to "own" the census, rather than approaching the census as an instrument that belongs to the government or to the nation as a whole. It is important to recognize how revolutionary "going local" on this scale would be.

At the same time, the survival of many community organizations depends on the census, because their funding is linked directly to the size of the populations they serve. If for no other reason than self-interest, many Native American, Haitian, African-American, Hispanic, and Pacific Islander social service agencies are eager to help. Grass-roots groups have infrastructures that can be of enormous assistance in the enumeration process; they know where to find their people, they have lists of their members, and they are trusted in the community. These are assets that cannot be acquired by outsiders, and they are directly related to a successful enumeration. One concern with grass-roots efforts, however, is the potential for increases in erroneous enumerations and consequent overcounting when the involved organizations may be interested more in the size rather than the accuracy of the count.

An interdivisional working group at the Census Bureau has suggested regional office activities that involve ongoing local contact. In particular, the working group has recommended that continuous outreach in hard-to-enumerate areas be undertaken at least two years before decennial Census Day (Bureau of the Census, 1994b):

> The outreach staff would engage in such activities as [developing] an on-going presence in the schools, establishing and maintaining rapport with local media, educating and gaining entree into local community groups, and making speeches and presentations to any groups [that] could help with the census enumeration in the area.

Recommendation 3.4: The Census Bureau should consider developing an extensive network of relations between field offices and local community resources, particularly in hard-to-enumerate areas, and should examine the cost-effectiveness of maintaining this infrastructure in continuous operation between censuses. The Census Bureau should develop and implement pilot programs in conjunction with the 1995 census test in order to gather information about the potential costs and benefits of a large-scale local outreach program.

Further Comparative Studies of Hard-to-Enumerate Populations

There is a tendency to assume that irregular households are the product of culturally specific notions of family, but the evidence from the case studies suggests a surprising degree of uniformity in the residence practices of the nation's poor, whether immigrant or native born. Further research is needed, and results must be incorporated into the targeting model and into any component of the census design that depends on comprehensive coverage (e.g., as part of integrated coverage measurement). A theoretical understanding of the distribution of hard-to-enumerate populations is needed, one that looks across ethnic and racial groups to the common characteristics of poor populations; that theoretical knowledge is of considerable practical value in directing additional resources to field offices where differential undercounts are likely. The same modeling may help in determining the most effective placement of the standing infrastructure discussed in Recommendation 3.4.

Recommendation 3.5: The Census Bureau should conduct further comparative studies of hard-to-enumerate areas, focusing on those parts of the country where three phenomena coincide: a shortage of affordable housing, a high proportion of undocumented immigrants, and the presence of low-income neighborhoods.

Strategies for Reducing Differentials in Coverage

Ethnographers who were involved in the 1990 studies generally believe that enumerators who reflect the racial, ethnic, and cultural composition of the target population are better able to conduct the census collection than those who are defined as outsiders. Some of the advantages are trust, communication skills (especially foreign-language skills), knowledge of the housing stock, and creation of the appearance (and reality) of "local ownership" of the census. Communities that are suspicious of the federal government or that see no reward from participation are more likely to be persuaded of the importance of the census if the words come from people they know and have reason to admire or trust. One potential disadvantage with community enumerators is that respondents may be reluctant to give accurate information about more sensitive items, such as income, to a friend or a neighbor.

Local enumerators are more likely to know the ins and outs of the neighborhoods that feature irregular housing, but further training and support for locating hidden housing units will be necessary. The ethnographic studies recommend making more systematic use of letter carriers, not to conduct the count, but as sources for identifying housing units. Rental offices and landlords turn out to be poor sources of information, but letter carriers are disinterested parties whose knowledge is currently underused.

Clearly a large-scale program of ethnic enumerators would require a significant change in traditional training methods. More resources would have to be available to train enumerators, and the process would take longer. It would be foolhardy to hire people and provide them with insufficient training. But the investment would be well worth it if the program contributed to reducing the differential undercount—particularly if it was tied to an ongoing organizational structure (which would not have to be reborn with every decennial census).

Ethnographers working in Spanish-speaking areas noted the importance of developing Spanish-language census forms based on a conceptual rather than a literal translation and distributing these forms more effectively than in 1990, when people were required to call a toll-free number to request a Spanish-language form. They reported frustration on the part of Spanish speakers who were unable to participate even though they are literate in their native tongue. This appears to be a relatively simple and cost-effective change. Every form that can be completed by mail saves on the cost of follow-up. Although this was the only non-English-language form suggestion, further research on the efficacy of translating the form into other languages might be useful. Further research is needed to assess whether the use of written information materials, foreign-language tapes, or interactive video might be effective ways of reaching individuals who are not literate in their native language.

Immigrant families working shifts and seasonal jobs are often difficult to enumerate because their schedules are irregular. Ethnographers recommend that enumerators conduct visits in the evening and on weekends, rather than in the middle of workdays, in order to find more people at home. They also noted the importance of moving Census Day so that it falls in the middle of the month; occupants of low-cost housing are more likely to move at the beginning and the end of a month (see also the discussion in Chapter 2). Hence, a change in the timing of the census itself will reduce differentials in coverage that are attributable to residential mobility (see Recommendation 2.3).[5] Canada has already changed its Census Day in 1996 from June 4 to May 14 for essentially the same reasons (Choudhry, 1992). Officials concluded that some coverage problems could be solved simply by shifting the census reference date from the beginning of the month.

> **Recommendation 3.6: In the 1995 census test, the Census Bureau should include a larger repertoire of foreign-language materials than those currently available in Spanish (both written and audio). In addition, the Census Bureau should conduct more aggressive hiring of community-based enumerators (with due consideration of local concerns about the confidentiality of census responses) and should accommodate greater flexibility in the timing of enumeration by personal visit (i.e., permitting contact during evenings and weekends).**

Enumerating Persons With No Usual Residence

Because of the methodological and operational problems encountered in the 1990 attempt to enumerate the street population (Martin, 1992), the Census Bureau is developing a service-based approach to the enumeration of persons with no usual residence (Bureau of the Census, 1994e). The development and testing of a service-based approach was recommended in a methodological review (Kalton et al., 1994) of studies of the homeless populations in several U.S. cities. The review was commissioned by the Census Bureau to evaluate possible strategies for enumerating persons with no usual residence in the 2000 census.

Similarly designed surveys of the homeless population have been carried out in several major cities—Los Angeles, Chicago, and the Washington, D.C., metropolitan area. The studies used multiple frames to sample places where people find social services (e.g., shelters and soup kitchens); coverage results ranged from approximately 51 to 92 percent of the estimated homeless population in these areas (Kalton et al., 1994). These findings suggest that canvassing shelters and soup kitchens may be more cost-effective than a street-based approach to enumerating persons with no usual residence.

Street enumeration might instead serve a supplementary role in estimating coverage in sample areas. Some type of coverage evaluation will be needed to judge the completeness of coverage of the homeless population that can be achieved by enumeration at service providers. It will also be important to assess

---

[5] We note that the 1995 census test is set for March 4. It is not clear whether the Census Bureau plans to analyze the impact of moving Census Day from April 1. We hope that some kind of evaluation will be considered, although the March 4 date may still be too early in the month to result in appreciably fewer problems with end-of-month movers.

the variation among communities in rates of service utilization because of the implications for census coverage of homeless people via a service-based approach. Results suggest that service usage rates vary considerably across geographic areas and across time of year; possible explanations for this variation include differences in weather and in the level of available services (Kalton et al., 1994).

> **Recommendation 3.7: We endorse the Census Bureau's plans to conduct, in the 1995 census test, enumeration at service providers (e.g., shelters and soup kitchens) as a method for counting persons with no usual residence (and possibly migrant workers). The Census Bureau should consider conducting enumeration of streets and other public places on a sample basis at each of the test sites for the purpose of coverage assessment.**

Further research will be needed to determine whether service-based enumeration is the most cost-effective approach to counting the homeless population. Finally, we observe that any enumeration method would likely benefit from greater community outreach to identify locations in which persons with no usual residence might be found.

Cognitive Research on Race/Ethnic Classification

The racial and ethnic categories used in the census must be consistent with federal standards established by the Statistical Policy Office of Office of Management and Budget (OMB). The OMB standards take into account legal requirements for race and ethnicity data, as well as user needs; the standards apply to all federal statistical agencies and to federal agencies that maintain administrative record systems. Information about race and Hispanic origin is collected on the short form of the decennial census; the long form collects additional information about such characteristics as ancestry or ethnic origin, country of birth, language, and citizenship status. Our discussion in this section is concerned primarily with the short-form questions that are asked of everyone in the census.

Ethnographers noted the increasingly outdated conceptualization of race and ethnic identity embodied in the census. America is becoming a multicultural society, and personal identities are changing along with this trend. The selection of single-race identifiers is proving particularly problematic under these circumstances. Are immigrants supposed to define themselves by nationality, ethnicity, language group, or physical appearance? Are individuals supposed to select a category that expresses how they view themselves or how others define them? This is a source of great confusion. Laotian nationals of Chinese descent and Hmong origin, for example, have difficulty in knowing how to respond. Spanish-speaking Filipinos are unsure whether they should check "Asian or Pacific Islander" for race and then "Hispanic" for origin.

Questionnaire items that apply OMB guidelines and ask respondents to claim a single race suggest a conceptualization of race (and ethnicity) as something fixed, inherited, and unambiguous. But contemporary racial and ethnic self-identification seems to be more fluid, situational, and continuum-like in its cognitive organization. The United States is starting to look more like Brazil or Tahiti, among the many places in the world where fluid racial and ethnic identity is the norm and where single-category identifications are not easily reconciled with personal conceptions of race. As immigration patterns bring more people from these societies (e.g., the Dominican Republic) to the United States, patterns of identification are shifting.

The Census Bureau should continue to support research on questions about racial and ethnic identity[6], and policy makers should clarify the purpose of such questions. Recent and ongoing activities have begun to address these issues. The Census Bureau and Statistics Canada jointly sponsored an international conference on the measurement of ethnicity in April 1992 (Statistics Canada and Bureau of the Census, 1993). OMB has convened an interagency committee to study federal standards on the collection and reporting of race and Hispanic origin data by federal agencies. At the request of OMB, the Committee on National Statistics held a workshop in February 1994 to review federal experience with these standards. Also, the Panel on Census Requirements in the Year 2000 and Beyond is investigating the subject of racial and ethnic classification with regard to content needs in the decennial census and other demographic programs.

The complexity of racial and ethnic identity causes methodological problems of racial and ethnic misclassification in the decennial census. The effects of misclassification on differential undercount are not well-understood. But the Census Bureau will continue to feel pressure to solve these problems as long as resource flows to ethnic community organizations depend on the accurate classification and counting of their members and as long as the Voting Rights Act demands single-race reporting. We recognize that these are extremely difficult methodological problems to solve; we suggest, among other things, that the Census Bureau consider experimenting with classification schemes that enable respondents to check off more than one race category. We further suggest that the Census Bureau sponsor additional research on the question of ethnic identity, utilizing the intellectual resources of cognitive anthropology (in which much relevant research has already been done) and sociology.

We note in passing the importance of the cognitive research that has accompanied the Living Situation Survey; this research is being conducted primarily to develop new ways of defining the residence rules (Gerber and Bates, 1994;

---

[6] The Census Bureau has conducted or sponsored studies of the effects of the order of race and Hispanic origin questions on item nonresponse and race reporting (see Bates et al., 1994).

Sweet, 1994). A similar program of research should be undertaken on the subject of racial and ethnic identity.

Recommendation 3.8: The Census Bureau should undertake a program of research in cognitive anthropology, sociology, and psychology that will contribute to the development of more acceptable racial and ethnic identification questions.

The policy recommendations that emerged from the ethnographic studies are potentially of great value for the 2000 census. We believe that the Census Bureau has made major progress in developing strategies of outreach and enumeration that are based on the ethnographic evidence—particularly strategies that involve localized, customized methods of recruiting enumerators drawn from minority populations, providing ongoing outreach support to local minority organizations, and using the greater trust and recognition of these organizations by hard-to-enumerate populations as a basis for a partnership in census-taking. Work must now continue to transform these policy recommendations into operational components that can be tested and evaluated in the 1995 census test.

TOOL KIT AND PLANNING DATABASE

The key census design components being developed to improve coverage and consequently reduce the differential undercount of hard-to-enumerate populations are the tool kit and the planning database. The tool kit comprises the set of special enumeration methods and such strategies as questionnaire assistance and targeted outreach and promotion efforts. Some tool-kit methods—for example, team enumeration, blitz tactics, and bilingual enumerators—would be available for deployment by regional offices in hard-to-enumerate areas. Use of the tool kit could also involve specialized outreach procedures and decisions at the headquarters level on mailout-mailback procedures, allocation of staff and resources, and differential pay rates and incentives for census workers.

The planning database (formerly called the targeting database in Census Bureau documents) would be used—either informally or with a predictive model (the targeting model)—in the 2000 census to preidentify geographic areas in which enumeration barriers are likely to be present and deployment of the special enumeration methods in the tool kit might particularly improve coverage. The planning database could be used, for example, to identify linguistically isolated areas to which Spanish forms should be mailed, to target recruiting messages, and to tailor promotion and marketing materials.

Development of the tool kit and the planning database draws on the findings of interdivisional working groups at the Census Bureau that were charged with identifying barriers to enumeration and special methods that might overcome these barriers. The final report of the Tool Kit Working Group (Bureau of the Census, 1994b) recommended tools for further consideration for research and possible use in the 2000 census. Seven candidate tools for use by district or regional offices have been identified for testing and evaluation in the 1995 census test (Bureau of the Census, 1994d):

1. *Blitz enumeration.* The district office would employ crews of specially trained enumerators who would conduct enumeration activities in a very compressed time schedule.

2. *Use of community-based organizations.* The regional office would identify local organizations that are willing to conduct questionnaire assistance or outreach activities.

3. *Use of rental companies.* In areas with high concentrations of rental units, regional offices would ask moving companies, resident managers, managers of temporary storage space, truck rental companies, and others who provide services to renters and movers, to participate in census promotion. Participants could display census posters and publicity materials, as well as distribute census promotional items, such as key chains and calendars, to their customers.

4. *Use of local facilitators.* The district office would have the option of using either paid or volunteer local facilitators, such as community activists, religious leaders, gang leaders, and other recognized local figures, to facilitate the enumeration—for example, by introducing enumerators to households, translating when necessary, convincing people to cooperate, and locating hidden living quarters.

5. *Promotion focus on confidentiality.* The regional or district office would identify geographic areas in which greater attention should be given to confidentiality concerns. In such areas, confidentiality would become the key theme in outreach and promotion efforts. The regional or district office would develop messages that speak to the specific fears and concerns of the local population.

6. *Assistance centers in large multiunit buildings.* District offices would open and staff booths in large multiunit buildings to enumerate residents and assist residents in completing their census questionnaires.

7. *Team enumeration.* More than one enumerator would work in an area because of concerns about safety or because additional enumerators could assist in locating the units or in persuading respondents to cooperate.

An eighth tool, multilingual telephone assistance, was identified but will not be used in 1995 because of insufficient need at the test sites. This method will be developed for use in the 2000 census. The 1995 census test will also include four tools requiring coordination by census headquarters:

1. *Urban update/enumerate.* Headquarters would work with regional offices to identify selected areas for urban update/enumerate methodologies instead of attempting to conduct regular mailout-mailback operations. Enumerators would canvass selected areas to update the address list and to enumerate people they find while canvassing.

2. *Questionnaires in languages other than English and Spanish.* Headquarters would develop questionnaires as well as guides in languages other than English and Spanish. Regional offices would be responsible for using these materials with appropriate populations during nonresponse follow-up and update/enumerate.

3. *Unaddressed questionnaires.* Census questionnaires in various languages would be available in places where the historically undercounted tend to congregate.

4. *Mailout of Spanish-language questionnaires.* Headquarters would mail questionnaires in Spanish to areas with high concentrations of linguistically isolated Spanish-speaking households.

We strongly encourage the Census Bureau to examine these tool-kit methods in the 1995 census test. Some of the above tools have been used in past censuses (e.g., blitz and team enumeration, use of community-based organizations), but their cost-effectiveness is not well documented. The Census Bureau has little or no research experience with most of the proposed tools, and testing in 1995 should therefore provide important imformation.

We note, however, that the application of the tool kit needs further specification. It should not be assumed, for example, that tools could only be used in efforts to improve the initial counts in particular geographic areas. Some tools, especially if they are expensive to implement, might be used most effectively during nonresponse follow-up or integrated coverage measurement. The application of tool-kit methods in different stages of census operations would require coordination. Similarly, some tools may be more appropriate for identifying and including housing units; others may be suited for motivating and reaching individuals.

The planning database has an important role to play in guiding application of the tool kit to ensure that tools are used systematically and only when needed and that their use is recorded so that, when relevant, this information can be taken into account in integrated coverage measurement. Current plans for the 1995 census test call for a tool to be assigned to a given area if that area exceeds predefined threshold values (e.g., mail nonresponse rates) that are set using judgments from experienced field personnel.

The Tool Kit Working Group's report (Bureau of the Census, 1994b) attempts to identify the role that the tools would play as components of a full census design and to suggest the need for their evaluation. But these suggestions are not yet fully developed, and there does not appear to be a formal evaluation plan for all of these methods or for the smaller set included in the 1995 census test. The need for formal evaluation of the components of the tool kit is similar to that for evaluating the effects of different instruments or modes. When multiple data collection strategies are used, particularly in conjunction with nonresponse follow-up and integrated coverage measurement, it is important to be able to estimate the impact of the different strategies.

The first step is more complete definition of the tools themselves. Subsequent evaluation of tool-kit methods should include information on their effectiveness (yield, impact on the differential undercount) and cost. Information on cost will be needed to choose among competing strategies. Although full experimental evaluation of components of the tool kit used in the 1995 census test is probably not possible, it should still be possible to plan comparisons and variation across sites or areas within sites. Posttest evaluation surveys that ask people whether they were aware of outreach and promotion efforts can help in evaluating the effectiveness of such efforts. Information on effectiveness and cost will be needed to inform decisions after 1995.

At present, the planning database includes block-level tabulations of 1990 census content, mail return rates, and information from administrative records. We understand that the Census Bureau intends to add recently acquired crime statistics (compiled at the census tract level) and more current administrative records data to the targeting database for the 1995 census test. The effectiveness of the planning database will depend on its being maintained with up-to-date information. Commercial databases and local administrative record systems may be good sources of block-level supplemental information.

Both the tool kit and the planning database represent substantial development efforts, and developing a formal predictive model for use with the database requires even larger investments. It seems very likely that the development and testing of the tool kit, planning database, and targeting model will continue after the 1995 census test, and planning should take this schedule into account. Experimental evaluation of some components of the tool kit (e.g., blitz enumeration) could be incorporated into census tests after 1995 or carried out in conjunction with special-purpose tests, special censuses, or current Census Bureau surveys.

OUTREACH AND PROMOTION

The outreach and promotion program for the 1990 census was the most intensive to date for a decennial census. For the first time, a multifaceted mass media campaign addressed several traditionally undercounted groups as well as the general public. The community-based Census Awareness and Products Program was enhanced and began operations farther in advance of Census Day than in 1980. Programs were conducted that worked through national civic and religious organizations, schools, Head Start agencies, governmental units, and business organizations.

Based on an analysis of the data collected in the 1990 Outreach and Evaluation Survey, Bates and Whitford (1991) concluded that the Census Bureau's 1990 outreach and promotion program achieved many of its goals. The Advertising

Council's mass media campaign received wide exposure, and it achieved significant media presence around Census Day in the six media markets in which the coverage was monitored. By Census Day, over 90 percent of the population had recently heard or read something about the census, although the campaign was less effective in reaching blacks than whites and Hispanics. Ironically, the differential success of national outreach in raising levels of census awareness may have had the unintended effect of exacerbating problems of differential coverage. This experience underscores the importance of outreach to local communities with hard-to-enumerate populations.

Outreach and publicity may also help the census mail response rate; data from the Outreach and Evaluation Survey indicate that in 1990 the mail return rates of respondents with high awareness of census operations and knowledge of census uses were 15 to 20 percentage points higher than respondents with low awareness and knowledge (Bates and Whitford, 1991). (We cite these results with the standard caution that the question of whether these associations reflect causal relationships cannot be answered without considering potential interaction effects and controlling for other variables in a designed experiment.) Nevertheless, the mail response rate in 1990 was 10 percentage points below that in the 1980 census, and the differential undercount between blacks and others was the highest since the Census Bureau began estimating coverage in 1940 (U.S. General Accounting Office, 1992). Although there are undoubtedly many social factors that contributed to the response rate decline, it is also possible that the Census Bureau's 1990 outreach and promotion campaign did a better job of announcing the census than it did of persuading people to participate. Regardless, it seems clear that an even more intensive—and effective—outreach and promotion program will need to be designed, tested, and successfully implemented in the 2000 census if the Census Bureau is to prevent further erosion of census participation rates that began declining in 1970.

Responsibility for Decennial Census Outreach and Promotion

The Census Bureau does not have a single, permanent office that is responsible for decennial census outreach and promotion. Instead, in the past two censuses, it has opened a temporary Census Promotion Office two years prior to the census and then closed the office after census operations were completed. It appears that the primary function of this office is to coordinate the media campaign with the Advertising Council and to oversee various national outreach programs conducted to promote the upcoming census. (The Census Bureau has a permanent Public Information Office, but it is not directly involved in decennial census promotion.)

In every census since 1950, the Census Bureau has relied on the Advertising Council to design and conduct the media campaign. (Working through advertising agencies that volunteer their time, the Advertising Council regularly conducts mass media advertising campaigns on a pro bono basis for government and nonprofit agencies.) In 1990 the Advertising Council for the first time designed multiple campaigns to target selected minorities (blacks, Hispanics, and Asian and Pacific Islanders) as well as the general public.

The principal national outreach program to undercounted groups is the National Services Program. Conducted by the Data User Services Division, the program is a continuing outreach and data dissemination program aimed at national organizations that represent undercounted minorities. Its goal is to secure the support of the national organizations and their local and regional chapters in efforts to encourage participation by the minority communities they represent. The Census Bureau also conducts a variety of national outreach activities close to Census Day; these include programs that target a variety of organizations, schools, governmental units and agencies, and private-sector corporations.

The principal program for local outreach in 1990 was the Census Awareness and Products Program. Administered by the Census Bureau's Field Division, this program was typically activated at least one year prior to Census Day in local areas and deactivated shortly thereafter. In 1990 there were about 280 staff across the country, working out of the regional field offices.

The Census Bureau's census outreach and promotion program does not include a structured plan for conducting research and development work. The absence of a permanent office responsible for census outreach and promotion militates against sustaining an ongoing research program during the decade between censuses. Also, the Advertising Council does not permit its clients to undertake or commission media research on their own. The Census Bureau does, however, undertake retrospective research to evaluate census outreach and promotion. Examples from the 1990 census include the Outreach Evaluation Survey, the Telephone Survey of Census Participation, the Survey of 1990 Census Participation, and the National Service Program Structured Debriefings.

The Census Bureau's Public Information Office has recently funded some focus groups with young black, Hispanic, and Asian males with the hope of identifying ways to reach these groups and motivate them to participate in the census. The Year 2000 Research and Development staff is also involved in outreach and is considering a joint venture with state and local governments to improve outreach at the local level.

We are concerned that the responsibility for outreach and promotion is split among several different units within the Census Bureau. We believe that the effectiveness and efficiency of the Census Bureau's census outreach and promotion program could be improved if a permanent office were established and staffed with advertising and public relations professionals. This office would be responsible for planning, researching, and developing all outreach and promotion activities and for overseeing the implementation of the decennial census program. It should be a permanent and nonpartisan office to provide continuity between censuses and to monitor an ongoing national and local outreach and promotion program during the decade. Because the Census Bureau already has a permanent Public Information Office, we suggest that the Census Bureau consider expanding the mission of this office to include responsibility for the decennial census outreach and promotion program.

Although the establishment of a permanent decennial census outreach and promotion office would centralize the overall responsibility for outreach and promotion activities, it does not follow that such activities would become more focused on the national rather than the local level. Nor should they, as we argue below; a principal objective of the new central office should be to enhance outreach efforts at the local level. Just as the centralized Field Division is responsible for all data collection operations conducted by the regional offices, so a centralized census outreach and promotion office would design, monitor, and support all field outreach activities conducted through those regional offices.

The one outreach and promotion activity that should not be consolidated under the purview of the new office is evaluation research. To preserve independence, this type of research should continue to be undertaken by other units within the Census Bureau, such as the Center for Survey Methods Research.

Recommendation 3.9: The Census Bureau should assign overall responsibility for decennial census outreach and promotion to a centralized, permanent office. The Census Bureau should consider expanding the mission of the extant Public Information Office to include this charge. Evaluation of outreach and promotion programs should be conducted by an independent unit within the Census Bureau.

National Media Campaign

An important issue confronting the Census Bureau is whether to continue to rely on the Advertising Council to design and implement the national media campaign. As noted above, the Advertising Council's rules prohibit clients from commissioning any media research on their own. It also does not permit clients to supplement the pro bono campaign with any paid advertising. Thus, the Census Bureau is entirely dependent on the Advertising Council's pro bono campaign for its media research and advertising.

Because the Advertising Council depends on volunteer labor, we are concerned that its pro bono campaign may not include the same level of media research that large commercial advertisers have found beneficial. For example, the leading advertising agencies evaluate commercials by using sophisticated technology that continuously measures a focus group's response to a proposed commercial message. However, this type of research is expensive and may not be included within the scope of a pro bono campaign.

We also understand that there is a growing feeling among certain charitable organizations that national public service announcement campaigns are losing their effectiveness. One theory about this change is that U.S. society has become so diverse and complex that people are increasingly narrowing their focus to the community in which they live. As a consequence, there is a movement among pro bono advertisers away from the national campaigns toward increased use of local campaigns.

Certainly, the Census Bureau must continue to rely on public service announcements run on a pro bono basis; it would be prohibitively expensive to launch an equivalent campaign on a strictly fee-for-service basis. However, it could discontinue use of the Advertising Council and instead work directly with local and regional agencies. This approach would allow the Census Bureau to undertake a paid media research program to identify the most effective advertising messages. It would also mean that the national campaign would include a collection of local and regional campaigns that might be more effective in reaching the communities to which they are directed.

Finally, this approach would allow the Census Bureau to supplement pro bono advertising with paid advertising—especially in hard-to-enumerate communities where a pro bono campaign may not provide sufficient or appropriate media exposure (Committee on National Statistics, 1978). We believe that the additional cost involved may be more than offset by the increase in response among the traditionally undercounted groups, with a corresponding reduction in the differential undercount. We note in this regard that Statistics Canada is a strong proponent of paid advertising; it was discontinued in Canada in 1986 as a cost-saving measure, but then promptly reinstated after a decline in participation.

Recommendation 3.10: The Census Bureau should evaluate the costs and benefits of alternatives to the use of the Advertising Council to conduct the 2000 census media campaign. Some alternative options are working directly with local and regional agencies, undertaking paid media research, and supplementing pro bono advertising with paid advertising in hard-to-enumerate localities.

Cooperative Ventures With State and Local Governments

The Census Bureau has undertaken a number of initiatives designed to improve the level of cooperation between its field operations and state and local governments, critical nodes in the Census Bureau's efforts to go local. These efforts span a range of tasks, from outreach and promotion of the decennial census to the use of state or locally maintained administrative records for the purpose of improving coverage (Collins, 1994). Some of these efforts will be put in place during the 1995 census test in order to assess their effectiveness, implemented by "census advisors" who will be placed in local offices in the test communities in order to oversee liaison programs of all kinds. We understand that, in the 1995 census test sites of Oakland, California, and the six parishes in northwestern Louisiana, the census advisors will be district office employees of the Census Bureau. Discussions are ongoing regarding whether the census advisors in the remaining two test sites—Patterson, New Jersey, and New Haven, Connecticut—will be district office staff or local people appointed by the mayor or city council.

With respect to outreach and promotion activities, current plans build on the 1990 experience, during which "complete count committees" formed in various localities to boost the coverage of the decennial census. These committees were responsible for tailoring local press coverage of the census and for maintaining contact with grass-roots organizations and advocacy groups with particular knowledge of hard-to-enumerate populations. For the 1995 census test, these activities will be expanded, formalized, and coordinated by the census advisors. This effort is of great importance, for the more effective the Census Bureau's ties to local organizations involved in service delivery to poor people, migrants, immigrants, and other groups traditionally undercounted, the better the coverage will be. Future census tests may provide an opportunity to assess how much complete count committees and other outreach activities cost and how much they contribute to better coverage.

Census advisors will also be responsible for coordinating local information and personnel resources that can assist in augmenting the Master Address File. Local officials will be sworn in so that they can be given access to Census Bureau address lists and held accountable for maintaining confidentiality.[7] Thereafter, the Census Bureau plans to (a) share census address lists with state and local governments officials, particularly those in city planning departments; (b) solicit block boundary suggestions from local officials familiar with the contours of neighborhoods; (c) hire city employees to work on address list verification; (d) work with knowledgeable local officials on administrative records that are locally generated and maintained that can be used to improve coverage; and (e) develop an effective program for office space procurement, a perennial problem for the census staff. These strategies will, we believe, capitalize on the knowledge base that resides at the local level, improving outreach, promotion, and the quality of address lists and encourage much-needed federal-state-local cooperation.

The Census Bureau plans to enlist the support of local officials to help in the planning of the 1995 census test, particularly where blitz enumeration is concerned. City employees who know the hard-to-count populations in their localities will be able to assist enumeration teams, making it more likely that poor people, immigrants, and internal migrants will be counted the first time. These individuals will be working under the direction of the census advisors during the test and will, in this capacity, become part of the planning apparatus for using the

---

[7] For the 2000 census, legislative changes will be required in order to make it possible to expand this cooperative program nationwide.

tool-kit strategies for hard-to-enumerate groups. Clear guidelines and role definitions may be needed to ensure that the involvement of local officials with enforcement responsibilities is accomplished in a manner that preserves the integrity of the census operation.

In an effort to evaluate the Census Bureau's program of cooperative ventures with state and local governments, a series of debriefings with participants are being planned for the 1995 census test. The debriefings will serve to obtain information from program participants, state and local government officials, and the Census Bureau staff from the regional offices on their reactions to the program and what effects they experienced on timing, operations, and logistics. The Census Bureau will also meet with representatives from localities that elected not to participate in the program to discuss their reasons for not participating as well as review the reasons why some decided to participate only in certain aspects of the program.

Cooperative ventures of this kind are responsive to our general call for a strategy of going local, in the sense that they make use of existing ties and local expertise to encourage cooperation with the census. We believe they should be seen as complementary to programs already in place (particularly the Census Awareness and Products Program), rather than substitutions for them.

Recommendation 3.11: The Census Bureau should evaluate the programs for state and local cooperation that will be overseen by census advisors in the 1995 census test areas in order to collect from these experimental initiatives those programs most likely to (a) reduce the cost of the decennial census (particularly by improving mail response rates) and (b) reduce the differential undercount. Preservation of the Census Awareness and Products Program should, however, be a high priority, not to be superseded by this new initiative for improving state and local cooperation.

4

Sampling and Statistical Estimation

This chapter discusses potential uses of sampling and statistical estimation to address the two main challenges of the 2000 census: reducing differential coverage and controlling operational costs. Why should the Census Bureau consider the use of sampling and estimation? Sampling and subsequent estimation offer two advantages over enumerating or surveying an entire population. The first, more obvious one, is cost savings. Trying to obtain data from everyone in a large population is usually prohibitively expensive. Drawing a sample can dramatically slash resources requirements and often yields adequately precise estimates for the population and major subgroups. Only when estimates are required for fine levels of detail, as in the U.S. census, does it make sense to even consider trying to obtain data from everyone in a large population. The second advantage of sampling is that it enables enhancements in data quality that would be too expensive or intrusive to apply to the entire population. A well-conducted sample survey will usually provide more accurate information than a program that attempts to collect data from an entire population but suffers from high nonresponse or biased responses. Indeed, the Census Bureau has traditionally used a sample survey to evaluate census coverage.

This chapter focuses on two major innovations that the Census Bureau is considering for producing population counts in the 2000 census. The first innovation is sampling for nonresponse follow-up. Instead of trying to enumerate all housing units for which there is no response during mailout-mailback operations, the Census Bureau would follow up only a sample of such housing units (most likely between 10 and 33 percent). Data from housing units sampled for nonresponse follow-up would allow estimation of counts and characteristics of mailback nonrespondents who are not sampled.

The second proposal, called integrated coverage measurement (ICM), is designed to measure and correct the differential undercount. In July 1990, the Census Bureau conducted the Post-Enumeration Survey (PES) in a sample of 165,000 housing units to allow measurement of the coverage achieved by the main census operation. Although the survey identified a net undercount of about 1.6 percent and substantial differential undercount by geography and demographic characteristics, the official 1990 census counts did not use the information obtained as part of the PES. During the 1995 census test, the Census Bureau plans to evaluate a new integrated coverage measurement method, CensusPlus, designed to run concurrently with the main census operations and thereby to facilitate production of official counts by the legal deadlines.

The Census Bureau decided not to use sampling during the initial mailout-mailback phase of the census because of concerns about the legality of that strategy and the adverse impact that it would have on the accuracy of counts (Isaki et al., 1993). We concur with that decision. Both nonresponse follow-up sampling and integrated coverage measurement use sampling to try to obtain more accurate responses than could be achieved in a census. Combined with statistical estimation, these techniques should improve the absolute counts and reduce differentials in census coverage across states, other large political divisions, and major demographic categories. At the same time, initial attempts to enumerate everyone should produce acceptable accuracy for smaller areas like minor civil divisions and census tracts. The likely combination of nonresponse follow-up sampling and integrated coverage measurement clarifies the need for statistical estimation in the 2000 census. Consequently, as Chapter 1 explains, the Census Bureau is planning for a "one-number census" that combines the use of enumeration, assignment, and estimation for production of the census counts.

The next three sections of this chapter discuss sampling for nonresponse follow-up, integrated coverage measurement, and statistical estimation, respectively. Although we discuss them separately, a recurring theme of the chapter is that decisions about each of these topics should be considered in light of the other two. Estimation methods clearly cannot be determined without knowledge about sampling methods. And, for example, ultimate evaluation of a design for integrated coverage measurement must refer to specifications of the plans for nonresponse follow-up sampling and estimation procedures.

NONRESPONSE FOLLOW-UP

Background

The 1990 census was substantially more expensive than the 1980 census, even after accounting for inflation and population growth. The largest single part of the expense was follow-up of housing units that had not responded during the mailout-mailback portion of the census. Estimates of the total cost of nonresponse follow-up operations in the 1990 census range from $490 to $560 million, roughly 20 percent of the $2.6 billion 10-year cycle cost of the census (Bureau of the Census, 1992b; U.S. General Accounting Office, 1992). Each 1 percent of nonresponse to the mailed questionnaire is estimated to have added approximately $17 million to the cost of the census.

Perhaps just as important, nonresponse follow-up (NRFU) took much longer than anticipated in some sites (in particular, New York City), pushing back the schedule for completion of the census. In turn, NRFU operations pushed back the beginning of coverage measurement by the Post-Enumeration Survey. The long delay between Census Day and the beginning of coverage measurement compromised the ability of the PES to operate accurately and was one of several factors making it impossible for the Census Bureau to incorporate the PES results into official counts released by the legal deadlines.

Even without delays in schedule, the latter stages of census operations typically suffer degradation of data quality. Ericksen et al. (1991) report that, for the 1990 census, the rate of erroneous enumeration on mailout-mailback was 3.1 percent. On nonresponse follow-up, the rate was 11.3 percent; on field follow-up, the rate was 19.4 percent.

Much of the problem in 1990 resulted from mailback response rates that were lower than expected. Item nonresponse also contributed to the follow-up work because additional contacts were required to complete missing items. Questionnaire simplification, reminder postcards, replacement questionnaires, and other innovations are expected to improve mailback rates, and the use of telephone interviews may speed NRFU operations. Even so, a 100-percent NRFU operation would certainly be very expensive. Thus, the Census Bureau has focused substantial efforts on ways to reduce the scope of nonresponse follow-up without undue sacrifices in the accuracy of the count or the content. The Census Bureau has studied three major innovations for nonresponse follow-up in the 2000 census: truncating NRFU early, following up only a sample of mailback nonrespondents, and using administrative records to replace or supplement traditional NRFU. In addition, it has considered combinations of these strategies— e.g., a two-stage NRFU consisting of a truncated operation aimed at all mailback nonrespondents, followed by continued nonresponse follow-up for only a sample of households.

The Census Bureau's cost models estimated very large cost savings with either a truncated NRFU or with sampling for NRFU. Estimated cost savings from truncation compared with the 1990 10-year cycle costs—(in 1992 dollars)—ranged from about $127 to $160 million (depending on assumptions) for truncation on June 30 up to $740 to $894 million for truncation on April 21 (no follow-up) (Keller and Van Horn, 1993). For NRFU sampling rates of 50 percent down to 10 percent, the models estimated cost savings compared with the 1990 10-year cycle costs ranging from approximately $300 to $750 million, even after increasing the sample size for ICM measurement (Bureau of the Census, 1993d).

However, those estimates do include some savings that could probably be achieved even with 100 percent NRFU. We have not seen any estimates for cost savings associated with the use of administrative records, presumably because no detailed plans have been proposed for their use in NRFU.

Either of these innovations would also offer timing benefits compared with the 1990 scenario. Either truncation or sampling for NRFU would accelerate the completion of ICM. Because one of the potential problems with the planned ICM method is difficulty with retrospective identification of Census Day residency, moving up the last cases could be an important benefit. Earlier completion of ICM would also make it easier for the Census Bureau to produce final counts in time to meet legal deadlines. However, we note that these potential benefits would be more important for a 1990-style PES than for the currently planned ICM survey, which would run concurrently with the main census operations.

In contrast to these cost and operational advantages, both truncation and sampling have negative implications for the precision of counts and other results, especially for small areas. Counts and attributes of persons in nonsampled, nonresponding housing units would need to be estimated, producing sampling variability roughly proportional to the number of cases being estimated (although the exact relationship would depend on the sample design and estimation method). As results are aggregated to larger geographic areas, the errors diminish in size relative to the population of the area.

The Census Bureau ran simulations with 1990 census data to evaluate the adverse impact on the accuracy of various counts from exclusively using either early truncation of NRFU or sampling for NRFU. Unfortunately, the simulation studies did not produce estimates that allow for direct comparison of the two methods. Even so, the Census Bureau concluded that sampling for NRFU seems the more promising option at this point. Studies of NRFU truncation indicated that, to achieve savings of $300 million (in 1992 dollars), truncation would have had to occur so early in the 1990 census that the residual nonresponse rate would have been 11 percent of all housing units. More troubling, the nonresponse cases would have been spread very nonuniformly across district offices and demographic groups. As a result, truncation would have greatly increased the differential undercount in the census enumeration, placing further burden on integrated coverage measurement.

Plans for the 1995 Census Test

On the basis of these conclusions, the Census Bureau decided to focus on evaluating sampling for NRFU in the 1995 census test. Households that do not respond to the mail questionnaire by 6 weeks after the initial mailout (14 days after mailing of a replacement questionnaire) will be considered mailback non-respondents, and one-third of these households will be sampled for NRFU. Current plans call for the collection of only short-form data during NRFU. No attempt will be made to obtain information from the other two-thirds of mailback nonresponding households. An attempt will be made to identify vacant housing units before selection of the nonresponse sample. Interviewers will visit units for which a postmaster returned the prenotice to the first mailing. Confirmed vacancies will not be included in the NRFU sample. A major purpose of testing sampling for NRFU in the 1995 census test is to learn more about the relative merits of sampling individual housing units (a unit sample) versus whole blocks (a block sample); in the test, the NRFU sample will be split evenly between the two types of samples. (Census Bureau documents refer to the former as a case sample design, but we prefer to describe it as a unit sample design.) In a random sample of one-half of the blocks not involved in ICM, the Census Bureau will sample 33 percent (one-third) of nonresponding housing units. In the other non-ICM blocks, block sampling will be used. That is, all mailback nonrespondents will be followed up in one-third of the block-sample blocks, and no NRFU activities will be conducted in the remainder of the block-sample blocks. Complete nonresponse follow-up will be conducted in all ICM blocks.

Decisions for the 2000 Census

The Census Bureau faces several important decisions in connection with sampling for NRFU in the 2000 census.

- Should sampling for nonresponse follow-up be used at all?
- Is a unit or a block sample preferable?
- What proportion of units or blocks should be sampled?
- Should the sampling probability be uniform across blocks (for a unit sample) or across areas (for a block sample)?
- How should the Census Bureau treat mail returns received after the beginning of NRFU?
- Should any nonresponse follow-up operations be conducted for all households before (or concurrent) with the sampling for nonresponse follow-up?

We discuss these questions in the sections that follow.

Should Sampling for Nonresponse Follow-up be Used?

Whether to use sampling for NRFU in the 2000 census is mainly a policy decision about whether the expected cost savings from the use of sampling outweigh the likely decreases in the accuracy of counts and other data, particularly for small areas. The 1995 census test will provide valuable data to inform that decision: more current inputs to the NRFU components of the Census Bureau's cost model and data on the relationship between NRFU and ICM. In particular, it will be important to identify all fixed components of the cost of NRFU sampling in order to obtain accurate estimates of the cost savings during the 2000 census. However, the most complete information about the effects of sampling for NRFU on the accuracy of the census would be gained from additional simulations with 1990 data, especially to the extent that these effects vary across geographic areas.

Ultimately, resolving whether to sample for nonresponse follow-up is likely to involve answering the question: How accurate does the 2000 census need to be for small areas? Although that question is more central to the charge of the Panel on Census Requirements in the Year 2000 and Beyond, we offer a pair of comments. First, counts and other tabulations are needed at the block level primarily to allow flexibility for redistricting and for aggregating results to various political jurisdictions and other territories. Thus, the success of the 2000 census should be measured by the accuracy of these aggregate statistics rather than by the accuracy of block-level data. Even so, we note that there will be no single answer to the question of accuracy because sampling for NRFU would affect various levels of aggregation in different ways.

Second, sampling variability is not the only source of error in census results. Incomplete counts and erroneous enumerations occur during both the mailback stage and the NRFU operation (even with 100 percent follow-up). Although sampling for NRFU would certainly contribute most to the error in block- and tract-level data, sampling error may be small compared with systematic error at larger levels of aggregation. Systematic errors have contributed most to the differential undercount in past censuses. If sampling for NRFU frees resources for taking steps to reduce other sources of error in the final results, it may produce a more accurate census by some measures.

Another concern associated with the use of NRFU sampling is that publicity about it may reduce the mailback response rate. If NRFU sampling is used in the 2000 census, that fact would certainly become public knowledge, which might dilute any positive effect that the mandatory nature of the census has on the mailback response rate. It is also conceivable that Census Bureau staff might be less committed to their enumeration efforts in the belief that sampling will take care of nonresponse. Unfortunately, there is no way to learn from census tests whether concerns about such reactions are warranted.

Whether sampling for nonresponse follow-up is used in the 2000 census will also depend on obtaining adequate answers to the other questions posed above.

Is a Unit or Block Sample Preferable?

The choice between a unit sample and a block sample for NRFU involves mainly a trade-off between the greater statistical efficiency of a unit sample and the operational and cost advantages of a block sample. An additional consideration is that a block sample would be easier to combine with the planned version of ICM. The 1995 census test will provide much of the information needed to compare the relative advantages of the two options.

Sampling for NRFU necessitates estimating the attributes of nonsampled (and nonresponding) housing units in a block from the information obtained (during mailback or NRFU sampling) about responding units in that block and in blocks judged similar in terms of geography and demographic characteristics. There is reason to expect that a unit sample would generally produce more accurate estimates than a block sample of the same size, because there is probably some within-block correlation in household size and other attributes of mailback nonresponse housing units, even within carefully selected strata.

Suppose, for illustrative purposes only, that information from sampled housing units in a 100-block area (roughly 1,000 nonresponding housing units) is used in estimating the characteristics of nonsampled mailback nonrespondents in the same blocks. To the extent that there is within-block correlation in the 100 blocks, data on a sample of nonrespondents spread evenly among the 100 blocks would be more valuable—by a ratio known as the design effect—than data from the same number of housing units concentrated in a smaller number of blocks. A unit sample would also provide the opportunity to use information from sampled mailback nonrespondents in the same block to improve the estimates for nonsampled housing units in that block.

Certainly, heterogeneity among blocks can be expected for such characteristics as race and ethnicity. However, the critical quantities to estimate may be differences in mailback response rates among groups cross-classified by race, ethnicity, and age; such differences may be relatively homogeneous among blocks. Initial Census Bureau simulations with 1990 census data have found advantages to both unit and block sampling under various circumstances (Fuller et al., 1994), but further investigation is needed to separate the possible effects of the estimation procedures from those of the design. Also, these simulations have been limited to a few district offices. More comprehensive simulations with more fully developed estimators are needed to precisely determine the size of the unit sample advantage.

Another potential advantage of unit sampling is that it would spread imprecision due to sampling and estimation among all blocks, thereby reducing the maximum amount of block-level error. However, because block sampling would eliminate the need for estimation in sampled blocks, the two methods would not differ in the total number of housing units where estimation is needed. Consequently, the relative accuracy of aggregate estimates based on unit sampling would not necessarily increase beyond the amount attributable to within-block correlation.

In contrast, block sampling might offer certain operational advantages. Enumerators would need to spend less time traveling between blocks. They might also be able to use their time in each block more effectively. For example, while visiting a complete sample of mailback nonrespondents in a block, enumerators might frequently observe occupants entering or leaving other units on the NRFU list. With a unit sample instead, enumerators might tend to finish and proceed to the next block too quickly for such contacts to occur. On the basis of very preliminary assumptions, the Census Bureau has estimated that, compared with a unit sample of the same size, a block sample would save from $14 million (for a 10 percent sample) to $42 million (for a 50 percent sample) more than the corresponding amounts saved by the unit sample. Therefore, it is not obvious in advance whether the unit sample or the block sample is more efficient in terms of accuracy for equal costs. Operational data from the 1995 census test should allow the Census Bureau to estimate the relative cost advantage more accurately.

Block sampling would fit better with any likely method of ICM, because 100 percent NRFU would be required in the ICM blocks (and, perhaps, in surrounding blocks). Complete NRFU is needed so that the block total from the ICM operation can be validly compared with the total from preceding census operations. In effect, ICM blocks would also be NRFU block-sample blocks. Thus, even if unit sampling is the primary strategy for NRFU, it may need to be mixed with some block sampling for ICM purposes.

A related consideration is whether the choice of sampling design affects coverage in NRFU housing units. For example, with the more concentrated effort involved in following up a block sample, enumerators might be more likely to discover housing units that had been omitted from the frame (e.g., garage apartments). And if they do, it will be easier to use the results, because such housing units will automatically be part of a block sample. Enumerators may also be able to collect better proxy information for difficult-to-complete cases under block sampling.

The Census Bureau plans to perform statistical tests for whether the average household size differs systematically between unit and block sampling in the 1995 census test (Bureau of the Census, 1994c). However, the size and design of the planned test are such that it could easily miss a coverage difference of 0.05 person per housing unit (about 2 percent of people in sampled units) between the block-sampling and unit-sampling design; a difference of this magnitude would be important to the decision on which sampling plan to use. If coverage differs under block sampling and unit sampling, then the viability of unit sampling for NRFU operations would be compromised, because ICM would measure coverage in block-sample NRFU and there would not be an adequate corresponding measure for unit-sample NRFU. Consequently, the Census Bureau should investigate other ways to compare the validity of the two methods, such as comparing the numbers of added housing units.

What Proportion of Units or Blocks Should be Sampled?

The Census Bureau appears to be considering sampling proportions in the range of 10 to 33 percent. Like the question of whether to sample for nonresponse follow-up at all, the choice of sampling proportion rests mainly on a trade-off between cost savings and accuracy of small-area data. Updated estimates of the cost savings available from various sampling proportions will be one critical input to the decision. The other critical input will be detailed simulation studies of the effect of the sampling proportion on the accuracy of various estimates. This decision should be made jointly with the decision about how large a sample to use for ICM (assuming that element is included). Thus, simulations need to account for the trade-offs between these two procedures.

Should Sampling Proportions be Uniform?

The Census Bureau will need to decide whether to sample all units or blocks with equal probability. Factors that might influence the sampling probability include the mailback response rate in the block, the size of the estimation post-stratum of the block, and the cost of sending an enumerator to the block (or housing unit).

How Should Late Mail Returns be Treated?

Inevitably, mail returns will continue to trickle in after selection of the NRFU sample. Because these returns will not come from a random sample of all housing units that failed to respond prior to sampling, use of data from these returns could bias estimates. However, ignoring the results might add unnecessary variance and be a public relations problem. Research is needed about the best use of such data from either sampled or nonsampled housing units. (In a later section, we discuss a similar issue and possible solution in the context of ICM.) The 1995 census test will provide information about the likely frequency of late mail returns for various cutoff dates. That information may suggest moving the date for beginning NRFU.

Operations to Supplement Sampling for Nonresponse Follow-up

In the panel's interim report, we recommended that the Census Bureau consider a two-stage strategy that combines a truncated NRFU followed by sampling first-stage nonrespondents. Although the Census Bureau chose not to directly try out a two-stage strategy in the 1995 census test, data collected as part of the test could provide valuable information about this option. If the response rate can be increased substantially during a brief effort directed at 100 percent of mailback nonrespondents, this strategy might reduce the magnitude of estimation required while retaining large cost savings. Although the 1990 census results are discouraging on this score, the computer-assisted telephone interview (CATI) system offers some hope for yielding a large number of responses in a cost-effective manner.

We also recommended that the Census Bureau investigate the value of administrative records as background information to make possible more accurate estimation of people in blocks not sampled for nonresponse follow-up. The idea (which could be applied equally well to a unit sample) is to use administrative records information to help estimate the count and characteristics of people in housing units about which there is no other direct information. The Census Bureau would neither accept the administrative records data at face value (too unreliable) nor require direct verification (too expensive). Instead, the same administrative records data would be compiled for housing units in the NRFU sample. The combination of administrative records that best predicted counts and characteristics in the NRFU sample would be used to estimate those same quantities in nonsampled households. Evaluating estimators on the ability to predict in sampled housing units would serve as an aggregate verification process for any administrative record. If some combination of administrative records is fairly accurate, then using such records in the estimation could substantially improve the accuracy of small-area estimates at relatively little increase in costs. Because administrative records data will be collected and processed independently from NRFU operations, the Census Bureau can evaluate the ability of these records to improve estimates for nonsampled housing units.

Recommendation 4.1: Sampling for nonresponse follow-up could produce major cost savings in 2000. The Census Bureau should test nonresponse follow-up sampling in 1995 and collect data that allows evaluation of (1) follow-up of all nonrespondents during a truncated period of time, combined with the use of sampling during a subsequent period of follow-up of the remaining nonrespondents, and (2) the use of administrative records to improve estimates for nonsampled housing units.

INTEGRATED COVERAGE MEASUREMENT

In addition to the use of sampling and estimation for nonresponse follow-up as described above, current census design plans call for a separate data collection effort in a smaller sample of blocks to measure the coverage of all census operations that precede it. The preceding census operations include address list development, mailout-mailback of census questionnaires, special enumeration methods, and nonresponse follow-up. In a one-number census, the coverage measurement survey and the estimation and modeling associated with it are conceived as an integral component of census-taking, not as a separate postcensal evaluation activity. Hence, this phase of census-taking is called integrated coverage measurement. In this section we focus on the ICM data collection methodology; we discuss coverage measurement methods used in the past, the data collection procedures planned for the 1995 census test, our concerns about those methods, and suggestions for evaluation. We turn our attention to the associated estimation in a later section.

Previous Coverage Evaluation Programs

The Census Bureau has evaluated coverage of census enumerations since 1950 (Coale, 1955; Himes and Clogg, 1992). Two methods of coverage evaluation have been used: demographic analysis (DA) and dual-system estimation (DSE).

Demographic analysis combines data from previous censuses, vital statistics on births and deaths, and other administrative records, such as Medicare data, to obtain national population estimates by age, race or ethnicity, and sex. DA relies on what is called the demographic accounting equation:

population = previous population + births − deaths + inmigrants − outmigrants.

DA has been useful in determining broad patterns of census coverage over time. Because of the lack of detailed information on internal migration and other state-level components of this accounting method, however, DA is regarded as reliable only for national-level estimates of population by demographic group and cannot provide estimates for subnational areas such as states. Uses and extensions of DA are discussed further in a subsequent section.

Dual-system estimation as used in recent censuses is based on data collected for a stratified sample of households in a coverage measurement survey. (DSE more broadly construed has taken many forms in problems of human and animal population estimation—see e.g., Marks et al., 1974; Seber, 1982; Chandrasekhar and Deming, 1949). In short, people "caught" in the survey are matched against the census enumeration in order to estimate the fraction of the population that was included in the census. Similarly, a sample of people enumerated in the census is followed up to determine whether these people should in fact have been included or whether they were erroneously enumerated. The DSE method allows estimation of census coverage—undercount or overcount—by combinations of demographic group, geographic area, and other variables available on the census form (such as owner/renter status); the degree of stratification is limited only by the sample size.

The coverage measurement survey may be conducted as a postenumeration survey, following the census and temporally and operationally separated from it, as in the 1990 census, but this is only one of several possible alternatives. In 1980, two panels of the Current Population Survey were used as the coverage measurement survey. Pre-enumeration surveys have also been proposed.

The 1980 Post-Enumeration Program was designed purely as an evaluation of the 1980 census enumeration. The possibility of using the 1980 coverage estimates for adjustment was proposed, debated, and litigated (Ericksen and Kadane, 1985; Freedman and Navidi, 1986, 1992). The 1990 Post-Enumeration Survey (PES) was designed not only to measure coverage of the census enumeration, but also to allow adjustment of the 1990 census counts if it was judged that PES data could be used to improve their accuracy. Eventually, however, a decision was made by the Secretary of Commerce not to carry out the adjustment (U.S. Department of Commerce, 1991; Fienberg, 1992; Bryant, 1993; Choldin, 1994).

All previous coverage evaluation programs (both DSE and DA) have demonstrated the existence of an overall undercount. These programs have also found that there is a differential undercount; i.e., certain groups, such as black males, and certain areas, such as inner cities, are systematically undercounted relative to other groups and areas in conventional census enumerations. Despite improved overall census coverage, the black-white coverage differentials have remained remarkably constant at about 4 percent since the 1950 census, when evaluation programs of this kind began.

The Census Bureau's research program since 1990 has studied methods that might lead to higher response rates to the census mail questionnaire. The available evidence indicates that mail response rates can be increased with the use of reminder cards, precensus notices, and user-friendly census forms, but there is no evidence that these techniques will reduce differential response rates. Other programs that target special, hard-to-enumerate subpopulations might reduce differential coverage to some extent, but it is unlikely that these innovations will close the gap completely, at least at acceptable costs. Rather, the effect of these programs may be primarily to prevent the coverage gap from widening and to maintain public confidence in the face of increasingly difficult census-taking conditions. (See Citro and Cohen, 1985:Ch. 5, for similar predictions concerning the 1990 census, which were borne out by the 1990 experience; see U.S. General Accounting Office, 1992, for similar evaluations or predictions pertaining to future censuses.) Therefore, the need for coverage measurement in 2000 promises to be at least as great as in previous censuses.

Current plans for the 2000 census are predicated on the use of integrated coverage measurement as an essential part of census-taking and not just as an evaluation of other census operations, although ICM would also produce valuable evaluative data. ICM is therefore not regarded as a method of producing a second set of population estimates that competes with population estimates obtained without the use of ICM. Instead, ICM would integrate coverage measurement—which includes the use of samples, statistical estimation based on these samples, and statistical modeling—with the other census-taking operations. This new use of ICM as an essential component of census-taking defines the one-number census concept referred to throughout this report.

In our judgment, the one-number census concept utilizing ICM in this fashion has several advantages. First, ICM can be used to remove or at least decrease differential coverage by estimating the magnitude of such differentials, making possible the use of estimators designed to correct for the resulting biases. Second, the design of all aspects of the census can be optimized using the knowledge that ICM is part of the design. Third, decisions on methodology for ICM data collection and estimation would be governed by statistical and scientific criteria such as bias, mean squared error, and risk with respect to various loss functions (see later section on statistical estimation). Therefore, the proper use of ICM would minimize political concerns about which group is positively or negatively affected by the estimation. Finally, it should be possible to garner wide support for a one-number census based in part on ICM given the overriding importance of reducing census cost and reducing differential undercount.

> **Recommendation 4.2: Differential undercount cannot be reduced to acceptable levels at acceptable costs without the use of integrated coverage measurement and the statistical methods associated with it. We endorse the use of integrated coverage measurement as an essential part of census-taking in the 2000 census.**

Major Criteria for Selection of an ICM Method

An ICM method should be chosen with the following set of criteria in mind.

1. *The method must control bias.* That is, the method must produce estimates that remove or greatly reduce coverage differentials by demographic group, by relevant socioeconomic factors, and by pertinent levels of geography. No method can control bias at all levels of geography without using very large samples, however, so the bias to be removed or reduced must be defined in terms of pertinent levels of detail, considering such geographic areas as major political jurisdictions.

2. *The method must give precise estimates of population for various pertinent levels of geography.* Sample size is the most important factor determining precision (or variance), and sample design is another important factor.

These first two criteria cannot be considered in isolation for several reasons. First, neither the bias nor the variance of an ICM method can be judged without reference to the estimation methods, including the use of models for combining information from "similar" blocks. Second, bias and variance reduction often conflict, making it necessary to strike a balance between these first two criteria (see also discussion in the statistical estimation section). Mean squared error provides a credible measure that balances the two objectives; it will be important to be able to estimate such measures of accuracy. Third, these criteria are not intended to suggest that an ICM method must improve the counts simultaneously for every area at a particular level of geography. A method should be judged by how well it improves overall accuracy for areas of a given size, because any kind of estimation is almost sure to make counts less accurate in a small fraction of areas.

3. *The method must be operationally feasible.* How well an ICM method could theoretically meet criteria 1 and 2 is irrelevant if operational or cost problems mean that it will not be conducted as designed. Operations such as computer matching and elimination of duplicate records, intensive telephone or personal interviewing, utilization of administrative records and other address lists, computer and clerical processing and checking of information, preparation of estimates, and so on, must be feasible given cost constraints.

4. *The method must produce estimates by legal deadlines.* Under current law, population totals for states are due by December 31 of the census year. Detailed files with counts for blocks by age, race, and Hispanic origin must be available by March 31 of the following year for use in legislative redistricting. The ICM method must be operationally feasible within these constraints. (In Chapter 2, however, we argue that a superior method should not be disqualified by this criterion alone.)

5. *Finally, it must be possible to demonstrate that the method can meet the above criteria when implemented on a large scale.* In practice, this means that the ICM method chosen must be thoroughly evaluated prior to going into the field in 2000.

Alternative Methods for Integrated Coverage Measurement

Since 1990 three basic designs for integrated coverage measurement have received serious attention: (1) a modified PES modeled after the 1990 methodology but taking account of experience gained in 1990 and subsequent analyses; (2) a new method called CensusPlus; and (3) another new method called SuperCensus. All three methods estimate census coverage using information collected by a coverage measurement survey conducted in a sample of blocks.

The 1990 PES consisted of two surveys—one to measure census omissions and one to measure erroneous enumerations—conducted in identical samples of 5,000 block clusters. Methods were developed for adjusting census data for all subnational geographic units and for demographic groups. The 1990 PES has been extensively documented (Hogan, 1992, 1993; Mulry and Spencer, 1991, 1993; Belin et al., 1993).

The DSE methodology used in 1990 is valid under the statistical assumption of independence between capture in the census enumeration and capture in the PES samples within each poststratum. Great efforts were taken to make the 1990 PES *operationally* independent of other census operations. Much of the statistical controversy over the use of DSE in 1990 focused on the accuracy of the assumption of independence and on the effect of lack of independence on the validity of the DSE (e.g., Freedman et al., 1993, 1994; Freedman and Wachter, 1994).

The assumptions and estimation methods associated with the PES operation have been subjected to much scrutiny. It is important to note that, in 1990, coverage evaluation using PES data and the DSE was studied more than any other coverage evaluation method applied to any other census in the world. The extensive program of research evaluating the 1990 PES methodology, including criticisms of that methodology, has played an important role in developing plans for integrated coverage measurement for the 2000 census. We believe that, with modifications, DSE based on a PES could be used in the 2000 census, satisfying the above criteria, if other methods are judged to be unreliable or infeasible. We also believe that the controversies that occurred in the 1990 PES program could be resolved if a larger sample were used and if past experience and criticisms of the 1990 PES were taken into account.

CensusPlus uses intensive enumeration methods and highly trained interviewers with the objective of obtaining a complete enumeration of the true population in a sample of blocks. As with the PES, regular census operations, including the mailout of census forms and NRFU, also take place in the blocks sampled for ICM.

CensusPlus is properly understood as an ICM field operation, and at least two estimation strategies could be applied to the data collected during CensusPlus. A ratio estimator (described below) is perhaps most natural, although a variant of dual-system estimation could also be used. Under ratio estimation, capture in the ICM blocks chosen for intensive enumeration is assumed to occur with probability one. That is, the ratio estimation methodology assumes that a complete enumeration can be obtained for the blocks included in the ICM sample. In subsequent sections, we consider possible problems and discuss evaluations related to this assumption.

The assumption of complete coverage replaces the independence assumption implicit in use of the DSE after a PES, although it would still be important that the CensusPlus operations be conducted in a way that does not make the sample blocks atypical with respect to the conduct of primary census operations. The ICM enumeration involves adding people found in ICM who were omitted from the census and deleting people who were included in the census but found by ICM to have been erroneously enumerated. The coverage rate for each estimation stratum may then be estimated as the ratio of the count obtained by pre-ICM operations in sample blocks to the corresponding count after completion of ICM.

The logic of the method can be illustrated as follows. We compare the CensusPlus count for a given stratum (e.g., black males ages 20-34 in urban areas in the Northeast who rent instead of own their home) in the ICM sample blocks with the count obtained from the census enumeration, assignment, and NRFU in those blocks. The ratio of these numbers is a coverage factor that can be applied to counts from non-ICM blocks. CensusPlus will be tested in the 1995 census test. Details of the implementation of CensusPlus are discussed below, and estimation methods are considered in a later section.

SuperCensus, like CensusPlus, would involve selecting a sample of blocks or block clusters and striving for a complete enumeration of all housing units and persons in those blocks. In the SuperCensus method, however, implementation of the special enumeration methods would begin on or before Census Day; no regular census-taking would be done in those blocks and no counts would be obtained there for non-ICM census methods. Coverage factors would therefore have to be based on a count that is available before the census—specifically, the number of housing units. The number of people per housing unit in SuperCensus sample blocks would be calculated, and this estimate would be applied to housing unit counts for other blocks in the corresponding area to estimate population in the nonsampled blocks.

Little evaluation of other census operations would be possible because census mailout would not take place in the SuperCensus sample blocks. For this reason and because of the possibility that ratios of people to housing units would be too variable to permit accurate estimates, the panel expressed reservations in its interim report about use of the SuperCensus method. The Census Bureau has subsequently rejected SuperCensus as a method for ICM in either the 1995 census test or the 2000 census.

CensusPlus in the 1995 Census Test

The Census Bureau has decided to test a version of the CensusPlus method in the 1995 census test. The proposed implementation involves conducting CensusPlus operations concurrently with regular census operations in the ICM sample block in order to facilitate identification of residence on Census Day and to improve the ability to produce final census results by legal reporting deadlines. The procedure has also been designed to distinguish housing unit coverage errors in the Master Address File (MAF) from coverage errors that occur during census enumeration of housing units.

The PES will not be tested in 1995 because much more is known about it than about CensusPlus in terms of implementation, operational feasibility, the empirical validity of the assumptions on which it is based, the degree to which the assumptions can be checked, whether bias and precision can be controlled at acceptable levels of cost, and whether it can produce results within time constraints. Current plans for implementing the CensusPlus ICM method in the 1995 census test are described briefly here; the proposed implementation for the 2000 census would be similar except in the extent of the operations.

First, the sample of ICM blocks or block clusters will be selected. Current plans call for a sample of 100 to 200 ICM sample blocks at each of the four 1995 census test sites.

Early in the year, prior to the census mailout, interviewers will canvass the ICM sample blocks to construct an independent listing of housing units (and addresses). This list will then be matched to the MAF, the frame for enumeration and NRFU in non-ICM census operations, generating two lists: (1) housing units that were found by the ICM canvass but missed in the MAF and (2) housing units that were included in the MAF. The two lists of units will be followed up in the housing unit coverage and within-housing-unit coverage portions of ICM, respectively.

The housing unit coverage operation is designed to check the completeness of the MAF and estimate: (1) the number of housing units that were omitted from the MAF (and therefore from the frame for mailout and NRFU) and (2) the number of people omitted because they were in these housing units. ICM interviewers will go into the field immediately after Census Day to check on the accuracy of the listing of these units in the ICM canvass and to enumerate the households living there or determine that the units are vacant. Housing units that appear in the MAF but not in the independent listing will also be flagged for attention as part of this operation.

Housing units in the within-housing-unit sample will be followed up as their census returns come in, whether by mailback, by other enumeration methods, or by NRFU interviews. (In order to avoid confusion over which households were included in the NRFU sample, NRFU will be carried out on a 100 percent basis in these blocks regardless of whether a block or unit sample is used in other blocks.)

Computer-assisted telephone interviews will be attempted first, and computer-assisted personal interviews will be used to follow up households not contacted by telephone. Each responding household will be given a two-part reinterview by an ICM interviewer. First, the interviewer will collect information similar to that on the census form (but possibly including more detailed and probing questions) to construct a roster of persons living in that household. The computer will then reveal to the interviewer the roster from the original census response, showing discrepancies from the reinterview. In the reconciliation phase of the reinterview, the interviewer will attempt to resolve these discrepancies in order to come up with an accurate roster, using information from both the original response and the reinterview. The use of the computer makes it possible to conduct both an independent reinterview and the reconciliation in the same telephone call or personal visit.

Some housing units will be resolved as vacant by NRFU; these will be rechecked by ICM interviewers in order to verify that the units are in fact vacant or, when a unit is not vacant, to conduct an interview in order to obtain information on the household living there. Conversely, ICM interviewers may determine that some households enumerated by mailback or NRFU were erroneously enumerated and should be removed from the roster.

The end product of these operations is a corrected or resolved roster of both housing units and people in the ICM sample blocks, from which resolved counts of units and of people by age, sex, race, and other variables would be calculated.

It should be clear from the above description that there are many general similarities between the CensusPlus methodology as outlined above and the PES.

The specifics of the implementation of CensusPlus, however, include several important differences from the PES as conducted in 1990:

1. ICM operations would be conducted simultaneously with other census operations, although any given housing unit should not be contacted for ICM until after other census operations for that unit have been completed. This would permit ICM to begin much earlier than the PES did (as early as Census Day), spreading out the workload and moving up the anticipated completion date for ICM. This is one of the most important potential benefits of the CensusPlus design. The temporal interpenetration of mailout-mailback, NRFU, and ICM is illustrated in Table 4.1. Control of these simultaneous operations is predicated on improved management capabilities and, in particular, on very good control of addresses using the TIGER geographical information system (see Chapter 2) in order to separate distinct operations that may be going on at the same time in adjacent housing units.

2. The ICM interview will not be completely independent of other census information, because names from the previous response will be available for matching and reconciliation on the spot, eliminating in most cases the need for an additional contact to resolve discrepancies as in the 1990 PES. The independence of the first phase of the reinterview, however, provides a useful check on the accuracy of both the reinterview and the original response. The same comment applies to the independence of the ICM housing unit listing relative to the MAF.

3. The ICM interview will attempt to establish an accurate roster for the household as of Census Day. The 1990 PES was defined to include people at the sample address at the time of the PES; this roster could be different from the Census Day roster because households moved in the intervening months. CensusPlus must be able to follow up people who move out of the ICM sample blocks after Census Day; this may be facilitated by the relatively short interval between Census Day and the time of the CensusPlus interview.

4. The 1995 CensusPlus (and any ICM methodology used in 2000) may benefit from research that has been conducted on enumeration methods and administrative records since the last census. In hard-to-enumerate areas, special methods from the tool kit (see Chapter 3), especially those judged to be effective but too expensive to use except in a sample of blocks, can be employed in order to improve the coverage of the ICM effort. Information from other sources, such as administrative lists, could also be matched with the census file and made available for the reconciliation phase.

Issues for Evaluation of CensusPlus Methodology

The CensusPlus procedures proposed for the 1995 census test have some very attractive new features. We congratulate the Census Bureau for developing this new design, which represents a many-sided rethinking of coverage measure-

TABLE 4.1 Interpenetration of Primary Response, Nonresponse Follow-up, and Integrated Coverage Measurement Operations

Date	Primary Response (mailout-mailback) Operations	NRFU Operations	ICM Operations—Housing Unit Coverage	ICM Operations—Within-Housing-Unit Coverage
Jan-Feb			Housing unit canvass, followed by list preparation and matching to the MAF	
March 1	Census mailout; unaddressed questionnaires are distributed			
Early March	Begin follow-up of postmaster returns (check that these are actually vacant); begin to receive responses by telephone call-in		Begin field reconciliation of independent listing addresses not matched to MAF; begin interviews for unmatched housing units that are valid addresses	
Mid-March	Begin to receive and process mailback returns, including unaddressed questionnaires			Begin ICM interviews for mailback returns (on flow basis)
Late March	Mail reminder card, followed by replacement questionnaire			
Early April		Begin NRFU by telephone and personal interviews		Begin ICM interviews for NRFU responses (on flow basis)
Late May	Close out mail response	Close out NRFU interviewing		
Late June			Close out ICM interviews for housing unit discrepancies	Close out ICM interviews for within-housing-unit coverage check
July			Final matching of ICM and census returns; duplicate and surrounding block search; late field work to resolve ambiguities	

Note: Dates are illustrative and somewhat conjectural; they may not correspond to deadlines that will actually be used in the 1995 census test or 2000 census. Many important operations have been omitted for simplicity of presentation; in particular, mailout-mailback (rather than update/leave) primary response is assumed. NRFU=Nonresponse Follow-up; ICM=Integrated Coverage Measurement; MAF=Master Address File.

ment methodology. At the same time, however, we believe that two critical issues about CensusPlus methodology must be evaluated in 1995 before it can be adopted for use in 2000:

1. Can CensusPlus be conducted without affecting the results of the regular enumeration in the CensusPlus sample blocks?
2. Can CensusPlus attain near-perfect coverage in the sample blocks?

The answers to these questions will determine the accuracy of the inputs from CensusPlus to the estimation phase of ICM (in particular, to calculation of the numerators and denominators of estimated coverage rates) and consequently the validity of final population estimates.

Some of the particular issues to be addressed by evaluations have been identified by Singh (1993) and Thompson (1993) and have been discussed by Census Bureau staff and panel members. Evaluations of these issues in the 1995 census test have been given high priority by the Census Bureau. These evaluations will also guide the formulation of the final plans for 2000; they may lead to incremental modifications (such as changing the scheduling of particular operations) or major revisions.

We focus attention first on the two key issues that must be addressed by these evaluations. These are of particular importance because they are fundamental to validation of the assumptions that underlie the CensusPlus methodology.

Can CensusPlus be conducted without affecting the results of the regular enumeration in the CensusPlus sample blocks? The census coverage rates measured in the ICM sample blocks can be regarded as valid estimates of the coverage rates in other blocks only if the conduct of the census is essentially indistinguishable in the sample and nonsample blocks. As noted above and in Table 4.1, the ICM operations will overlap in time with other operations. It is therefore possible that the conduct of the ICM operations will have some direct effect on the pre-ICM census counts obtained in the sample blocks, causing them to be systematically either larger or smaller than what they would have been if ICM had not occurred there. This effect is referred to as *contamination* of the census by ICM. Contamination can lead to bias in CensusPlus estimates, because, if there is contamination, coverage rates measured in sample blocks will differ systematically from coverage rates in other blocks. A number of potential forms of contamination have been identified.

• The precensus canvass for housing units conducted in ICM blocks may affect awareness of the census and consequently response to the regular census in those blocks—particularly if census personnel knock on doors to verify the existence of housing units.
• The responses of residents in sample blocks may be affected by their awareness of the presence of ICM interviewers, particularly if an ICM inter-

viewer accidentally approaches a household that has not yet made its mailback or NRFU response.

• It may be difficult to determine that a household that has not responded to the census at a particular time will probably never respond and can therefore be approached for an ICM interview; if the treatment of the cutoff date for response is different in ICM blocks than in other blocks, then ICM contaminates the census.

• NRFU interviewers may become aware of the presence of ICM interviewers and make special efforts in ICM sample blocks to obtain more complete follow-up results than in other blocks.

• We expect that some housing units missed by the MAF in non-ICM blocks will still get counted (census adds) due to fortuitous contacts by census interviewers or respondent-initiated responses (possible through unaddressed questionnaires). Early ICM interviews could forestall some of these responses in ICM blocks.

These issues are particular salient if more intrusive and public ICM tool-kit methodologies such as team or blitz enumeration are employed.

Several evaluations may be directed at this issue in 1995. The Census Bureau should compare the results from the enumerative part of the census in ICM blocks with those from non-ICM blocks. These comparisons should be disaggregated to focus attention on effects on distinct aspects of primary data collection, such as census adds or late mail returns, that are particularly likely to be affected by ICM. Due to the small ICM sample size in the 1995 census test and the lack of direct measures of some of the effects, it will be hard to conclude that there are no significant biases due to contamination on the basis of purely quantitative comparisons. Further evaluations could look for direct evidence of contamination by debriefing of enumerators and ICM interviewers and re-interview of respondents. If these evaluations identify problems with contamination, they may be addressed through changes in the timing of ICM operations— or other operational changes—to keep them more strictly separated from enumerations.

Can CensusPlus attain near-perfect coverage in the sample blocks? The proposed ratio estimator, described above, is based on the assumption that the resolved roster in ICM blocks can be treated as the truth for those blocks. First and foremost, there is the problem that many individuals in our society are difficult to count. Comparisons of 1990 coverage measurement results to DA suggested that at least in some groups, a substantial number of people were missed by both the PES and the regular census, and that the number of these people was underestimated by DSE (Bell, 1993). CensusPlus may be no more successful at finding the very toughest households and individuals; hence, the resolved roster will probably be incomplete. However, we caution against using this concern by itself to dismiss any ICM method. Even if no method can totally eliminate the differential undercount, which is probably the case, ICM may well lead to substantially better estimates.

We see several other challenges to this coverage assumption that apply more specifically to CensusPlus.

• Does the reconciliation phase of the reinterview give an accurate roster? The two-phase reinterview and reconciliation envisaged for CensusPlus provides important operational advantages, but it also is a new and as yet untested methodology. The technical aspects of the computer-aided reconciliation will challenge the capabilities of matching technology to support integration of two or more lists on the fly, but the deepest issues may lie in the dynamics of the reinterview process itself. Previous research on reinterview methodologies (Biemer and Forsman, 1992) suggests that a respondent confronted with discrepancies between two interviews may tend to seek a resolution that is consistent with the most recent responses; the interviewer may also prefer to obtain an outcome at reconciliation that is consistent with information recorded just before by the same interviewer.

• Can the CensusPlus methodology identify erroneous enumerations? In particular, one form of erroneous enumeration is duplication, i.e., the listing of one person in more than one place. Detection of duplications must involve at least some searching in blocks adjacent to the blocks that were sampled. How should the search area be defined? What information should be used to define matches or mismatches? There is a trade-off between improved accuracy and increasing cost as the size of the search area is increased; it may be possible to reduce bias at minimal cost by using an extended search area for a sample of the cases.

• Is it possible to resolve place-of-residence ambiguities, for example, when true residence is close to a block included in a given CensusPlus sample block, or when a person could plausibly be regarded as resident at any of several addresses?

• Can the ICM instrument find the people who lived in the sample blocks on Census Day, even if they have moved since then? And can it distinguish them from people who moved in after Census Day? Because in ICM blocks the ICM sample is accumulated on a flow basis as the census enumerations and NRFU are accumulated, it becomes important to determine whether information added actually pertains to residence on Census Day. If, for example, enumerations in the ICM samples add people who moved into the blocks in question after Census Day, then this would create an upward bias in the population total, with an obvious effect on the validity of estimates.

• At least two modes and instruments will be used in the ICM interview: the CATI and CAPI versions. The possibility of mode effects, systematic differences in responses to the different interview modalities, in enumerating people in ICM blocks should be considered and their effects on estimates analyzed.

Recommendation 4.3: The Census Bureau should investigate during the 1995 census test whether the CensusPlus field operation can attain excellent coverage in CensusPlus blocks without contaminating the regular enumeration in those blocks. If substantial problems are identified, CensusPlus should not be selected as the field methodology for integrated coverage measurement in the 2000 census unless clearly effective corrective measures can be implemented within the research and development schedule.

Evaluations should be designed to respond to these issues. The following suggestions address particular concerns in CensusPlus evaluation and are among the ideas that could be implemented in 1995 or later tests.

• It will be quite difficult to demonstrate perfect coverage of the resolved CensusPlus roster, but some evaluations are possible that would help to assess the quality of its coverage. One would be to find a third source of names and perform triple system estimation (Marks et al., 1974; Zaslavsky and Wolfgang, 1993) to evaluate the number missed in both of the original lists. Possible sources would be an administrative list that was not used either in the original enumeration or in constructing the ICM roster, or a list from a particularly intensive form of enumeration, such as observation by a resident ethnographer. The objective would be to seek out people who are particularly hard to count.

• It would be useful to conduct some experiments to evaluate the effect of the design of the ICM reinterview. For example, the reconciliation phase for some fraction of the cases could be carried out by experts different from the original ICM interviewers, and the results compared with those obtained in similar households when the interview and reconciliation are carried out in the same session. A careful study of these dynamics under cognitive laboratory conditions may also be helpful.

• Some information will be gained by carefully monitoring particular ICM operations, such as follow-up of movers.

• It may be possible to deliberately salt some of the data with information that is incorrect (enumerations or deliberate omissions) but plausible, in order to measure the success of the ICM reinterview in detecting and correcting these cases.

Other Issues for ICM Methodology

In addition to the two major issues addressed above, there are many others to be considered in design and evaluation of the new ICM methodology. We mention several of them here.

• The Census Bureau intends to experiment with use of administrative records as part of integrated coverage measurement (see Chapter 5). Administrative records can be used to provide additional addresses for the independent address listing and also as a source of additional names to be checked in the ICM reinterview. The Census Bureau should study whether administrative records can contribute to the accuracy and completeness of ICM.

• Other innovations in census-taking, including the use of forms to be received from nontraditional sources and returns received by phone (reverse CATI), need to be examined in relation to their effects on assumptions used in ICM.

• How will the use of tool-kit methods be integrated with ICM? The use of special tool-kit methods for hard-to-count populations has been endorsed by the panel as a way to increase response rates and improve the reliability of data. These methods also hold promise for improving coverage of the ICM survey. Some decisions must be reached as to which tool-kit methods should be used in primary enumeration and which in ICM. Some consideration must also be given to the effect of the former on the conduct of the ICM survey, since tool-kit methods may involve very different schedules of census activities from those in most areas.

• What sample size is required to obtain acceptable ICM estimates? Simulations based on the 1990 PES, together with information from field tests, can be used to determine optimal design and sample size. We anticipate that a block sample for ICM that includes at least 300,000 households—double the number of households included in the 1990 PES—would be required for ICM to succeed in 2000. Considerations in selection of sample size are taken up again in the next section in the context of estimation.

Recommendation 4.4: Whatever method for integrated coverage measurement is used in 2000, the Census Bureau should ensure that a sufficiently large sample is taken so that the single set of counts provides the accuracy needed by data users at pertinent levels of geography.

STATISTICAL ESTIMATION

Estimation and the One-Number Census

Census design features being considered for 2000 will create new demands for statistical estimation methods. Each of the methods described previously in this chapter—sampling of nonresponse follow-up and integrated coverage measurement—requires a corresponding estimation strategy and research on particular aspects of implementation, as do some uses of administrative records and other additional sources of information. We briefly summarize these areas here and provide further details below.

• *Nonresponse follow-up sampling.* Estimates must be obtained of numbers and characteristics of people and households who would have been found in each block during nonresponse follow-up had all households been included in the nonresponse follow-up sample. The information that can be used in this estimation process includes the number and characteristics of people found during nonresponse follow-up in sample blocks or households, the number of unresolved nonresponse addresses in the nonsample blocks or households, and the number and characteristics of people found during unsampled census operations (mailback and other presampling responses).

- *Coverage estimation.* Methods such as models or poststratification schemes must be developed for summarizing patterns of undercoverage. Formulas must be developed for estimating net coverage rates from ICM data.
- *Additional information sources.* Inclusion of new information sources into the census, such as administrative records and multiple response modes, may create new demands on estimation methodologies.
- *Population estimates for small areas.* Results from NRFU sampling and ICM must be combined to produce estimates of population for small areas, down to the level of individual blocks. At the most detailed level, methods will be required for incorporating estimated persons and households into individual blocks, creating units with realistic characteristics in such a way that additivity is maintained across levels of geography (i.e., the total of counts for a collection of smaller areas equals the count for the larger area that they constitute.)

The fundamental principle of the one-number census, as described above, is that a single set of population numbers will be produced, incorporating estimation as well as counting and assignment. Although in a sense the reported census counts have always been estimates, in the 2000 census for the first time the role of estimation as part of the census process will be made explicit.

Fundamental Criteria for Estimation Methodologies

A number of criteria should be considered in the choice of estimation methodologies; in considering these, estimation is inextricable from sample design.

1. *Reduction of variance for given cost.* The variance of estimates depends on the sample design, the sample size, and the estimation procedure. Efficiencies gained in estimation may be used to reduce variance (improve precision), to reduce cost, or some combination of the two.

2. *Reduction of bias.* The term *bias* is used here in its strict statistical sense, meaning that an estimate does not, even on the average over hypothetical repeated surveys, give exactly the value that would be obtained if the entire population were observed. This does not imply intent or unfairness. Some biases will inevitably exist in a survey like this one, which is directed at a complex and heterogeneous population and designed to be very sensitive to nonresponse.

Estimation decisions require trade-offs between bias and variance. Procedures that reduce variance through modeling may create biases at some level, even if the models are very simple. For example, if an attempt were made to calculate unbiased ICM estimates for very fine levels of detail, the variances of the estimates would be very large because each area might have only a few sample blocks. However, estimators that reduce variance by sharing information across wider areas risk creating bias for small areas if some parts of the larger area actually had poorer coverage during the census enumeration than did other parts. This example illustrates that it is important to consider different levels of geography because variance tends to predominate for small areas, but, since variance is inversely proportional to sample size, bias becomes more prominent in larger areas. Thus, different estimators may look best depending on the level of geography considered important. "Loss measures" such as weighted mean squared error are credible ways of combining estimated bias and variance into a single measure at any selected level of geography.

3. *Simplicity and explainability.* Other factors being equal, a method that is simple and can be explained is preferable to a more complicated method. This objective may conflict with the first two criteria, because complex statistical methods may be required to optimize the bias-variance trade-off. Note, however, that methods that are not used for *estimation* because they are regarded as too complex may still be used for *evaluation* of simpler estimators. One aspect of simplicity is directness, the use of data from an area to produce estimates for the same area; some issues about directness are discussed below.

Specific Issues in Estimation Methodology

It appears likely that estimation will be divided into two stages. One stage is concerned with estimating the population in nonsample nonresponding households, i.e., those that did not respond by mail and were not included in the NRFU sample. The other stage uses ICM data to estimate the difference between the numbers and characteristics of households and people estimated by all stages preceding ICM and the true population and characteristics. ICM estimation may be further divided into two aspects. The first aspect concerns the way in which ratios or factors are estimated based on data in sample blocks. The second concerns how these estimates are applied to pre-ICM census counts (i.e., those based on direct enumeration, assignment, and estimation from the NRFU sample).

Estimation Methods for NRFU Sampling

If NRFU is conducted in a sample of households, it will be necessary to calculate estimates of numbers and characteristics of households at addresses that were not included in the NRFU sample. In other words, estimates must be obtained for numbers of households with various characteristics and for the number of addresses that are vacant. Under a block sampling design, if households are added through NRFU field operations that are not at addresses on the pre-census address list (census adds), it will also be necessary to estimate the number of census adds that would have appeared in the NRFU nonsample blocks. Several sources of information are available for use in estimation of these numbers for each target block for which estimation is required: (1) numbers and characteristics of households that responded to the mailback census in the target block and every other block, (2) numbers and characteristics of households in addresses that did not respond by mail but were included in the NRFU sample, in other blocks, and (under a unit-sampling design only) in the target block, (3) administrative list or other auxiliary information for the target block, and (4) other block-level covariates. The Census Bureau has used relatively simple estimators so far in research to contrast unit and block designs (Fuller et al., 1994). More sophisticated estimators that try to optimize use of the various information sources may lead to improved estimation. Some of the relevant concepts and considerations involved in use of these more complex estimators are discussed below in the context of ICM.

The main basis for considering estimation methods and accuracy will be simulations using 1990 data, even after 1995 census test results become available. Only simulations using data with complete follow-up can provide data for evaluating the accuracy of various estimation schemes under various sample designs. The 1995 census test results will primarily answer questions about operational and cost issues associated with NRFU sampling.

Estimation Methods for ICM: Estimating Factors

In the 1990 undercount estimation program, adjustment factors were calculated for domains or cells defined by geography and population characteristics that cut across state lines. These factors were initially estimated using dual system estimation. With this estimator, the estimated adjustment factor for a domain takes the following form:

$$A = \left(\frac{C_0 - I_0}{C_0} \right) \left(\frac{C - E}{C} \right) \left(\frac{P}{M} \right)$$

$$= \frac{\text{Actually enumerated persons in census}}{\substack{\text{Census totals} \\ \text{including imputations}}} \times \frac{\text{Estimated correctly enumerated persons}}{\substack{\text{Estimated actually} \\ \text{enumerated persons}}} \times \frac{\text{Estimated number of persons actually in area}}{\substack{\text{Estimated persons} \\ \text{correctly enumerated by} \\ \text{the census}}}$$

The product of these three factors, by cancellation, is the estimated ratio of people actually in the domain to the census totals including imputations. The first factor is the fraction of the census counts (C_0) that represent people actually enumerated, excluding imputations and other cases for which matching and follow-up are impossible (I_0). The second factor is an estimate of the fraction of the people enumerated in the census (C) who were not erroneous enumerations (E).

The third factor is the inverse of the estimated fraction of people in the whole population (represented by P, the P-sample or PES count) who were included in the census (M, or matched, part of the P-sample). The first factor is calculated from the complete census (up to but not including coverage measurement), while the second and third factors are based on the coverage measurement survey (hence the distinction between C and C_0).

This estimator is valid under the assumption that (within any given estimation cell) people in the P-sample are included in the census at the same rate as those who are not in the P-sample (the assumption of independence). It therefore implicitly includes an estimate of the number of people who would be missed by both census and PES even if their block were included in the sample, the so-called fourth cell (in the two-by-two table of inclusion in the census by inclusion in the ICM survey). Some research conducted prior to and around the 1990 census suggests that the number of people in this cell may be larger than the number predicted under independence, at least for some demographic groups, causing the estimated adjustment factors to be biased downward compared with the correct adjustment factors (ratio of true to census population) (Bell, 1993; Zaslavsky and Wolfgang, 1993). This bias may be explained by heterogeneity in the probability of enumeration among people in the same adjustment cell, the problem of the hard-to-enumerate population (Alho et al., 1993; Darroch et al., 1993), but such effects can only be estimated using supplementary information of some kind.

The estimation method that would be used with the proposed ICM methodology has not been determined. One possibility would be an estimator similar to the DSE used in 1990, treating the census (including NRFU) as the first source and the ICM interview (before reconciliation) as the second source. Another estimator, which we call the resolved population ratio estimator, would treat as the truth the counts in ICM blocks after enumeration of missed addresses and reconciliation of discrepancies between census and ICM enumerations (Wright, 1993). (This is the estimator assumed in the descriptions in the preceding section.) Adjustment factors would then be estimated as the ratio of these resolved counts to pre-ICM census counts. The resolved population ratio estimator is valid under the assumption that the reinterview and reconciliation process attains near-complete coverage. In the 1995 census test, the statistical robustness of the ratio estimator should be assessed by determining the effects of modest departures from complete coverage on the accuracy of ICM estimates. This estimator would tend to produce estimated factors that are smaller than those obtained from the DSE, but the differences should be small except for poststratum cells with large omission rates.

An important issue is the choice of cells or poststrata for which adjustment factors are calculated. In order to make the final stage of estimation as accurate as possible, the cells should be internally homogeneous but different from each other with respect to coverage rates. Cells for the 1990 PES were defined by age, sex, race, type of place, tenure (owner/renter), and geographical region. Analyses of 1990 census data led to some changes in cell definitions for the 1992 decision on adjustment of postcensal estimates, with greater emphasis on the owner/renter distinction. With improved data processing in 2000, it may be possible to define cells using census process data, such as mailback rates and NRFU completion rates, which have been found to be strongly related to omission and erroneous enumeration rates.

The development of a new ICM methodology may provide an opportunity to consider variations on the estimation procedure other than alternative methods of calculating adjustment factors for cells. The fact that omitted addresses will be located in an operation distinct from that which identifies missed persons in listed addresses suggests the possibility of calculating an adjustment factor for number of addresses or for number of households. It would also be possible to distinguish between people omitted from the pre-ICM census in enumerated households and people omitted in households that were omitted from the census. Finally, models could be used to describe the omissions and erroneous enumerations in ways that are more complicated than simple estimates of ratios of true to enumerated counts in a cell, such as models with covariates for individual or household omissions.

Another feature of the estimation procedure in the 1990 effort was "smoothing" of the estimates through an empirical Bayes model (Hogan 1993). In effect, this model combines the direct estimates based on sample data for each cell with estimates from a regression model fitted to data from all cells, weighting the direct estimates more heavily when they are more precise. This methodology holds the promise of giving smoothed estimates with smaller variance than the direct estimates, but it also was a source of much controversy in evaluation of the 1990 estimates. This methodology was not used in calculation of the proposed 1992 adjustment of postcensal estimates. The smoothing methodology bears further consideration, especially if an attempt will be made to calculate estimates for a refined set of adjustment cells. Further research will be required to make it sufficiently robust to stand up against possible criticisms of model bias or arbitrariness.

Estimation Methods for ICM: Carrying Estimates Down to Lower Levels

Let us assume for the moment that adjustment factors for cells have been calculated. Because the geographic detail for cells will almost certainly be much coarser than many of the units for which estimates are required (such as census tracts or small political subdivisions), there must be a procedure for carrying estimates down to lower levels. A synthetic estimation procedure was used for this purpose in the 1990 undercount estimation program, meaning that the population for each area was estimated by disaggregating the enumerated population for that area into the parts falling into each adjustment cell, multiplying the part in each cell by the corresponding adjustment factor, and then summing the adjusted counts.

The validity of these synthetic estimates was criticized on the grounds that undercount is not in fact uniform across each adjustment cell. The question of how this lack of uniformity affects the accuracy of synthetic estimates of population (in absolute terms, and in comparison to unadjusted enumerations) has been a subject of lively debate (Freedman and Navidi, 1986; Schirm and Preston, 1987, 1992; Freedman and Wachter, 1994; Wolter and Causey, 1991; Fay and Thompson, 1993). This question has been approached through theoretical investigation and through simulations based on coverage measurement data and census data for other variables than the undercount. Further research in this area before the 2000 census would make a useful contribution to design and validation of the estimation methodology.

Other methods have been proposed for carrying estimates down to small areas. One alternative, for example, is a simple regression methodology, with proportions from different adjustment cells as covariates (Causey, 1994) or with other variables as covariates (Ericksen and Kadane, 1985). Like the synthetic approach, these methods should be subjected to testing through simulations before a final decision is made.

Direct and Indirect Estimates

Direct estimates are defined as estimates based entirely on data from the domain for which the estimates are calculated. Indirect estimates make use of data from outside the domain. Simple survey estimates are direct estimates, whereas model-based estimates may be indirect. In particular, synthetic estimates are indirect because they apply factors calculated over an estimation cell to geographic areas that are smaller than the geographic extent of that estimation cell. Empirical Bayes smoothing models are also indirect because the model component of the estimates is estimated across a large number of cells.

In the 1990 undercount estimation program, almost all cells cut across state lines. Consequently, estimates of population for states and subdivisions of states were synthetic and therefore indirect. This fact was grounds for some controversy over whether it was accurate and fair to estimate one state's population using data from another state, if conditions might in fact have differed among states. Evaluation studies directed at this question were inconclusive (Kim et al., 1991).

The Census Bureau is now considering requiring that direct estimates be obtained for all states. This would have major implications for design of the ICM sample, because even the states with the smallest populations would need substantial ICM sample sizes to obtain direct estimates of acceptable accuracy. The calculations of sample sizes could vary greatly, however, depending on the criterion of accuracy that is adopted. At one extreme, a criterion of equal coefficient of variation of direct population estimates in every state (equal standard error of estimated ICM adjustment factors) would imply roughly equal sample sizes in every state, despite the 100-fold ratio of populations between the most and least populous states. Such a design might be drastically inefficient for estimation of adjustment factors for domains other than states. At the other extreme, a criterion of equal variance of direct population estimates for every state would imply larger sampling rates (and therefore disproportionately larger sample sizes) in larger states. Considerations based on minimization of expected loss (Spencer, 1980; Zaslavsky, 1993) would lead to other sample allocations with higher sampling rates but smaller absolute sample sizes in small states compared with large states.

A decision to require direct state estimates must be considered in light of its implications for accuracy of estimated population shares for other domains, such as urban versus suburban areas within states and white, black, and Hispanic populations in a region. We recommend that alternative ICM designs should be prepared with and without direct state estimates and that the added costs or loss of accuracy for other domains of interest should be made clear at a policy-making level before it is decided whether this feature is essential. Compromises may also deserve consideration, such as requiring direct estimation only for states and cities larger than some minimum size.

Use of direct estimation for some or all states would not preclude calculation of indirect estimates for subdomains within states, down to a level of detail similar to the poststratification in the 1990 PES. For example, the total population of Idaho might be obtained from a direct estimate, but the estimate for urban Idaho (compared with suburban Idaho) might be based in part on adjustment factors calculated from data for Idaho, Wyoming, and Montana, and the estimate for Native American reservations in Idaho might use nationally estimated adjustment factors for Native American reservations. This could be accomplished, for example, by calculating synthetic estimates for all domains and then ratio adjusting them or raking them to match direct state estimates. Selection of estimators must be guided by an awareness that, although for some purposes state estimates are the most important product of the census, for other purposes the distribution of population within states, for example by race and urbanicity, is paramount.

Recommendation 4.5: The Census Bureau should prepare alternative sample designs for integrated coverage measurement with varying levels of support for direct state estimation. The provision of direct state estimates should be evaluated in terms of the relative costs and the consequent loss of accuracy in population estimates for other geographic areas or subpopulations of interest.

What Form Will Final Population Counts Take?

The Census Bureau has placed a high priority on making all census products consistent internally and with each other. Consistency requires that, when several published cross-tabulations share a common stub or margin, or when such a margin can be calculated by summing numbers from several tables, the margins of various tables should agree with each other. For example, the total of the number of white males over age 18 in a state should be the same regardless of whether it is read off the state totals or calculated from tables by county, by tract, or by block. Similarly, published means or proportions should agree with quantities that might be calculated from tables.

A wide variety of census products are produced, and it is impossible to foresee all tabulations that will be generated as part of regular data series or special tabulations. Therefore, the surest way of guaranteeing this consistency is to produce a microdata file that looks like a simple enumeration of people and households but includes records for people estimated through NRFU sampling and ICM as well as those directly enumerated. Then tabulations and public-use microdata samples may be produced from this microdata file. There are two difficulties inherent to this approach. First, simple estimation methods such as those described above for ICM estimation produce adjustment factors that can be used to calculate expected numbers of people. They do not, however, describe the full detail required to create a roster of households that include the estimated number of people in each estimation cell. Therefore, procedures must be developed that predict household structure for the "estimated" part of the population. These procedures could take various forms, ranging from arbitrary grouping of people to full probability modeling.

Second, the rounding inherent in imputation of complete households adds noise to the estimates. For example, if calculations based on the adjustment factors indicate that 0.15 person should be estimated in a block (beyond the enumerated roster) in each of 9 cells, then the total number of people added will have to be rounded to either 1 or 2, and the number in each cell to either 0 or 1. The requirements of creating realistic households may require even more rounding, since it may not be realistic to assume that the estimated people were necessarily in households of only one or two people, even if that is the average number estimated per block. A further complication is that there would be a stochastic element in this calculation. Both the rounding and stochastic components of error would be most noticeable at the most detailed levels of geography. At more aggregated levels, rounding could be controlled to area totals, and the stochastic component of error would tend to average out. This problem is another research area that will have to be considered in the years before 2000.

Weighting presents an alternative to imputation that avoids the above difficulties. But weighting possesses the disadvantage that it produces noninteger counts. Rounding must therefore be performed after the weighted tables are created, thus complicating the task of maintaining consistency in all census products.

A minor, but possibly sensitive, issue is the treatment in estimation of counts associated with census forms that are collected late, after the implicit reference point of ICM. In principle, these should not be counted because the factors derived from ICM do not include these forms in their base. Simply ignoring these forms might be a public relations disaster, however. One appealing solution would be to substitute these forms for households that would have been imputed for ICM without changing the total number estimated for any geographical area. Similar issues may arise with respect to late mailback returns that come in after NRFU sampling and data collection have taken place.

Acceptable Accuracy for Estimates

The design of NRFU and ICM samples is motivated by considerations of desired accuracy at various levels of geographic aggregation. Under all designs within the current range of consideration, the NRFU sample will be much larger than the ICM sample (10-33 percent versus less than 1 percent), but the portion of the population that will be estimated and imputed on the basis of NRFU sampling (on the order of the mail nonresponse rate, about 30 percent in 1990) is also much larger than the portion estimated through ICM (of the order of 1-2 percent of pre-ICM totals, on the average). Therefore, issues about the accuracy of estimates under NRFU sampling are concerned primarily with small levels of aggregation, such as blocks, tracts, and minor political divisions, and issues about ICM accuracy are concerned primarily with larger levels of aggregation, such as states, demographic groups in broad geographic regions, and cities.

Early research (Fuller et al., 1994) suggests that coefficients of variation for block population estimates under NRFU sampling will be high. Research may lead to improved estimators that reduce variance for small areas, but it is unlikely that any estimator can make major gains in precision at this level. Precise block-level counts are rarely if ever needed, however, except as a means for building up estimates for larger levels of aggregation. Therefore, evaluation of NRFU sampling should focus on accuracy at the level of minor civil divisions, state legislative districts, and similar-sized units.

Conversely, evaluation of ICM should focus on accuracy at broader levels of aggregation. There are important interactions between ICM sample design, estimation methods, and the units for which ICM accuracy is measured. The ICM sample must be designed to give acceptable accuracy for important units such as those listed above. It would be desirable to attain a level of accuracy such that error for these units is smaller than the differential coverage of the pre-ICM phase of the census, but this may not be attainable within acceptable limits for the scale of ICM.

The Role of Demographic Analysis

Demographic analysis refers to the estimation of population using the basic demographic identities relating population to birth, deaths, immigration, and emigration (e.g., Robinson et al., 1993, 1994). In practice, demographic analysis can be used to obtain population estimates at high levels of aggregation. Traditional methods for demographic analysis yield estimates of the national population cross-classified by age, sex, and race.

In the 1990 census, demographic estimates were used as a check on the aggregate accuracy of dual-system estimates of undercount by age × sex × race group (Robinson et al., 1993). They are particularly suited to this purpose because most of the components of demographic estimates are quite accurately determined, although estimates of undocumented immigration remain controversial (see, e.g., Bean et al., 1990). In addition, demographic estimates of sex ratios have been used to check the internal consistency of dual-system estimates from the 1990 PES (Bell, 1993). For this purpose, the DA estimates of sex ratios were regarded as more reliable than DA estimates of population totals, and the results suggested a substantial undercount of black males, even after dual-system estimation. Demographic estimates were also used to evaluate the face validity of subnational dual-system estimates in the decision on adjustment of the 1992 postcensal estimates base.

More recent and ongoing efforts have attempted to develop improved demographic estimates at subnational geographic areas for the youngest and oldest segments of the population. Estimates for the population age 65 and over have been produced using state-level Medicare records, with allowance for state-by-state variability in Medicare enrollment rates and in percentages of eligible members of the population age 65 and over (Robinson et al., 1993). State enrollment and eligibility rates are affected by such variables as citizenship status and the proportion of retirees who have held federal government jobs. The Census Bureau has also worked to develop subnational estimates for the population under age 10, using vital statistics and estimates of interstate migration (Robinson et al., 1994). These estimates require assumptions about the state-to-state variability in migration patterns, the completeness of birth records, and the use of valid residence definitions during hospital birth registration.

These research programs are breaking important new ground, but it would be premature to judge the credibility of these estimates. As noted above, the estimates are based on a number of assumptions that require further evaluation. Also, a major limitation of demographic analysis is that the uncertainties in estimates provided by the method are largely unknown (see Clogg and Himes, 1993; Robinson et al., 1993).

Demographic analysis possesses a number of potential strengths as a method for coverage evaluation in the 2000 census: operational feasibility, timeliness (estimates could be available early in the census year), low cost, independence of

ICM, and comparability to historical series (Robinson et al., 1993, 1994; Clogg and Himes, 1993). But, in addition to the problem of measuring uncertainty, there remain significant difficulties associated with the use of demographic analysis that currently limit its role in the decennial census: the lack of reliable data on international migration, particularly for emigration and undocumented immigration; questionable measures of interstate migration, which limit the accuracy of subnational estimates; and problems with racial classification in birth and death records and their congruency with self-identification in the census, which affects estimates for all groups (especially Hispanics, Asians and Pacific Islanders, and Native Americans).

Because of the limitations of foreseeable progress on these methodological problems, we expect that demographic analysis will be useful primarily as an evaluation tool for ICM in the 2000 census. We assume that, as in recent censuses, national estimates of the population cross-classified by age, sex, and race will be produced for this purpose. It may also be possible and worthwhile to incorporate some demographic information—e.g., estimates of sex ratios—into the estimation procedure for integrated coverage measurement. However, based on the current state of research, we doubt that demographic analysis could be used in the 2000 census to adjust (or benchmark) final population estimates as part of integrated coverage measurement.

Nonetheless, the panel believes further research on demographic methods is a cost-effective investment that could pay long-term dividends beyond the contributions to census coverage and evaluation. An exciting new development is the convergence of demographic analysis, the postcensal estimates program, and the Program for Integrated Estimates in connection with the proposed continuous measurement system (see Chapter 6). The common ground of these programs is that each of them uses a variety of data sources to improve estimation of population counts and characteristics without relying on the census itself. Demographic analysis traditionally has depended primarily on demographic data, as described above, in order to obtain very aggregated estimates; administrative records such as Medicare registrations have also begun to be used in this program. The postcensal estimates program (Long, 1993) combines census-year population counts with a variety of indicators of change of the population at local levels, such as school enrollments and changes in housing stock, to obtain estimates of the population at a fairly detailed level. The Program for Integrated Estimates (Alexander, 1994) would make use of a wide variety of sources, including data from a new survey and a variety of administrative records with coverage for people, households, or housing units, to produce detailed estimates of counts and characteristics down to the block and tract levels (see Chapter 5 for a discussion of the potential of health care records in this regard).

The three programs described above can be seen in a progression according to time of development (from several decades ago to the present and future), cost (from least to most expensive), operational difficulty (from easiest to most challenging), use of localized sources (from purely aggregate analysis to integration of microdata sources), and degree of small-area precision (from least to most detailed). Each step in this progression has been justified by contemporary needs, but each step also brings us closer to having the technical capabilities and experience required to be able to obtain adequate information from administrative records without having to mount a full-scale census.

> **Recommendation 4.6: The panel endorses the continued use of demographic analysis as an evaluation tool in the decennial census. However, the present state of development does not support a prominent role for demographic methods in the production of official population totals as part of integrated coverage measurement in the 2000 census. The Census Bureau should continue research to develop subnational demographic estimates, with particular attention to potential links between demographic analysis and further development of the continuous measurement prototype and the administrative records census option.**

Other Uses of Estimation

As discussed in Chapter 3, current proposals (Kalton et al., 1994) for enumeration of the homeless population call for service-based enumeration. Under these plans, persons making use of services, such as shelters and soup kitchens, would be enumerated on several different occasions. The lists from these enumerations will then be matched so that the degree of overlap in the service population from day to day can be determined. These data will be the basis for estimation of the total homeless population that makes use of these services. These estimation methods are related to dual-system estimation, but there are special complications because one site might be enumerated on several different occasions and because the same person could appear for services at more than one site.

Statistical modeling and estimation may also play a role in the use of quality assurance (QA) data to monitor and evaluate the coverage measurement survey (Biemer, 1994). Evaluation of this survey is difficult, expensive, and controversial, because it requires replication and reconsideration of judgmental decisions made during the original coverage measurement operation. For example, the most skilled and experienced matching staff may reanalyze data and obtain additional data from the field long after the census to check the accuracy of matching determinations made during the CensusPlus operation. Because these studies are difficult and depend on skills that are in short supply, they will almost certainly be small compared with the coverage measurement sample itself. If research over the next few years can identify QA measures of the census and coverage measurement *process* that are correlated with evaluation *outcomes*, the QA data will provide useful auxiliary variables for evaluation of the distribution and consequences of errors in the coverage measurement operation.

Prespecification and Documentation of Procedures

In the year 2000 census, increased reliance on estimation makes it essential that the Census Bureau's choice of estimation methodologies should inspire general confidence. It is unrealistic to hope that there will be total unanimity in support of any full set of methodologies. Census methods have always received criticism insofar as they have had a discernible effect on an identifiable geographic area or a particular group. For example, the local review process during the 1990 census led to inclusion of units that were determined to have been omitted from address lists and to recanvassing of some areas. Many procedural decisions, however, are invisible to those outside the Census Bureau and have consequences that are obscure. Decisions about estimation methods have been, and in all likelihood will continue to be, especially controversial (1) because they are open and explicit and (2) because their effects on totals for identifiable areas can be determined, at least after the fact. We address each of these considerations, taking the second first.

Past experience (for example, with adjustment of the 1990 census and with adjustment of the 1992 base for postcensal estimates) has shown that the majority of the public comments received on an estimation methodology are motivated by concerns for its effects on particular political jurisdictions (Bryant, 1993). Another common concern was that confusion would be created by having two sets of results, those before and after adjustment. By prespecifying estimation methods as much as possible, the Census Bureau makes it clear that decisions have been made on good statistical principles and judgment, rather than being motivated by any consideration of how they will affect particular areas. Adopting such a policy avoids the 1990 experience of placing estimation choices before decision makers who could perceive the political consequences of different procedures. In this way, the Census Bureau obtains some protection against criticisms directed at the particular effects of methods.

A proper balance must be struck that gains these benefits of prespecification without committing the Census Bureau to a rigid set of procedures that permit no leeway for handling unforeseen circumstances in the conduct of the census or adapting estimators to unanticipated features of the data. Therefore, an appropriate level of prespecification includes a positive statement of areas in which judgment may be exercised as well as areas in which decisions are made before the census. For example, the general form of the estimators to be used and the flow of information in processing should be prespecified, but it may be recognized in advance that judgment will be exercised in deletion or downweighting of outliers, variable selection in regression models, or splitting of poststrata.

The openness and explicitness of estimation methodologies make it possible to begin to build consensus in support of them, both technically and politically, before the census even begins. To make this possible, the Census Bureau should release a publication describing the main steps in data collection and processing and the estimation methods that will be used in the census, including a description of estimators, of evaluations that will be applied to these estimators, and of points at which the use of professional judgment is foreseen.

The process of consensus-building continues after the census through the release of suitable technical documentation. This documentation, as well as describing in general terms the estimators that were used, should present in aggregate terms the calculations that produced population totals reported for major geographic areas (states and large cities), as well as for major demographic groupings. It must be emphasized that this documentation would be released *after* the publication of census population figures used for apportionment and redistricting, and that the intermediate totals in these calculations should not be interpreted as competing estimates of population. The procedures should be regarded as an integrated whole, not a menu of options from which various parties can pick and choose to find the treatment most favorable to their local area. The postcensal documentation should also contain a summary of evaluation results. Summary measures of accuracy for various levels of aggregation, such as those calculated through the total error model in the evaluation of the 1990 PES, may be a suitable format for summarizing these evaluation results.

Recommendation 4.7: Before the census, the Census Bureau should produce detailed documentation of statistical methodology to be used for estimation and modeling. After the census, the Census Bureau should document how the methodology was applied empirically and should provide evaluation of the methodology.

Reporting of Uncertainty

Official statistics have progressed over the century from a narrow focus on simple tabulations of population characteristics to provision of a range of census products, including complex tabulations and sample microdata files. Analytical uses of these data require availability of both point estimates and measures of uncertainty. When complex statistical methods, such as complex sampling schemes, indirect estimation, and imputation are used in creating census products, users will not be able to derive valid measures of uncertainty by elementary methods, and they may not have adequate information in the published or available products to derive these measures. It therefore becomes the responsibility of the data producers to facilitate estimation of uncertainty.

Total error models have been used by the Census Bureau to measure uncertainty in the outcomes of the census and the contributions of the various sources of error to this uncertainty (Hansen et al., 1961). More recently, a total error model was developed for estimation of uncertainty in adjusted estimates based on the 1990 census and PES (Mulry and Spencer, 1993). Such models take into account both sampling errors in the estimates and potential biases stemming from the regular census and from coverage estimation. Bias can arise, for example, from use of several response modes or from differences among response times. Similar models may be a useful tool for evaluating uncertainty in integrated estimates from a complex census in the year 2000.

After uncertainties have been estimated, they should be described in a manner that allows users to incorporate them into their data analyses. A variety of methods for representing uncertainty are familiar from the world of survey sampling. Summary measures of uncertainty (such as average coefficients of variation or variance functions) may be published as a supplement to published tabulations, or standard errors may be published for quantities of particular interest. A number of imputation methodologies are available (Rubin, 1987; Clogg et al., 1991) that enable users of public use microdata samples to estimate the effects of sampling and nonsampling variability on their analyses.

Recommendation 4.8: The Census Bureau should develop methods for measuring and modeling all sources of error in the census and for showing uncertainty in published tabulations or otherwise enabling users to estimate uncertainty.

Research Program on Estimation

Necessary research on statistical estimation divides roughly into three phases. In the first phase, which is now under way and continues until the major design decisions have been made for the 1995 census test, estimation research focuses on broadening the range of possibilities for the use of sampling and other statistically based techniques. In this phase, preliminary assessments can be obtained of the expected precision for various designs.

In the second phase, roughly coinciding with the planning, execution, and processing of the 1995 census test, the emphasis shifts to developing methods needed for the selected designs and methodological features. Although it is not necessary during this phase to decide on all the estimators that will be used, it is critical that enough progress be made on NRFU sampling and ICM estimators to avoid making decisions about design based on estimators that will later be replaced.

In the final phase, beginning with assessment of the 1995 census test and continuing through the decade, the selected estimation methods will have to be consolidated, optimized, validated, and made both theoretically and operationally robust. This last process will ensure that they can stand up to critical scrutiny and to problems that may arise in the course of the 2000 census. In this phase, work will also continue on selecting estimation procedures required for the production of all census products, including measures of uncertainty, and on more complex procedures that will be used in evaluation of the census estimates.

Recommendation 4.9: The Census Bureau should vigorously pursue research on statistical estimation now and throughout the decade. Topics should include nonresponse follow-up sampling, coverage estimation, incorporation of varied information sources (including administrative records), and indirect estimation for small areas.

5

Administrative Records

In a chapter of the panel's interim report called "Administrative Records: Intriguing Prospects, Formidable Obstacles" and in an earlier letter report, we outlined some basic requirements for more effective use of administrative records and recommended several actions to explore and develop new uses of administrative records in the 2000 census and beyond. In the letter report, we recommended that the Census Bureau "undertake a planning study . . . that would develop one or more detailed design options for a 2010 administrative records census." The Panel on Census Requirements in the Year 2000 and Beyond, in its interim report, gave strong support to the recommendations in our letter report and also urged greater attention to enhanced uses of administrative records in the Census Bureau's current estimates programs.

In this report, we focus on many of the same issues, illuminated by the light of some significant developments since the interim report was issued. The prospects for a national health care information system and legislation to govern the use of health records, a July 1993 Interagency Conference on Statistical Uses of Administrative Records sponsored by the Census Bureau, increased interest in continuous measurement, and other developments have served to heighten the prospects for expanded uses of administrative records. November 1993 brought the publication of the final report of the Panel on Confidentiality and Data Access of the Committee on National Statistics, with several recommendations relevant to statistical uses of administrative records.

In this chapter we examine uses of administrative records not only in census operations, but also in other demographic programs. Although some of the obstacles associated with administrative record uses are indeed formidable, we believe that the prospects are more intriguing and promising than ever before. The recommendations in this chapter are designed to take full advantage of these prospects.

Some of the topics covered here are of such central importance in improving the census (e.g., the development of a Master Address File and improved record linkage techniques) that they have been discussed in a broader context in Chapter 2. Here we address the particular relevance of these issues for uses of administrative records.

The panel is encouraged by the progress that has been made in response to its earlier recommendations about the use of administrative records. In particular, the Census Bureau should be commended for taking a major step in initiating government-wide discussion of the use of administrative records by convening an Interagency Conference on Statistical Uses of Administrative Records in July 1993 and subsequently issuing a report on the conference. We also commend the Census Bureau for its initiation of a cooperative arrangement with the Statistics of Income Division of the Internal Revenue Service (IRS) to support and extend the latter's research on the population coverage of IRS and Social Security Administration records. We believe that the Census Bureau's announced plans for using administrative records in the 1995 census test are consistent with the relevant recommendations in our interim report, subject to certain reservations discussed later in this chapter.

Other recommendations made at the time of the interim report pertain to longer-term goals, such as the call for a long-range research and development program relating to the use of administrative records for demographic data, and the need for ultimate coordination and oversight for statistical uses of administrative records through the Office of Management and Budget (OMB). In this chapter, we reemphasize these recommendations and stress the importance of a proactive policy aimed at overcoming the formidable obstacles and taking full advantage of the intriguing prospects.

Early in its deliberations, the panel concurred with the Census Bureau's judgment that a 2000 census based entirely or primarily on administrative records would not be feasible. We recommended, therefore, that exploration of census uses of administrative records follow a two-track approach. The 2000 census track would identify and test possible uses of administrative records in the 2000 census as an adjunct to the more traditional modes of data collection; the long-range track would develop and test procedures for a possible administrative records census in 2010 or beyond, as well as uses of administrative records in other demographic data programs. We remain committed to this two-track approach. We believe that an administrative records census in 2010 is a live option that should be thoroughly examined and evaluated during the current decennial census cycle, in order to avoid putting off the question of its feasibility for yet another decade.

The next section of this chapter addresses some of the fundamental questions associated with the use of administrative records in statistical programs. Among them are those associated with access to administrative records for statistical and research purposes, the importance of public acceptance, and how best to address some of the specific technical requirements associated with the use of administrative records. Key recommendations in this section are that health care legislation should not preclude uses of new health care records in the decennial census and that the Census Bureau should be invited to participate in the design of new health care record systems to help ensure their suitability for statistical uses.

We then proceed to a description of the main features of an administrative records census and a discussion of the many issues that arise. We identify privacy, coverage, geography, content, and cost as considerations that need to be properly addressed. This section also emphasizes the crucial need for a Master Address File—without it, an administrative records census would be virtually impossible to conduct.

In the next section we examine the uses of administrative records in the 1995 census test and the 2000 census. Although a census based primarily on administrative records is not feasible for 2000, there are still many ways in which administrative records can be used to improve the quality and reduce the costs associated with the 2000 census. In addition, both the 1995 census test and the 2000 census provide rare opportunities to learn more about the potential benefits and the potential problems arising from an administrative records census.

Administrative records have current and potential uses not only in decennial census operations, but also in other demographic programs. They play a major role, for example, in the Census Bureau's current population estimates program, and they also have a potentially significant role to play in a continuous measurement system. In the next to last section, we stress the importance of this broader view of the role of administrative records in demographic programs.

In the final section of the chapter we summarize the different ways in which administrative records have been or might be used to help satisfy needs for small-area demographic data. We identify the major components of a proactive policy to develop enhanced statistical uses of administrative records. We urge the Census Bureau to follow such a policy and we call on other executive branch agencies and the Congress to lend their support to it.

BASIC REQUIREMENTS FOR MORE EFFECTIVE
USE OF ADMINISTRATIVE RECORDS

The panel believes that there are significant benefits to be obtained from greater use of administrative records both in the decennial census program and in the programs that provide current demographic data. For example, tabulations of birth and death records and extracts from tax and Social Security records are important inputs to the Census Bureau's current population estimates program and in the demographic analyses that have played a significant role in the evaluation of census coverage for several decades. However, the potential benefits of using administrative records, especially to produce more frequent and timely data for small geographic areas, are far from being fully realized. In this section we discuss major policy and technical issues that must be addressed in order to be successful in efforts to develop effective new uses of administrative records.

As indicated above, these issues were addressed in our interim report, and some of the relevant background presented in that discussion is repeated here. We also take note of some important developments over the past few months that are relevant to this discussion.

Access

Effective use of administrative records by the Census Bureau requires a legal right to access, the establishment of close and mutually beneficial ongoing relationships between the Census Bureau and the custodians of administrative records, and reasonable assurance of continued access to data that are suitable for the intended statistical uses. The value of administrative record systems for statistical uses will be enhanced if custodians are willing to consider making modest additions to or changes in content, when this can be done at a reasonable cost and without detriment to the program uses of the data.

By a legal right to access we mean at least the absence of legal prohibitions on access for statistical uses, and, preferably, positive statutory recognition of statistical uses as a permissible secondary use of the records. The Census Bureau probably has greater legal access to administrative records than any other U.S. statistical agency, but its access is by no means universal, especially to systems maintained at the state level, for which access is controlled in part by state laws.

Currently, the question of Census Bureau access to health records is of special interest. Under the Clinton administration's proposal for health care reform, virtually everyone would be covered by one of the available health care plans. Administration of the new system will require the creation and continuous updating of enrollment records for all participants with information about their identities, current addresses, characteristics, and plan affiliations. Potentially, these health care enrollment records could provide more complete coverage of the U.S. population, with current information about each person's location and demographic characteristics, than any other national system of administrative records. The records are likely to include information on each person's race and ethnicity, data elements that are lacking or incomplete in other administrative record systems with broad national coverage.

The potential usefulness of such a record system for the decennial census and other demographic data programs is obvious. The extent of its actual usefulness will be determined by decisions about the specific content of health care records and about legislation governing use of and access to them. The schedule for reaching these decisions is difficult to predict, but relevant legislation on the privacy and confidentiality of health records is being actively considered and may be enacted in the current session of the U.S. Congress. Also being considered is more general legislation that would modify and extend the scope of the Privacy Act of 1974 and establish a privacy protection commission.

The Committee on National Statistics, over the past several months, has paid close attention to the implications of health care reform for federal statistical activities. In March 1994, it approved and transmitted a letter report (Bradburn, 1994) to several members of the Congress who have played major roles in the development of legislation on the confidentiality of health care information. The position taken by the committee in this report can be summarized by the following excerpt:

> The Committee has two concerns. The first and foremost is that privacy and confidentiality of health care information be adequately protected. The second is that the U.S. health care system, individual health care subscribers, and the public as a whole benefit from access to that information for research and other statistical purposes in ways that protect confidentiality. It is not necessary to sacrifice either confidentiality or the benefits of information: both are possible if legislation provides for responsible access and demonstrated, effective means to protect confidentiality.

In the report, the committee identifies ways in which access to health care enrollment information would permit the Census Bureau to reduce the cost of decennial census operations and improve the quality of current population estimates.

A recommendation of the Panel on Confidentiality and Data Access of the Committee on National Statistics (Duncan et al., 1993) called for expanded access to administrative records for statistical uses, subject to appropriate constraints: "Greater access should be permitted to key statistical and administrative data sets for the development of sampling frames and other statistical uses. Additional data sharing should only be undertaken in those instances in which the procedures for collecting the data comply with the panel's recommendations for informed consent or notification" (Duncan et al., 1993:99, Recommendation 4.1).

Legal access is necessary but not sufficient for effective use. Access in specific instances is often arranged only with great difficulty. These difficulties will continue unless statistical agencies and the custodians of record systems develop new ways of thinking about statistical uses of administrative records. The custodians need to regard satisfying the statistical requirements of the nation as one of the responsibilities on which they will be judged, not as an inconvenience or an intrusion on their territory. Some flexibility is needed on the part of both statistical and program agencies in adapting their operating procedures and schedules to meet basic statistical needs. There must also be willingness by the statistical agencies to assist administrative agencies in every possible way, for example, by providing technical support to the latter for the production of small-area tabulations of administrative records, to the extent that this can be done while ensuring a one-way flow of administrative records for statistical uses. Statistics Canada's access to administrative records, which makes possible the demographic data system that is described later in this chapter, may provide a useful model.

These conditions might be more readily created if the Office of Management and Budget were to adopt a strong leadership position, as part of the current administration's campaign to reinvent government, in efforts to maximize the utility of information collected by federal government agencies. A 1976 policy statement of the Social Security Administration (U.S. Department of Health and Human Services, 1976:17) suggests a principle that might guide such efforts:

> The operation of the social security system produces a vast and unique body of statistical information about employment, payrolls, life-time earnings histories, retirement, disability, mortality, and benefit claims and payments.
>
> The Social Security Administration has an obligation to develop these data according to the best scientific standards and with maximum economy and minimum delay, and to publish them in a form useful both to the program administrator and to social scientists generally. It also has an obligation to encourage the linkage of these data with other bodies of statistical information and to make the data available for research uses by other organizations, subject always to careful safeguarding of the confidentiality of information relating to individuals.

A similar policy would be appropriate for all major systems of administrative records that have potential statistical uses.

The Census Bureau's initiative in organizing the July 1993 Interagency Conference on Statistical Uses of Administrative Records and its intention to hold a similar meeting with custodians of state record systems are important steps. As indicated in the proceedings of the first conference (Bureau of the Census, 1994h), many of the custodians of administrative record systems recognize that sharing their records for statistical uses would have benefits. Several officials said they would feel more comfortable sharing the records if specifically authorized to do so by their legislative authority. They were all conscious of the need to inform data subjects about how their data would be used and to inform the public about the benefits and risks associated with data sharing. They felt the need for some mechanism, such as an individual ombudsman, an expanded role for OMB or a data protection board, "to develop and oversee policies on data sharing, and to provide a balance between the interests of data providers and data users."

The panel also applauds the Census Bureau's initiative to establish and maintain its Administrative Records Information System, which now provides detailed information about major federal and state administrative record systems that may have potential statistical and research uses beyond those that are directly related to the programs for which they were established. The coverage, content, and structure of administrative record systems changes frequently, and it is important that the information system be periodically updated. The system, which is publicly accessible in electronic form, can be a valuable resource for all agencies and organizations wishing to explore possible statistical and research applications of administrative records.

Effective use of IRS records in the decennial census and other Census Bureau programs requires a close working relationship between the two agencies. In the past, the two agencies have occasionally had difficulty in agreeing on their respective roles and in developing and maintaining smooth working arrangements. Nonetheless, statistical uses of IRS records have led to major improvements and efficiencies in Census Bureau programs, especially in the quinquennial economic censuses, in which IRS and Social Security Administration records are a major input to the census mailing lists and eliminate the need to collect separate data for most of the small establishments. The negotiations between the two agencies for access to IRS records for use in the 1995 census test and the 2000 census will be an important test of this ongoing relationship.

The panel has been greatly encouraged by recent arrangements whereby the Census Bureau has funded work by a contractor to develop comprehensive methodological documentation of the IRS's research to compare estimated 1990 population counts based on a sample of linked individual income tax and informational return records with 1990 census counts, with and without adjustment (Czajka and Schirm, 1994). In a second phase of this project, the contractor will analyze the potential for using the same IRS data sets in the context of a census or a program of current population estimates. Census Bureau, IRS, and contractor personnel meet periodically to review the work and develop specific objectives.

The Census Bureau cannot commit itself to substantially greater reliance on administrative records unless it can have reasonable assurance of continued access. Proposed legislation that calls for the establishment of major new administrative records systems should be carefully monitored to ensure that possibilities for important statistical uses of the records are recognized and are not unnecessarily foreclosed.

We believe it is especially important for the Census Bureau, other statistical agencies, and the Statistical Policy Office of OMB to play a role in the development of new record systems in connection with health care reform. These agencies should have the opportunity to participate in decisions about content of the records, so that standard concepts and definitions that are suitable for both administrative and statistical purposes can be adopted. In our interim report, we recommended that the Statistical Policy Office recognize statistical uses of administrative records as one of its major areas of responsibility and assume an active role in facilitating effective working relationships between statistical and program agencies and in tracking relevant legislation.

Recommendation 5.1: Legislation that requires or authorizes the creation of individual record systems for administrative purposes should

not create unnecessary barriers to legitimate statistical uses of the records, including important uses not directly related to the programs that the records were developed to serve. Preferably, such legislation should explicitly allow for such uses, subject to strong protection of the confidentiality of individual information. The panel urges Congress, in considering legislation relevant to health care reform, not to foreclose possible uses of health care enrollment records for the decennial censuses and other basic demographic statistical programs.

Recommendation 5.2: To facilitate statistical uses of new health record systems, the responsible executive branch agencies should invite the Census Bureau and other federal statistical agencies to participate actively in the development of content and access provisions for these record systems.

Recommendation 5.3: The Office of Management and Budget should review identifiers, especially addresses, and demographic data items currently included in major administrative record systems with a view to promoting standardization and facilitation of statistical uses of information about individuals both in these record systems and in new ones that may be developed.

Public Acceptance

Expanded statistical uses of administrative records in the census will require at least the tacit acceptance of those who provide information about themselves to the program agencies. Greater use of administrative records could reduce the number of requests for individuals to provide information about themselves to the government and also has the potential for improving coverage and substantially reducing the cost of censuses. The key issues, however, are consent and confidentiality. Do people accept the use of information about themselves for statistical purposes that are not directly related to the purposes for which they supplied their information? Should they be able, as individuals, to prevent such uses? Will the confidentiality of their data be adequately protected? Effective use of administrative records for census evaluation, coverage improvement, and supplementation of content may require that one or more identifiers, such as full name, date of birth, and Social Security number, be collected in the census and entered into census electronic files, along with addresses. Will this be acceptable? These questions are not easy to answer.

As already noted, the final report of the Panel on Confidentiality and Data Access called for increased sharing of data among federal agencies for statistical and research purposes, with greater access to "key statistical and administrative data sets for the development of sampling frames and other statistical uses"

(Duncan et al., 1993, Recommendation 4.1). That panel specified that such uses should be conditional on strong protection of the confidentiality of the data and the use of suitable informed consent or notification procedures. It also recommended that statistical agencies undertake and support continuing research to monitor the views of data providers and the general public on data sharing for statistical purposes and on several other aspects of federal statistical activities (Recommendation 3.4).

We believe that it is necessary to proceed with public debate about the ethical, legal, and policy issues associated with statistical uses of administrative records. The Census Bureau has had contacts with privacy advocates in connection with previous censuses and has informed us that it plans future discussions that will focus specifically on statistical uses of administrative records in the 1995 census test. However, there has been some reluctance on the part of the agencies involved to enter a public debate for fear that calling attention to these questions might lead to discontinuance of important existing activities, such as the use of income tax return and Social Security data in the Census Bureau's intercensal population estimates programs. We believe it is better to face these questions directly. Discussions are likely to be more productive if they focus on specific uses of administrative records, such as improvement of coverage in the 2000 census and the implications of an administrative records census in 2010, rather than on broad philosophical questions.

Carefully designed surveys and focus group interviews can help provide background for public discussion of these issues. The views expressed by data providers and the public in surveys do not always coincide with those of privacy advocates as reflected in congressional testimony, panel reports, and other public venues. For example, some privacy advocates have expressed strong objections to the possible use of the Social Security number as an identifier for participants in health care plans. But in the 1993 Harris-Equifax Health Information Privacy Survey, about two-thirds of the respondents favored the use of the Social Security number for this purpose in preference to a new identifier (Louis Harris and Associates, 1993).

Relevant information on taxpayers' opinions about possible uses of their tax information in the census of population and for other statistical purposes has been collected in a series of surveys conducted for the IRS, most recently in the 1990 Taxpayer Opinion Survey. In that survey, the results suggested that the majority of taxpayers support the idea of their tax information being released to other agencies for statistical purposes, but that a minority, generally about 1 in 5, are strongly opposed. When they were specifically asked about the use of administrative records in a decennial census, 70 percent of the survey respondents favored the use of Social Security information on their date of birth and sex and 15 percent were strongly opposed. A smaller proportion, 61 percent, favored the use of income tax return information on their place of residence and income in the census and 23 percent were strongly opposed (Internal Revenue Service, 1993).

Another kind of evidence about people's feelings on this subject is provided by the responses of survey respondents to requests for their Social Security numbers or other identifiers, so that information about them residing in administrative record systems can be obtained and linked to their survey responses. When Social Security numbers have been requested in surveys sponsored by the Census Bureau, relatively small proportions of respondents, usually well under 10 percent, have refused to give them to the survey interviewers (Beresford, 1992). Response to these surveys and to individual survey items is voluntary.

Survey respondents' willingness to give permission for such linkages can be influenced considerably by the manner in which permission is sought. Common practice is to request the needed identifiers at some point in a survey, following a brief explanation of the purposes for which they will be used. Recent experiments conducted by Statistics Canada (1994) tested two different procedures for obtaining health insurance numbers from respondents to a national health survey, so that data from provincial health ministry administrative files could be linked to their survey responses. The common practice of asking for the numbers near the end of the survey, with an explanation of their intended use, resulted in a low refusal rate. However, a procedure that required a signed consent form was successful for only about one-half of the respondents.

The results of opinion surveys and experiments like the ones cited are sensitive to variations in many features: sponsorship and purpose of the survey; the population covered; the sample design and selection methods used; the wording, format, and order of questions; the context in which questions are asked; the mode of response; the level of nonresponse; and others. To obtain more information for developing its findings and recommendations on this topic, the panel commissioned a review of relevant research (Blair, 1994). Some of the preliminary findings of this review, which includes extensive analysis of the data from the most recent (1990) national Taxpayer Opinion Survey sponsored by the IRS, are reflected in our conclusions on this topic.

Data from different surveys and other sources are difficult to compare. Only the IRS Taxpayer Opinion Survey series specifically addressed statistical uses of administrative records, and that was done in the context of surveys dealing primarily with the experience and views of knowledgeable taxpayers (not the general adult population) relating to tax compliance issues. The series of U.S. surveys about privacy issues sponsored by Equifax, including the 1993 Health Information Privacy Survey, has focused almost entirely on people's concerns about administrative (nonstatistical) uses of and access to information about them in a much more general context. Nevertheless, analysis of the data from these two sets of surveys suggests a certain amount of consistency in identification of the population subgroups that are most concerned about privacy issues. Women, blacks, people with less education, and, somewhat less clearly, middle-aged people exhibit the highest proportions with general and specific privacy concerns.

It is our view that surveys and other research undertaken to date have not yet provided a sufficiently clear picture of the public's understanding of and views on statistical uses of administrative records. The issues are conceptually complex, requiring care in both explanation and attitude measurement. Most people have given little thought to this subject, so responses to questions about it may be based mostly on generalized feelings about privacy issues and may be sensitive to minor variations in question wording and context. Experience in the series of taxpayer opinion surveys has shown that asking people how they feel about specific kinds of uses leads to results that are substantially at variance with responses to broad philosophical questions. More information is needed about the specific concerns of those who express strong resistance to secondary uses of their administrative record information. Opinions may change if administrative record uses in the decennial census should enter the arena of broad public debate. For these reasons, the panel believes that further research on public views about the use of administrative records is needed.

Recommendation 5.4: The Census Bureau, in cooperation with other agencies and organizations, should support a program of research on public views about statistical uses of administrative records in government. The research should focus on public reaction to very specific administrative record use scenarios, rather than on general questions of privacy.

Possible biasing effects of the sponsorship of such research need to be guarded against. Survey designs, instruments, protocols, and procedures should by reviewed by qualified independent experts not associated with the sponsoring organizations. If legislation is passed that establishes a privacy protection commission or board, we believe it would be appropriate for such a body to sponsor research of this kind or to provide external advice on research plans to other organizations sponsoring such research.

Technical Requirements

Several of the central themes that are discussed in Chapters 1 and 2—including address list development, record linkage research, the need for long-term planning, and the need for greater interagency cooperation and coordination—are critical to making better use of administrative records in the decennial census and in other programs that produce small-area population and housing data. The first two of these are technical requirements, and in this subsection we discuss briefly their particular relevance to statistical uses of administrative records.

As stated in Chapter 2, the panel believes that a geographic database that is fully integrated with a Master Address File is a basic requirement, whether for a traditional census or for one making greater use of administrative records. To be cost-effective and available for noncensus uses, the system should be continuously updated. Its coverage should be extended to rural areas, and conversion of rural-type addresses to street addresses should be promoted by all means possible. We were pleased to note that the Census Bureau and U.S. Postal Service are collaborating on efforts to do this (Bureau of the Census, 1993a: November). Appendix B to the interim report of the Panel on Census Requirements explained clearly how such a system could serve as the keystone for using administrative records data to provide small-area data more frequently and inexpensively.

In our interim report, we recommended (Recommendation 1.1) that the transition to a continuous, integrated system begin immediately, at least for the 1995 census test sites, so that it could receive its first major tryout in the 1995 census test. We note that the Census Bureau recently expressed its intentions in the following terms: "The Census Bureau is committed to having a continuously updated, permanent address list linked to the TIGER database. . . . We plan to use the MAF [Master Address File] in the 1995 census test" (Bureau of the Census, 1994a:25).

Record linkage—that is, the identification of records belonging to the same unit, either within a single data set or in two different data sets—is critical to enhanced uses of administrative records, whether in the context of a full administrative records census or a more traditional design. If different administrative data sets are to be used to improve the coverage of the Master Address File or of persons at known addresses, duplicates must be identified and eliminated. Uses of administrative records to supply missing data or to evaluate the coverage and content of the census enumeration all require some type of record linkage for persons or addresses.

Record linkage, like any element of census data collection and processing, is subject to error. The Census Bureau and other organizations have developed effective techniques for linking large data sets, but many aspects need further research and development as the techniques are applied in specific circumstances. How can the inputs be standardized to facilitate linkages? Over how wide an area should initial computerized matches be undertaken? What are the best keys (e.g., name, address, date of birth, Social Security number), alone or in combination, and what are the costs and other considerations for capturing these items in the computerized files for a census or evaluation survey? Additional research on these questions is a prerequisite to success in making more effective use of administrative records. As discussed in more detail in the next two sections of this chapter, testing should be carried out in conjunction with the 2000 census and the tests leading up to it and also in separate initiatives to explore the possibility of a 2010 census based primarily on administrative records.

Another technical requirement for enhanced uses of administrative records is knowledge about the quality of the data that they can provide. How well do administrative record systems, individually or in combination, cover the target population for a census? Recent work in the United States (Sailer et al., 1993; Czajka and Schirm, 1994) and in Canada (Standish et al., 1993) indicates that well over 90 percent of the respective countries' enumerated populations can be identified in their tax systems, not supplemented by any other source. How much could this coverage be improved by adding records from other systems, and how would the coverage of subgroups defined by geography or other characteristics (differential coverage) be affected, both in absolute and relative terms? To what extent do the record systems proposed for use include information that makes it feasible to identify addresses and persons that are not members of the target population for the decennial census?

Besides coverage, the accuracy and relevance of data available from administrative records need to be considered. For example, suppose there are administrative data for persons whose census responses are incomplete. Is enough known about the quality of these data to make an informed choice among alternatives: further nonresponse follow-up, imputation based on similar persons, or substitution of the administrative data? To what extent could tax data be used either to evaluate or substitute for income data collected in a census? What are the implications of conceptual differences? Opportunities and resources should be sought to pursue questions like these.

Evaluation of the quality of information from administrative records should take into account the purposes for which the data may be used and the quality of comparable information that can be obtained in censuses and surveys. If data of equivalent or perhaps somewhat lower quality can be obtained from administrative records at a substantially lower cost, their use may be acceptable. Failure of administrative data to duplicate exactly the concepts used in the decennial census does not necessarily rule out their use for any statistical purpose. As discussed later in this chapter, IRS data on taxable income may provide useful indicators of change in total money income as defined in the census.

AN ADMINISTRATIVE RECORDS CENSUS:
KEY FEATURES AND ISSUES

As noted above, we agreed, at an early stage of our work, with the Census Bureau's conclusion that a census based primarily on administrative records was not a feasible option for 2000 (Bureau of the Census, 1992c). However, we also recommended that the Census Bureau initiate a separate program of research on uses of administrative records focusing on the 2010 census and on the current estimates program. This recommendation stemmed from our belief that research work must start now if an administrative records census is to be a possibility for 2010. Without an early start, the Census Bureau will miss the important opportunity provided by the 2000 census to try out and evaluate many aspects of this new approach. In this section we examine what a census based primarily on administrative records might mean, and consider the main political, managerial, and technical issues raised by this possibility.

In essence, an administrative records census represents a reversal of the roles of enumeration and administrative record use in the census. In the traditional census, and even with the innovative changes proposed for 2000, the census depends first and foremost on enumeration of the population, with administrative records available for use as an aid and supplement to the enumeration process. In an administrative records census, the administrative records become the primary source of information, supplemented when necessary by enumeration or other methods of data collection.

In our view there are five primary issues to be addressed in assessing the feasibility and benefits of an administrative records census.

1. *Privacy*: Is the American public prepared to accept the use and linkage of administrative records for the purposes of a census?

2. *Coverage*: Can administrative records deliver the level and distribution of overall coverage needed from a census?

3. *Geography*: Can administrative records allocate individuals accurately by place of residence as required by a census?

4. *Content*: How much of the traditional content can we expect an administrative record census to deliver, and with what quality?

5. *Cost*: How would the cost of an administrative record census compare with other alternatives?

These are the issues on which a research program must focus. We examine each of them in more detail below, but first we will sketch out some possible scenarios, and potential record sources, for an administrative records census.

Definition of an Administrative Records Census

There are many approaches one could envisage for an administrative records census. We will sketch out here a generic approach that seems to fit the current statistical and administrative record infrastructure in the United States. This scenario, which is illustrated in Figure 5.1, would start with a geocoded Master Address File purporting to contain all addresses in the country. Administrative sources would probably be used to some degree in the construction of this initial Master Address File.

Selected administrative files of individuals (or families or households) would be matched individually by address to the Master Address File. This would result in an enhanced file with a set (maybe an empty set) of individuals associated with each address. There would also be a set of addresses from administrative records that do not appear to have a match on the Master Address File.

The next step would be an edit that would apply specified checks to each address to identify cases in which the set of individuals linked to the address fails internal consistency tests, or no individuals are linked to the address. These would be the addresses for which some form of follow-up and resolution is required.

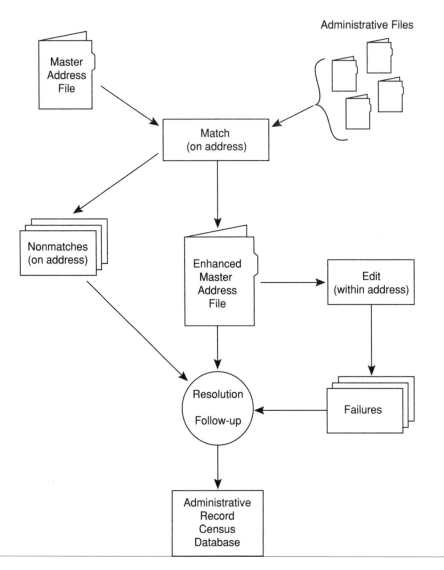

FIGURE 5.1   Schematic diagram of an administrative record census.

The next step would be resolution, in which cases referred from the edit, as well as addresses from administrative records that do not match to the Master Address File, are investigated and resolved. The precise form of this investigation can depend on the nature of the inconsistency found, but might include automated correction or imputation, manual review and decision, supplementary matching to additional sources, and telephone and field follow-up. The application of these resolution decisions to the enhanced Master Address File produces the census database.

This generic scenario leaves much room for variations. One important possibility would be to investigate and resolve only a sample of unmatched cases. This would be analogous to the use of sampling for nonresponse follow-up in a conventional census. Even if a combination of administrative files is used to produce the census data base, we would not want to assume that coverage is sufficiently complete and uniform to require no further correction. Like a conventional census, a census based primarily on administrative records would require the fourth step that was identified at the beginning of Chapter 1: a coverage measurement process that estimates the size of the population not covered through the initial and follow-up processes. The coverage measurement, which would be undertaken for a sample of areas, could take various forms, such as field enumeration, more intensive investigation of unmatched cases, verification of household composition for matched addresses, or some combination of these. Estimation procedures would be applied to the results to produce a one-number administrative records census.

Other crucial issues are the choice of administrative records to match to the Master Address File, specification of the checks or edits to be applied to the individuals who are linked to a particular address, and the nature of resolution measures for those cases that fail the checks. The choices in these areas will depend on the results of research into the quality and coverage of administrative record sources, and the costs and effectiveness of different resolution measures. The closer one can move to the situation in which resolution through field follow-up is unnecessary, the greater the benefits from the administrative records approach.

Another crucial issue is timing. As long as the concept of a specific Census Day remains, it is important that any follow-up take place soon after that date. This implies that the administrative records to be used must be available before or soon after Census Day. Most administrative records have some time lag, so versions that predate Census Day will probably have to be used.

Variations of an administrative records census that do not require a Master Address File do not seem promising. Whereas the administrative records themselves could be used to develop an address list, there would still need to be some bonding of these addresses to a precise geographic location.

In fact, if we look at what other countries have done, those that have carried out an administrative records census have had not only the equivalent of a Master Address File, but also a permanent population register, i.e., a requirement that individuals register all changes of address with a local or central authority. For example, Denmark, which is the leader in administrative records censuses, having conducted them in 1981 and 1991 (Redfern, 1994), has a network of permanent registers of population, dwellings, and enterprises. Other Scandinavian countries that have a population register, such as Sweden and Finland, have nonetheless conducted censuses that combine administrative records use with traditional enumerations in order to improve the quality and extend the content of the administrative record sources. Outside the Scandinavian countries, to our knowledge, only the Netherlands has conducted a census based primarily on administrative records. Therefore, in moving toward an administrative records census, the United States would be joining a select group of countries and would be breaking new ground by taking a census based on administrative records in the absence of a population register.

Record Sources for an Administrative Records Census

Three major requirements emerge when one considers what types of administrative records would be most suitable for use in a census based primarily on administrative records. First, the census should have as its core a nationally consistent set of administrative records. These could be held federally or could be decentralized but should be subject to precise national standards of content, quality, and timeliness. Although state or local administrative records can be very useful for local follow-up or supplementation of a traditional census, an approach that uses administrative records as the primary data source must start from a set of records that have broad and consistent coverage over most of the country. The prospects of trying to bring 50 or more independent administrative systems into conformity for a census, if they are not already following common standards, are not attractive. This preference is not meant to preclude the use of state and local record systems to supplement the basic administrative record set(s) used for the census. However, care should be taken to avoid the use of supplemental record systems in ways that would clearly lead to inequitable treatment of different localities or population groups.

The second requirement is, insofar as possible, to use administrative record systems that are updated on a continuous basis, rather than records that are subject only to periodic updating. Fulfillment of this requirement allows a snapshot to be taken at any point in time, in particular on Census Day, rather than being restricted to specific points in time when a file update has been completed. It is also almost certain that the average lag between real changes and their appearance in the file will be much less with a continuously updated system. For example, a record system for administering the provision and financing of health care may be updated every time there is a change in status affecting coverage, and every time there is a transaction with the health care system. In contrast, a record system for collecting income taxes may be updated for most people only once a year, following filing of their annual tax returns.

It is unlikely that the administrative record set(s) chosen as the basic source for the main collection phase of the census will provide equivalent coverage of all population subgroups defined in terms of geography or demographic and socioeconomic variables. The third requirement, therefore, is to supplement the core administrative record set(s) with other types of records that are expected to be promising sources for improving coverage of addresses or persons most likely to be missed by the basic administrative record sources. Some of the supplementation efforts could be made part of the main collection phase of the census; additional efforts could be part of special procedures analogous to the integrated coverage measurement survey that is proposed as a means of producing a one-number conventional census.

To illustrate some of the considerations that must go into the choice of administrative record systems, but without meaning to restrict consideration of other potentially useful sources, we next review two major contenders for the role of core administrative record system in an administrative records census: the individual taxation system and the health care system.

Income Tax and Social Security Records

About 65 percent of the population files a tax return either as primary or secondary taxpayers (Sailer et al., 1993). Children and other dependent individuals are claimed as exemptions by tax filers. In addition, many nonfiling individuals are known to the tax system through informational documents covering particular sources of income. By carefully combining and unduplicating these various sets of individuals, estimates of population can be developed from the individual tax system.

Research along these lines is under way at the IRS and has produced estimates of population that are 97.5 percent of the 1990 census population at the national level (Sailer et al., 1993). Coverage of males (99 percent) is higher than of females (96 percent). At the state level these ratios vary between 91 and 104 percent. Similar results have been obtained from comparable work in Canada. These results are encouraging but not yet good enough to stand alone—especially when we remember that these percentages are in relation to a census count that is itself probably 1-2 percent below the true population count. The variation in coverage between states may be due partly to the problem of counting tax filers at the appropriate location, a problem that is likely to become more apparent as one tries to make estimates for smaller geographic areas. Moreover, the observed net coverage rates may mask levels of offsetting under- and overcoverage higher than those estimated to have occurred in the 1990 census.

It is also the case that these high coverage rates have been achieved without any explicit attempt to adapt the tax system to become a source of population estimates. Further analysis of coverage rates should help to pinpoint sectors of the population that are not well covered and to identify measures that might be taken within the tax system to improve both coverage and geographic precision. Changes to tax rules themselves, particularly changes that encourage low-income individuals to file to receive tax credits, may also help to fill some of the coverage gaps.

Information in IRS files can be and for some purposes has been linked with information in files of the Social Security Administration, using Social Security number as the primary match key. Such linkages have made it possible for Sailer and colleagues to develop national estimates of the 1990 population by gender and age group. The key Social Security file, the NUMIDENT file, also contains information on race and ethnicity, determined at the time each person's Social Security number was issued, but the race/ethnic data are incomplete and of questionable quality.

Continuing this line of research appears worthwhile. If its potential materializes, it should eventually result in a policy decision that the production of population estimates become a recognized objective of the tax system, rather than just an incidental by-product. This would serve to justify any changes to the administrative system needed primarily for the purposes of population estimation. Even if this approach does not develop into a replacement for the census, it will surely lead to valuable intercensal estimates of population change.

Recommendation 5.5: Research on the production of population estimates from Internal Revenue Service and Social Security Administration records should continue as a joint initiative of these agencies with the Census Bureau and should focus on identifying measures that could serve to reduce coverage differentials and improve geographic precision.

Health Care Records

In contrast to the well-established individual tax system, comprehensive uniform health care records do not yet exist. But, as discussed in the preceding section, they may soon, and that presents a statistical opportunity that should not be missed. Given the coverage objectives for health care, one can expect that the records needed to support the system will provide very high coverage of the population. Furthermore, and again in contrast to the tax system, the health care system should have the advantage of being a system that almost all people will wish to be in rather than one they wish to avoid. The basic enrollment records are likely to include race and ethnicity information, based on the latest OMB requirements, for nearly all persons, something that is now lacking in the Social Security Administration and Internal Revenue Service record systems. This is potentially an extremely valuable source of population data.

There is a window of opportunity as a health care record system is put in place, but two important principles must be accepted. First, there must be recognition of the legitimacy of use of these records for census-type purposes. Second, there has to be statistical input to their design to enhance their value for this purpose by, for example, inclusion of appropriate information on geographic location, individual characteristics (especially race and ethnicity), and family relationships.

Given the legitimate privacy concerns that surround health care records, it is important to distinguish the demographic and socioeconomic enrollment information from the medical information that reflects general health status and specific encounters with the health system. It is only the former that is relevant to consideration of census alternatives. The latter is certainly of interest for medical research and health policy, but its access should probably be subject to different rules than those for the basic demographic data.

Other Major Record Systems

An administrative record census would not necessarily have to be based entirely on a single core system. Supplementation of the core system with records from other systems that have national coverage and are consistent content across states might prove cost-effective, especially if these additional record systems tend to cover populations that are more likely to be missed in an enumerative census. In the 1995 census test, the Census Bureau is planning to experiment with the use of several such files, including those maintained for the Food Stamp, Aid to Families With Dependent Children, and Medicaid programs. It is important to recognize, however, that ongoing initiatives for welfare reform are gathering strength, with the result that these programs and the associated record systems may soon undergo substantial change. The panel's Recommendations 5.1 and 5.2, which have singled out expected changes in health care records, could apply equally to new or modified record systems for welfare programs; that is, appropriate Census Bureau uses of records from these systems should not be precluded and the Census Bureau should have an opportunity to participate in the design of new record systems.

Summary of Key Factors Affecting Feasibility

We now return to the five primary issues identified earlier on which we feel a research program needs to focus if an administrative records census is to become a reality.

1. *Public acceptance.* The issue of public acceptance of the use of administrative records has been addressed in general in the preceding section. Because the census is the best known of all government statistical activities, the issue becomes paramount in the case of an administrative records census. The public benefits of using administrative records for a census, primarily in saving money and reducing respondent burden, have to be seen to outweigh any perceived invasion of privacy or violation of confidentiality from their use. A significant

public information effort would be needed to make clearer the distinction between statistical uses and administrative uses and the public benefits and benig-
nancy of the former.

We believe that it is important to pursue actively the public debate about an
administrative records census. (Some aspects were covered in a March 16, 1994,
hearing of the House Subcommittee on Census, Statistics and Postal Personnel on
uses of health information for research and statistical purposes.) If the idea is to
be rejected on political grounds, it might as well be rejected before significant
investment is made. And if the idea is to be judged on cost-benefit considerations, with some cost ascribed to the rights of individuals to control uses of
information about themselves, then a debate on these costs and benefits, with
an element of public education in it, should begin in parallel to technical
developments.

2. *Coverage.* Because one of the prime objectives of census redesign is to
reduce differential undercoverage, while at least maintaining overall coverage
levels, the level of coverage that an administrative record census can achieve is a
primary issue. We have reported above on work by the Internal Revenue Service
to begin to assess what overall coverage rates might be achievable from tax
records without any adaptation of tax reporting for purely statistical ends. We
have recommended that this work continue.

Assessing differentials in coverage by demographic characteristics requires
these characteristics to be available in the administrative files. For age and sex,
and maybe marital status, this is not a problem, but for race, one of the primary
correlates of undercoverage, it is. Options for associating a race variable with tax
records would have to be developed. A complete refiling of Social Security
numbers to eliminate duplicates, add personal identification numbers, and serve
related purposes would offer one option. Another would be to make greater use
of the birth registration system, possibly including parents' Social Security numbers on the certificates.

In the case of health care records, the opportunity still exists to ensure that
the required variables are included in the basic health care enrollment records. A
recent news article (Vobejda, 1994) indicates that the main advocacy organizations for racial and ethnic minorities are in favor of this.

3. *Geography.* The importance of an up-to-date Master Address File to a
successful census has already been stressed. For an administrative record census
it is crucial. Three other areas of research are important to the geographic dimen-
sion of an administrative record census. If the census requires persons to be
counted at their usual residence, administrative records must contain residential
addresses. The extent to which this is the case and the accuracy of de jure address
recording need to be assessed.

Addresses themselves must reflect geographic location. In many rural areas
this is not yet the case. The creation of urban-style addresses for rural areas is a
prerequisite for an administrative record census, and the Census Bureau is work-

ing with the Post Office to bring this about (Bureau of the Census, 1993a: November). Postal codes could be very helpful in matching addresses, especially if they are detailed and reported accurately in the administrative records. Liaison with the Post Office in the future development of the postal code system should aim at making the system as consistent with census needs as possible.

Finally, as discussed in the preceding section, efficient address and person matching software will be crucial to the large-scale matching operation that will be required by an administrative record census.

4. *Content.* Administrative records will not be able to match the richness of content of a long-form census. In terms of replicating short-form content, the gaps are likely to be race and family relationships. If administrative records are to become a basis for statistical uses, including the census, it would be helpful to specify a core set of demographic variables that should be maintained on all administrative files.

Particular administrative files will be rich in certain variables (e.g., income tax files are rich in income variables); other variables will not be available through any administrative record system and would have to be the subject of a follow-on or postcensal survey if they are to be linked directly to the census. Alternatively, estimates for these variables could be obtained at a fairly low level of geography from a continuous measurement system, as discussed in Chapter 6.

The fact that a variable is contained in an administrative record system does not ensure its relevance and quality. As noted earlier in Recommendation 5.3, we believe the Office of Management and Budget should take the lead in promoting standardization of identifiers and basic demographic variables that are commonly included in administrative records. Such standardization would benefit both statistical and program agencies. The latter would find it easier to relate aggregate program data to Census Bureau population data to analyze coverage and other features of their programs. The quality assurance procedures that are used within each administrative record system will have to be assessed in determining usability in a census.

5. *Cost.* A major reason for considering an administrative record census is its potential to be cheaper than a revised traditional methodology. It is difficult to cost an administrative record census without a clearer idea of the record sources and the methods to be used. Nevertheless, a costing model framework should be developed so that initial crude cost estimates can be derived and subsequently revised as the features of a practical administrative record census methodology are tied down.

Recommendation 5.6: The Census Bureau should continue its development of a cost model for an administrative record census and should use the model to maintain current cost estimates for several versions of this option as they are developed.

Modelled costs for several versions of an administrative record census should be compared with the costs of the alternative proposed census methodologies for 2000, not with 1990 costs. If the supposed significant savings do not materialize as research proceeds, the rationale for further pursuit of the administrative records option should be reexamined.

Testing an Administrative Records Census Approach

The previous section has identified a series of research issues to be addressed. Adequate exploration of these issues will require a series of tests that progressively expand the administrative record census process through the stages illustrated in Figure 5.1. For example, the following type of research program could be envisioned:

1. Pilot test(s) to construct a census purely from administrative records in a defined and limited geographic area—primarily to learn of the problems;

2. Test(s) as in (1), but in conjunction with a conventional census test to allow evaluation of coverage;

3. Test(s) that incorporate follow-up activities to investigate missing addresses and households for which the administrative data fail to meet standards for completeness and consistency—primarily procedural tests;

4. Test(s) as in (3), but in conjunction with a conventional census test (or a coverage measurement survey associated with a census test) to allow evaluation of coverage. This will require careful design to ensure that the administrative records test and the conventional census do not affect each other; and

5. Full stand-alone dress rehearsal(s) of an administrative records census in chosen areas, using the procedures found to be most effective in steps (1) to (4).

Since the 2000 census represents the last chance before 2010 to compare an administrative records census approach to the traditional approach under full census conditions, it is essential that research should by then have advanced to the stage at which a meaningful test (probably of type (4) above) can be undertaken in conjunction with the 2000 census. To meet this timetable will require an immediate start to the research program whose elements have been identified above.

Recommendation 5.7: During the 2000 census the Census Bureau should test one or more designs for an administrative records census in selected areas. Planning for this testing should begin immediately.

As stated at the start of this chapter, the panel believes that the Census Bureau should treat the possibility of a 2010 administrative record census as a live option, to be carefully explored and evaluated during the current decennial census cycle. The option may be rejected later in the cycle on the basis of new developments in legislation that governs coverage and content of and access to administrative records or public opinion about secondary statistical uses of the records. Research may show that the cost reduction and other advantages are smaller than expected, that the quality of administrative records data is inadequate, or that there are other unforeseen problems. However, we don't know enough now to reach a firm conclusion. Even if a 2010 administrative records census should prove to be out of the question, the research necessary to evaluate its feasibility may facilitate and accelerate other beneficial uses of administrative records to produce small-area demographic data.

USE OF ADMINISTRATIVE RECORDS IN THE 2000 CENSUS

We have recommended that the Census Bureau follow a two-track approach to expanded uses of administrative records. The 2000 census track, which is the subject of this section, would identify and test new uses of administrative records considered feasible for use in the 2000 census. Possible uses include coverage improvement, content improvement, evaluation of the census, and measures to improve operational efficiency. The long-range track would develop and test procedures for a possible administrative records census in 2010 or beyond and uses of administrative records in other demographic data programs, such as current population estimates and current sample surveys, including any new surveys that might be started as part of a continuous measurement program (see Chapter 6).

The preceding section of this chapter discussed the administrative records census part of the long-range track. The section that follows this one will discuss the current estimates and surveys parts of the long-range track. Tests of administrative record uses prior to the 2000 census and uses of administrative records in the 2000 census, if designed with the long-range track in mind, can contribute in important ways to progress on that track. Such progress requires that the Census Bureau take advantage of favorable opportunities to acquire knowledge about key administrative records systems and gain experience with their use.

The 1995 Census Test

A Census Bureau memorandum describing plans for testing various uses of administrative records in the 1995 census test was made available to the panel in January 1994 (Knott, 1994). A more widely distributed document, the "1995 Census Test Design Plan," which was issued in February, describes some of the uses of administrative records that the Census Bureau plans to evaluate in the test. The Census Bureau's plans call for the development of an administrative records database for each of the test sites, using records from several federal, state, and local record systems. Negotiation for acquisition of these records is already under way.

Several different uses of the administrative records database will be tested directly as part of the 1995 census test or simulated and evaluated by comparison with the census test results. The primary activities for which uses of administrative records will be tested or simulated are coverage improvement for the count portion of the test and integrated coverage measurement. Administrative records, along with data from the 1990 census and other sources, will also be used to develop a targeting database for use in the identification of areas with specific barriers to enumeration and efficient stratification of samples for nonresponse follow-up and integrated coverage measurement operations. It is anticipated that new software for matching and unduplication of persons will be developed to support all of these uses. These plans are consistent with the panel's recommendations in its interim report (Chapter 4, Recommendations 4.3 to 4.5) and we hope that they can be successfully implemented.

Privacy and confidentiality aspects of the research will require close attention. Census Bureau staff have been working on the development of respondent notification statements for the census test questionnaires and on the language that will be included to describe planned uses of administrative records (response to the census test will be mandatory, so it is not appropriate to refer to informed consent procedures in this instance). These uses will also have to be described in the Privacy Act record systems notice or notices for the census test that are required to be published in the *Federal Register*. Staff also plan to meet with organizations and individuals who are interested in privacy issues to explain and discuss their plans for administrative records uses in the 1995 census test.

Maintaining the confidentiality of the identifiable record extracts that will be obtained from several different administrative sources is also an important consideration. To maintain the continued trust and confidence of the public and of the federal and other agencies that supply these records, the Census Bureau will need a detailed plan for physical security and for control of access to the records at all stages—who will use them and for what purposes. An audit trail to record all instances of access should be part of the plan.

Because of the timing of this report, the panel was not in a position to comment in depth on technical details of plans for testing administrative record uses in the 1995 census test. What we have seen so far is encouraging. At this time, we have one general recommendation and comments on two specific features of the test plan.

Recommendation 5.8: The Census Bureau should plan its uses of administrative records in the 1995 census test and other tests leading up to the 2000 census and in the census itself in a manner that will also provide knowledge and experience of value for a possible administrative records census in 2010 or beyond and for uses of administrative records in demographic programs other than the census.

The primary reason for testing administrative records uses in the 1995 census test is unquestionably to determine what kinds of uses are most likely to be effective in attaining the main goals for the 2000 census, namely, to reduce differential undercoverage and unit costs of enumeration. However, with careful planning, much can also be learned about other potential uses of the records, whether for current programs or for a future administrative records census. One implication of this strategy is that attempts to obtain specific administrative record files should not necessarily be abandoned as soon as it becomes evident that they cannot be obtained in time for operational use in the 1995 census test. If obtained later, these files can still be used to simulate their use in the test or for other purposes, such as improving current population estimates. We believe that these considerations are especially important for major federal and state record systems.

In keeping with this general theme, we have two specific suggestions. The first is that birth records for a time period surrounding the 1995 census test enumeration date should be obtained for at least some of the test sites. Birth records could play a role in integrated coverage measurement procedures or, failing that, in the evaluation of those procedures.

Second, as mentioned in our interim report (p. 77), we suggest that Social Security numbers be obtained, on a voluntary basis, for a sample of people in one or more of the test sites. Doing this would contribute to general research on record linkage techniques by providing a basis for evaluation of the relative effectiveness of the Social Security number as a match key compared with other identifiers like name, address, and exact date of birth. A second reason would be to facilitate a full two-way match of people counted in the test sites by conventional census methods with those identified by one or more administrative records sources. In particular, it would be useful in an attempt to determine whether people enumerated but not identified in administrative records for the test sites were covered by administrative records for areas outside the test sites.

The 2000 Census

Earlier in this section we identified four kinds of administrative record uses that are worth considering for the 2000 census. We now consider each one in somewhat more detail.

1. *Measures to improve coverage.* Coverage improvement measures are of two kinds: those aimed at improving the Master Address File and those aimed at improving the coverage of individuals. The former can be used throughout the decade, or at least prior to the census, to ensure a good starting address list. The latter needs to use records current at the time of the census and will tend to focus on administrative sources that are rich in data on hard-to-enumerate subpopulations. Both kinds of uses of administrative records could be made either across the board or for a sample of blocks as part of a built-in adjustment process designed to produce a one-number census. Administrative records would be a

logical element of an integrated coverage measurement procedure (see Chapter 4) in which close to 100 percent coverage is sought for a sample of areas.

2. *Measures to improve content.* Administrative records have already been used to some extent to evaluate census responses, for example, in record checks with tax data to assess income reporting. A next step could be to use them as a source of data to replace data that are missing due to nonresponse or data that failed edit tests. The final level would be to use administrative records as the initial source of data for some variables, with some form of follow-up for missing data cases as necessary.

3. *Measures to improve operational efficiency.* The use of administrative records as a source of telephone numbers for use in nonresponse follow-up is one example of use for operational efficiency. Administrative records data could be used prior to the census to identify hard-to-enumerate areas for which special enumeration methods might be appropriate or as a basis for stratification of samples selected for nonresponse follow-up or integrated coverage measurement.

4. *Measures to evaluate the census.* Uses of administrative records for evaluation will depend very much on how the 2000 census methodology develops with regard to integrated coverage measurement processes that are designed as part of a one-number census. In this context, special attention would be given to the use of administrative records sources believed to offer the best coverage of hard-to-enumerate subpopulations. As in the past, administrative records are also likely to be one of the inputs to the demographic analyses that have traditionally played a role, along with postenumeration surveys, in evaluation of decennial census coverage. To the extent that administrative records are not used to improve content, they could be used to evaluate content.

Uses of administrative records for coverage and content improvement and evaluation can occur in three phases of the census: in the conduct of the main census operations (those activities that are carried out everywhere, i.e., without any use of sampling, and in sample nonresponse follow-up); in the acquisition and use of data for an integrated coverage measurement sample; and in evaluation activities. Development of the final design for the 2000 census will require decisions about what uses of administrative records (and other special techniques) are appropriate for each of these phases. Such decisions will depend partly on the relative costs of specific procedures and partly on complex technical considerations. Especially important among the latter are the nature of the sample designs and estimation procedures to be used for integrated coverage measurement and the potential effects of lack of independence on the estimation procedures.

Successful implementation of the Census Bureau's plan for construction of an administrative records database for the 1995 census test sites is a necessary prerequisite for obtaining the information needed to make well-informed design decisions about uses of administrative records in the 2000 census. In addition, significant resources will be needed to undertake simulation studies and other kinds of analyses of the role administrative records may play in the 2000 census program and elsewhere. We hope that the Census Bureau will have the will and the resources to take full advantage of this unique opportunity.

As noted earlier in this chapter, new health record systems that are expected to emerge over the next several years will be automated and are likely to have close to universal coverage. It is unlikely that such systems will exist for all states in time for significant general use in the 2000 census. However, it is expected that some states will have their reformed health care systems in place fairly soon, presenting opportunities to explore the characteristics and potential uses of health care enrollment records for demographic data programs. One possibility would be to simulate an administrative records census in one or more of these states in 2000.

Recommendation 5.9: In maintaining and updating its Administrative Records Information System, the Census Bureau should give high priority to the acquisition of detailed information about record systems that are being developed to support health care reform at the state level. The Census Bureau should seek early opportunities to obtain and use health enrollment records in one or more states and should plan for experimental uses of these records as part of the 2000 census.

USE OF ADMINISTRATIVE RECORDS IN OTHER DEMOGRAPHIC PROGRAMS

Administrative records already play a major role in various demographic programs of the federal statistical system. In fact, the system is highly dependent on the outputs of different record systems, whether regulatory or administrative in nature. A glance at any edition of the *Statistical Abstract of the United States* shows the extent and wealth of information now available. Statistical information based on aggregated data has always been forthcoming as a natural by-product of administrative record reporting systems. These aggregated data are an important ingredient in federal, state, and local information systems.

Even at the aggregate level one can distinguish between the mere summarization of data on a particular subject or program and the extension to secondary analysis or indirect measures of change in other social, economic, and demographic variables. For example, small-area population estimates for postcensal periods are heavily dependent on aggregated administrative record data that are deemed to be symptomatic of population change. Examples of uses abound at all levels of government at which programs are in place for producing current small-area population estimates carried forward from the last decennial census. Some examples: the Census Bureau uses school enrollment, housing units (building permits), vital records (births and deaths), immigration statistics, federal income tax returns and exemptions, and Medicare data in various ways in their population estimates programs; states and localities, use data on utility hookups, employment (from the federal-state unemployment insurance program), and drivers' licenses. At the local level the most widely used indicator or variable is building (and demolition) permits and similar types of information (e.g., certificates of occupancy and utility connections) to measure population change (Bureau of the Census, 1993g).

Extensive programs exist in other areas, but we need not belabor the point. The main purpose of the above litany is to clearly separate and distinguish such uses of aggregated administrative records from our current focus on the more intensive use of administrative records centered on individual records with the potential for matching, merging, linking, and geographic coding. It is at the micro level that the uses of administrative records discussed in this chapter are most effective for census-taking purposes and where they can have the greatest impact on current and future programs of population and other demographic estimates.

Uses in Current Population Estimates

The Census Bureau's Population Division has an extensive program of population estimates producing figures for the nation, states, counties, and places (cities, towns, and townships). These estimates represent updates from the last decennial census. Estimated population counts are provided for all levels of geography and counts for a few demographic subgroups at the higher levels only. The estimates serve many important uses, a major one being the allocation of federal and state funds. Examples of other uses are as denominators for vital rates and as benchmarks for survey estimates. Furthermore, many states also use the postcensal subnational estimates (produced by the states and cooperatively with the Census Bureau) to allocate state funds to counties, townships, and incorporated places within states (Long, 1993).

The history of the development, preparation and publication of population estimates for all places in the country and the role of administrative records in that process demonstrates how administrative records can be used to address major data needs and methodological challenges created by the demands of public policy and legislation. In the 1970s, general revenue-sharing legislation created a requirement for population and income estimates for all general-purpose units of government at a time when existing methodologies and available data sets were inadequate for such an undertaking. Fortunately, research in progress at about that time into possible statistical uses of individual income tax returns suggested the viability, validity, and credibility of their use as a primary input to estimates of population and income change. Considering the large amounts of money being allocated and distributed on the basis of the estimates, it was extremely important for the methodology to have a reasonably sound statistical basis and face validity—that elusive quality that says the system sounds right.

The IRS individual income tax records contained the necessary ingredients for a viable and sophisticated estimation process—one that permitted a separate estimate of population change through net migration, the major unknown component in the population change estimation process. The important characteristics of the records were: (1) a unique identifier, the Social Security number, that permitted matching records (within the system) over time and (2) a residential address whereby each record could be coded to an appropriate level of geography. Another important feature was the consistently relatively high coverage: at that time about 80 to 85 percent of the population was regularly covered on tax returns, with some geographic differential. Most important, the legislation provided for Census Bureau access to the individual records (actually an extract of each record with selected information required by the Census Bureau for the estimation process) on a continuing, annual basis and permission to request periodically a modification of the basic individual tax form to obtain information on specific place of residence to supplement the address information. This latter change was needed to provide a means of geographically assigning each record to the appropriate local jurisdiction—one of some 39,000 governmental units to which funds were to be distributed. This type of accommodation through modification of administrative records to meet program needs suggests a precedent for possible modification in tax returns or other administrative records to accommodate to specific statistical needs of other programs. The feasibility of a census conducted primarily through administrative records could be substantially increased by adjustments in both the content and format of the source records.

At present the Census Bureau regularly uses micro-level administrative records in its demographic programs only to generate estimates of the total population for all areas of the country. (With the ending of revenue sharing, estimates of income—per-capita income—are no longer produced.) However, a useful by-product of the methodology is estimates of gross migration flows for geographic areas of the population covered on tax returns. These are important proxies of population migration patterns and provide states and localities important insights into the characteristics of in- and out-migrants.

Data Enhanced Through Linkages

In recent years the Census Bureau has researched and experimented with estimation of population by age, race, and Spanish origin for selected large geographic areas by linking a 20 percent sample of the Social Security Administration's NUMIDENT file, which contains such demographic characteristics as age, sex, race, and Spanish origin, to the basic IRS record extract. Estimates of population classified by these characteristics are generated using the same methodology as for the total population. The extension of the estimation process to age, race, and Spanish origin illustrates how a significant enhancement to an existing program can be accomplished through linkages with only a modest use of additional resources and time.

However, the 20 percent sample used for assigning these characteristics imposes a lower limit on the size of areas for which sufficiently reliable estimates can be produced. Consideration might be given to expanding the sample or obtaining a complete file to permit more detailed estimation. In addition, although methodologically there are no significant problems in generating such estimates, there has been significant erosion of the completeness and quality of the race/ethnicity data in the Social Security file. Under the recently initiated enumeration at birth program, Social Security numbers and birth certificates are now being issued simultaneously for nearly all newborn infants. The Social Security Administration continues to capture the age and sex information for inclusion in the NUMIDENT file, but the standard race and ethnicity items from the Social Security number application form are not being asked. Federal and state laws and policies prevent the Social Security Administration from obtaining the birth certificate information on the race and ethnicity of the mother. If no action is taken to resolve this problem, the proportion of people in the NUMIDENT file lacking race and ethnic data will continue to grow, with negative consequences not only for uses of the NUMIDENT file by the Census Bureau but also for the Social Security Administration's ability to determine how its own programs affect different racial and ethnic groups. Until there is wider recognition of the benefits of using administrative records for statistical uses beyond those directly related to the administrative programs they serve, statistical programs that depend heavily on administrative records will continue to be at risk to changes beyond their control.

The foregoing illustrates only one type of expansion in program output through file linkage. Recent research by the Internal Revenue Service also suggests that significant improvement in population estimates may be achieved by merging and unduplicating files that now exist as part of the income tax collection system. As mentioned above, the basic 1040 individual income tax return file extract now used to generate population estimates covers somewhat less than 90 percent of the population, with considerable variance by state and county. Increasing overall coverage would have a significant positive effect on the accuracy of the estimate. Internal Revenue Service research with informational documents—forms 1099, W-2s, etc.—suggest that matching, unduplicating, and merging these records with the individual tax return files could raise coverage to the high 90s (98 percent according to one study) with concomitant increases in coverage for all geographic areas and reduction in geographic differentials. The first stage of the research has been fully documented and evaluated. As noted in Recommendation 5.5, the panel supports and encourages additional research aimed at resolving a number of technical and administrative issues involved in matching, unduplicating, and merging the various files so that the Census

Bureau's current population (and eventually income) estimates could be based on data covering a substantially greater proportion of the total U.S. population.

Estimates of Income and Poverty

For the past several years the Census Bureau has been considering ways to provide income and poverty estimates for counties, cities, and places. Although still in the research stage, the methodology would depend heavily on the availability and access to data from the IRS Individual Master File—the same file extract the Census Bureau now uses to prepare its population estimates (described above). Another set of files that would be used in methods development are those that can be created by linking the Individual Master File extract with sample survey data from the March Income Supplement of the Current Population Survey and the Survey of Income and Program Participation. Linking the sample survey individual and household records to the specific tax return would bring together the information on tax returns with the detailed demographic and socioeconomic data collected in those surveys for a substantial sample of the population. These enriched files for a sample of the population—essentially Census Bureau data and tax return data—would provide a basis for modeling small-area estimates (Bureau of the Census, 1993c).

New impetus for the development of small-area income and poverty estimates would be provided by the enactment of proposed legislation, the Poverty Data Improvement Act of 1993, calling on the Census Bureau to provide estimates of the number of children in poverty for states, counties, local units of general purpose government, and school districts. The legislation does not specifically call for access to additional administrative records (access to the IRS files mentioned above is assumed), but it would certainly improve the prospects of the Census Bureau's ability to prepare reliable estimates for the poverty universe if access to other administrative records were possible. Specifically, access to files of programs directed toward people and families at the lowest end of the income scale, e.g., Aid to Families With Dependent Children and Food Stamps, would be an important addition to the administrative record armamentarium useful for small-area poverty estimation. Poverty estimates based on a combination of IRS and Aid to Families With Dependent Children (or Food Stamp) files may provide more realistic and credible estimates than those based solely on IRS files linked to national sample survey data.

Use of Administrative Records in Surveys:
The Survey of Income and Program Participation

The Survey of Income and Program Participation (SIPP) is a Census Bureau panel survey that provides detailed information on the economic situation of people and families in the United States and how public transfer and tax programs affect their financial circumstances. SIPP was designed to obtain improved and more comprehensive information on the distribution of household and personal income in the United States. Hitherto, the main source of such information—the March Income Supplement of the Current Population Survey—had limitations that could be overcome only by making substantial changes in the survey instrument and procedures (Bowie and Kasprzyk, 1987). From the beginning, the SIPP was conceived as an instrument that would combine household survey data and administrative records through linkages based on Social Security numbers obtained from survey respondents. Some of the major goals anticipated for the use of administrative records in SIPP included:

1. *A supplemental sampling frame* to increase the reliability of estimates for selected subgroups (e.g., old age, survivors, and disability insurance recipients, supplemental security income recipients);

2. *To evaluate quality* of the survey data by comparing items collected in the survey with comparable items available from administrative records; and

3. *A supplemental source* for items difficult to obtain by a survey (e.g., earning and program benefit histories).

Other potential gains include data enhancements through linking demographic data from the survey with economic data sets from establishment and enterprise reporting in the economic census and other data files maintained by the Census Bureau (Herriot et al., 1989a).

During the development phases of SIPP, the Income Survey Development Program experimented with a large number of administrative records sources, including the Aid to Families With Dependent Children master file maintained by the Texas State Department of Welfare, the Supplementary Security Record, the Master Beneficiary Record, the Basic Educational Opportunity Grant applicant file, the Veterans Administration's Pension and Compensation file, the Internal Revenue Service's Individual Master File, and state record files for Unemployment Insurance and Workers Compensation. A planned match to the Summary Earnings File, which contains a history of covered earnings for each worker, was never implemented.

The SIPP program has a continuing commitment to the use of administrative records for statistical purposes, and the ability to match survey and records information with a minimum of error is of prime importance. The Social Security number, a unique key identifier, is collected and its quality benefits from the fact that special measures are taken by the Census Bureau to ensure that each number reported in SIPP is complete and valid. The wealth of other data—last name, first name, house number, street name, apartment designation, city, zip code, state, and date of birth—adds to the quality of any matching and linking of SIPP to other administrative records. In summary, SIPP is an example of a survey program designed to take advantage of administrative records to provide the highest-quality, comprehensive data on a specific subject. In addition, the potential exists for developing a substantially enhanced database by supplementing costly survey data with information already existing in administrative records systems. A recent Committee on National Statistics panel report on the Survey of Income and Program Participation (Citro and Kalton, 1993:90) said "we strongly support an increased role for administrative records in the SIPP program. However, there are many operational and technical problems, in addition to concerns about confidentiality, that impede ready use . . . . Nonetheless, we urge the Census Bureau to seek innovative ways for SIPP to benefit from the extensive information that is available on income and programs from administrative record sources."

This last suggestion, that the Census Bureau seek innovative ways for SIPP to benefit from administrative records, need not be limited to SIPP. The post-censal demographic/economics estimates program activities should also be encouraged to continue research into the use of administrative records files for program expansion and enhancement. Indeed, the federal statistical system in general could benefit by devoting some effort to looking for innovative ways to take advantage of information already available from administrative records.

Postcensal Estimates: State Programs

The foregoing discussion dealt only with the use of administrative records available at the national level across all areas of the country. There are large numbers of files maintained by and under the auspices of state authority. In at least one state, California, an administrative record file is used to generate population estimates at the substate level—counties. Data from the driver's license file maintained by the state's Department of Motor Vehicles are used to estimate gross intercounty (and interstate) migration of the population 18-64 years of age. The basic ingredient in the estimation process is the availability of driver's license change-of-address forms maintained by the Department of Motor Vehicles. Holders of driver's licenses are required to report any change of address to the department, and there are a number of incentives to do so within a reasonable time. These change-of-address forms are processed by the department and given to the Demographic Research Unit, California Department of Finance, which is charged with the responsibility of preparing postcensal population estimates. The change-of-address forms are coded to counties, and aggregated data showing gross in and out moves by county are provided to the Demographic Research Unit for its population estimates program (Hoag, 1984).

In this particular application, the statistical agency (Demographic Research Unit) does not obtain the actual micro-record but depends on the program agency, the Department of Motor Vehicles, to provide a special tabulation of its files. This model of interagency cooperation is instructive in that it permits program agencies that may be reluctant or legally prohibited from transferring individually identifiable administrative records to other agencies to still expand their use by carrying through special operations or tabulations to meet other agencies' statistical needs. One problem with this procedure is the total dependence on the originating agency to provide the material in some timely fashion. There may be legitimate reasons for delays and interruptions to occur. Another procedure would be for the originating agency to provide the basic file (extract or mini-record with confidentiality protection) on a regular basis and leave the processing to the receiving agency. But this may involve a number of legal and technical constraints that would have to be addressed. The California program illustrates an important use of state administrative records for population estimates that could be emulated by other states depending on the nature and scope of their own driver's license files.

Canada's Use of Administrative Records

Statistics Canada has been doing extensive research into the potential use of a variety of administrative records for small-area estimation and at present makes intensive use of the personal income tax records, i.e., Revenue Canada Taxation files (corresponding to our own Internal Revenue Service Individual Income Tax Returns) for this purpose. Statistics Canada had also been doing research on linking various files, on a sample basis, to provide an appreciably enhanced individual tax record for improved population coverage and expanded character-istic variables. However, this research has been set aside for the time being, primarily because changes to the tax system that will cause more low-income Canadians to file returns are expected to make it easier to address the main coverage issues without embarking on further record linkages with their atten-dant privacy concerns.

Canada's program of postcensal population estimates is similar to that of the United States but somewhat more elaborate in the characteristic detail available. Estimates of total population by age group and sex are prepared for geographic areas down to the census division (or county) level; data on age, sex, marital status, and number of families by type are provided for provinces and territories (Statistics Canada, 1987)

The main administrative record file used to generate population estimates is the Revenue Canada taxation file. The Tax Act provides for the transmission of copies of records held by Revenue Canada to Statistics Canada to meet the needs of the latter's estimation program. (Such legal and continuous access to the file is a basic underpinning of any postcensal estimate program dependent on admin-istrative records.) The methodology for measuring net and interarea migration is essentially the same as that for the United States. Individual tax records are matched for successive periods using Social Insurance Number as the main match-ing key. Migration of tax filers and their dependents to and from geographic areas is determined directly from the addresses on the tax file. The dependents are enumerated from information reported by the tax filers: exemptions for dependent spouse, exemptions for dependent children, claims for refundable tax credits for children, reporting of child care expenses, and the receipt of family allowance benefits. These imputations are made while creating the T1FF (T1 Family File, see description below) and are taken directly from it. Finally, an adjustment is made to the interarea migration estimates to benchmark them to an estimate of migration for the total population.

Another administrative records file used extensively in the estimates program, at least until recently, was the family allowance program file, administered by Health and Welfare Canada. This program provided monthly payments to every eligible child under age 18 (with certain limitations). Until very recently, the program file covered essentially all children under age 15, and well over 90 percent of those ages 15-17. The main use of the file was to measure net interarea migration of the population under age 18 (the adult population was not covered) through reporting of change of address. To continue receiving their family allowance checks, recipients had to notify the regional office of Health and Welfare Canada of any change of address. These notifications, which were assumed to be fairly accurate and comprehensive, became the vehicle for measuring net interarea migration for the universe coverage. Family allowance files were also used as symptomatic indicators in a regression model to generate preliminary estimates of total population for census divisions.

Recent legislation on the New Child Tax Benefit System—which took effect on January 1, 1993—eliminated both the Family Allowance Program and the Child Tax Credit program. Extensive research is under way on the use of the new system as an input to migration estimation. An important lesson is that a program that depends on administrative records is always at risk of new legislation and other program changes that can affect consistency with the past, adequacy of coverage, and continued relevance of the new file to statistical program needs.

The income tax system file is the backbone and main underpinning of Statistics Canada's administrative record work. Some other research projects under way and proposals for expanding uses of the basic individual income tax record file have included: (1) Expanding the individual tax record file to a tax filer family file, thereby creating families from the individual tax file. This is accomplished by a six-step process of matching and imputation using information from each record within the tax file system, such as Social Insurance number, postal code, and surname, to name a few. (2) A proposed pilot study to compile an administrative record consolidation file by linking a number of records to the individual tax record or the tax filer family file. The files to be linked (20 percent sample) included Old Age Security, Social Assistance, Unemployment Insurance, and Family Allowance. The linking might improve population coverage as well as expand and improve characteristics variables. However, the project is not being pursued because the statistical benefits were not seen to outweigh privacy concerns. (3) Development of a longitudinal administrative database. In early 1988, discussions were undertaken to assess the conceptual feasibility of building a longitudinal database from administrative records. Plans were developed for a pilot study to determine whether it would be feasible to use administrative records to build a longitudinal database for social research and policy analysis. Initial plans called for use of a 10 percent sample created from tax filer families plus a 10 percent sample of Social Assistance recipients in two provinces, Quebec and Nova Scotia, that were not on the tax filer database. The longitudinal administrative database had been created for a 10 percent sample of those two sources for a 5-year period, 1982-1986. However, again because of privacy concerns about linking files from more than one source, this project was shelved in favor of a 1 percent longitudinal administrative database created entirely from the tax file with no other linkages (Leyes, 1990).

In summary, the Canadian experience illustrates that the unidimensional use of administrative records is extremely useful for postcensal estimates programs. The further potential benefits that can be achieved by matching, merging, and linking files of administrative records have to be weighed against privacy concerns associated with such activities and can be realized only if the privacy issues are satisfactorily resolved and public concerns alleviated.

Matching and Informed Consent in Canada

As stated, the value of administrative records for programmatic purposes can be increased significantly if different program records containing supplementary and complementary data can be linked to form larger databases. At the moment, such linkages are cause for concern by those who perceive such actions by the government as an invasion of privacy. As noted, linkage to administrative records can also be used to improve data quality and reduce respondent burden in censuses and surveys. In this context, Statistics Canada is considering the feasibility of obtaining income information by linking Revenue Canada tax records with records of respondents to Statistics Canada income surveys (Greenberg, 1993).

As part of this investigation, a question about permission was asked of a subsample of respondents to the August 1993 Labor Force Survey. Respondents were asked whether they would give permission for Statistics Canada to get their income information directly from Revenue Canada, if they were asked to participate in a Statistics Canada income survey. The results showed that 55 to 62 percent of respondents would be willing to allow access to their files under the stated conditions. The permission rate varied little by geographic area or demographic group. An analysis of the results suggested that there would be benefits if a mixture of interviewing and linkages were used, particularly since many nonrespondents (to the Survey of Consumer Finances) said they would give permission to access their income tax records (Greenberg, 1993). More research is warranted into this area of permission and informed consent for linking individual records.

Summary

In this section, we have identified several new ways in which administrative records might be used for statistical purposes not directly related to the decennial census. A vigorous effort to explore and develop some of these uses would serve two important purposes. First, such an effort would bring knowledge and experience that would greatly assist the Census Bureau in future decisions about a greater role for administrative records in the decennial census. Second, it could add substantial value to the Census Bureau's current demographic data programs by providing data more frequently and with greater geographic and subject matter detail.

These two purposes were described in a convincing manner by the Panel on Census Requirements in the Year 2000 and Beyond (Committee on National Statistics, 1993a) in its interim report. Concerning the first goal, the panel said (pp. 25-26):

> We recommend (see above) that an important first step in examining administrative records is to begin working with them now. If administrative records are to have an expanded use in the decennial census, then there is an urgent need to start to exploit them more heavily for intercensal estimates. . . . Although the Bureau of the Census has been using administrative records for years, their expanded use for intercensal estimates would provide the necessary experience that is needed for assessing their potential for the decennial census.

Concerning the second goal, the panel's view was expressed (p. 26):

> Another rationale exists for using administrative records for intercensal estimates. Census data are available only every 10 years. . . . On average . . . U.S. small-area estimates are approximately 8 years old over the decade of their use [taking account of the 3-year lag between the census date and initial availability]. Administrative records have the potential to provide much more frequent information for small geographic areas, on important variables such as population and housing counts, poverty, and income.

In the final section of this chapter, this panel advocates adoption, by the Census Bureau, of a proactive policy for increased statistical use of administrative records. Uses not directly related to the decennial census should be an important component of that effort.

Recommendation 5.10: The Census Bureau should substantially increase the scope of its efforts to use administrative records to produce intercensal small-area tabulations, either through stand-alone tabulations of data from one or more administrative record sources or by combining such data with data from current surveys.

One step that could bring immediate benefits would be to begin supplementing the individual tax return extract data, which the Internal Revenue Service has been providing annually to the Census Bureau, with data from informational documents submitted to the Internal Revenue Service. Although tabulations of merged files of tax returns and informational documents prepared by the Internal Revenue Service would be of some value, transmission of extract files to the Census Bureau would be preferable, for the reasons described above. Important benefits would also result from any steps that can be taken to add race and ethnic information to the Social Security Administration's NUMIDENT file for all newborn infants and for other persons for whom it is missing or incomplete.

As opportunities present themselves, new health care enrollment records should be brought into the picture. The timetable for development of standardized national health care enrollment records is uncertain at this writing, but it is quite possible that some states will lead the way by developing their own automated health care information systems. Experience working with state record systems will give the Census Bureau an opportunity to judge their suitability for statistical uses and to develop recommendations for national standards that will facilitate statistical uses.

SUMMARY AND CONCLUSIONS

The mission of statistical agencies is to meet the information needs of government and society as effectively and efficiently as possible, using all available sources of information. The primary sources of statistical information about people are censuses, statistical surveys, and a large and diverse set of administrative record systems that have been created primarily for nonstatistical purposes.

There are several ways in which administrative records have been or might be used to help satisfy needs for small-area demographic data:

1. As an adjunct to a conventional decennial census of population, to improve coverage, reduce costs, make collection operations more efficient, and evaluate census coverage and quality.

2. As the primary source of census information, to be supplemented by other sources of data only to the extent necessary.

3. To produce stand-alone tabulations of small-area data from a single administrative records system or a combination of systems, as discussed by the Census Requirements Panel in Appendix B of its interim report and in the preceding section of this chapter.

4. As inputs to a system of current population estimates designed to provide periodic counts of people classified by age, sex, and race/ethnic status for geographic units defined in as much detail as possible. To the extent that the necessary data are available from administrative records, other variables, like income, might be included.

5. As part of a continuous measurement system of surveys designed to provide estimates of census long-form data on a continuing basis for areas down to the tract or block-group level. Small area counts based on an administrative

records could be used in the sample design and estimation process to reduce the sample sizes needed for the surveys to provide small-area data at acceptable levels of reliability.

For the first category, using administrative records as an adjunct to a conventional census, we have identified and discussed several possible uses in the 2000 census and plans for testing and evaluating them in the 1995 census test. The second possibility, a census based primarily on administrative records, has been realized in a few western European countries, but is clearly not feasible for the 2000 census in the United States. We believe, however, that it should be seriously considered as an option for the 2010 census and that the Census Bureau should continue to explore and evaluate it in a systematic way. In this context, the Census Bureau should give special attention to new health care records that may be developed to implement the reform of the health care system in the United States.

However, simply shifting from a twentieth century conventional decennial census to a twenty-first century model based on administrative records is not the only possible and perhaps not the most promising paradigm for counting people in the information age. It is unlikely that an administrative records census could provide all of the content items that have been included on the long-form questionnaire in recent censuses. Alternative paradigms should be identified and evaluated. One long-range goal might be to establish an integrated demographic data system consisting of 3 elements:

1. Annual small-area population counts based entirely on administrative records. People would be classified by age, sex, and the official race/ethnic categories.

2. Continuous measurement surveys to provide long-form data for areas down to the census tract, block group, and school district levels. Data would be available annually for areas with more than 250,000 population and moving multiyear averages would be provided for smaller areas.

3. Integrated coverage measurement surveys, similar to those that have been proposed for the 2000 census, at least once every 10 years, possibly more often. The results of these surveys would be used to adjust the annual population counts and the estimates based on the continuous measurement surveys.

The development of such a system is a pipe dream only if we limit ourselves to looking for reasons why it can't be done, rather than asking ourselves what steps would be necessary to accomplish it.

To start moving in the direction of such a goal, it may be desirable to give increased attention and priority, for the time being, to uses of administrative records in the third, fourth, and fifth categories enumerated at the beginning of this section, all of which aim at enhancing the scope and content of intercensal demographic data programs. The potential benefits for current data programs are substantial, and such initiatives would provide much-needed experience in using existing and new administrative records systems for statistical purposes. The costs for uses of administrative records in categories 3 and 4 would be relatively low compared with the cost of a decennial census or a continuous measurement system with a large survey component.

To the extent that continuous measurement and other programs are successful in better meeting user needs for small-area data and providing data more frequently, the pressures for long-form data on the decennial census should abate, thereby opening up the possibility for a relatively smooth transition to the kind of integrated demographic data system we have just outlined.

We believe it is a mistake to think of administrative records only in terms of how they might be used to replace a traditional version of the decennial census, duplicating all of its major design features. This kind of thinking can be a straitjacket that inhibits creativity about how to develop an integrated demographic data program that makes effective use of all available sources of data, taking into account relevance to user needs, cost, accuracy, frequency, and timeliness. It is somewhat akin to the frequently observed phenomenon that new technologies are often used at first only to replicate the uses of the old technologies.

We have discussed some major federal and state administrative records systems, existing and in prospect, that appear to have the greatest potential for demographic statistical uses. Internal Revenue Service and Social Security Administration record systems have been used for statistical purposes for many years, but now have substantial potential for enhanced use, as demonstrated by recent research on the coverage of merged files of tax returns and informational documents. The movement for health care reform brings the prospect of a new national system of records that may have close to universal coverage and may include some of the basic variables, especially race and ethnicity, that are not adequately represented in other systems of administrative records. Reforms to welfare programs may lead to better coverage, in the associated record systems, of people who tend to be more difficult to enumerate by conventional methods. Finally, the continuously updated Master Address File/TIGER system, to which the Census Bureau is now committed, will provide a hitherto unavailable capacity for using administrative data from different sources and assigning units to their correct geographic locations.

The future holds attractive prospects for using administrative records as the keystone in developing a greatly improved small-area demographic data system that can provide data more frequently at no increase and possibly a significant reduction in costs over the decade. However, these prospects can only be realized if the Census Bureau, with support from the Office of Management and Budget's Statistical Policy Office, other federal agencies, and the Congress, adopts a proactive policy to explore expanded uses of administrative records. To maximize the likelihood of success, a proactive policy should include the following elements:

- A determination, not just to make use of existing administrative records systems, but to play an active part, in cooperation with program agencies, in the development of new systems and in modification of existing systems to improve their utility for statistical uses.

• A suitable organizational unit and adequate resources for research and development activities not tied directly to ongoing census and survey programs. However, some of the exploratory research should be directed at existing programs, especially at the use of administrative records to improve current population estimates and small-area data for use in funds allocation. Hands-on experience is an essential part of learning to use administrative records effectively. Resources devoted to this effort should support work done by contractors and census fellows or under other external arrangements as well as in-house research and development activities.

• A determination to take advantage of every possible occasion to explore the long-range as well as immediate potential for using administrative records. For example, the 1995 census test should be seen as an opportunity, not only to test uses that are being considered for the 2000 census, but also to acquire information about administrative records that will be of value for uses in current population estimate programs or censuses after 2000. Similarly, forward-looking experiments with the use of administrative records should be part of the research program associated with the 2000 census.

• Access to a national integrated, continuously updated MAF/TIGER system.

• Full and continuing awareness of the concerns of individuals whose information is contained in administrative records that are being used for statistical purposes and recognition of the importance of their views about what kinds of uses are acceptable.

Since its beginnings, the Census Bureau has been in the forefront of many important advances in information technology, including the development and application of sampling theory in censuses and surveys, automation of data collection and processing operations, development of response error models, and application of tools from cognitive psychology and social anthropology to understand and improve data collection procedures. A proactive policy to develop enhanced uses of administrative records would be in keeping with the Census Bureau's tradition of innovation and adaptation to the technical and social environment in which it carries out its mission as fact-finder for the nation.

Recommendation 5.11: The panel urges the Census Bureau to adopt a proactive policy to expand its uses of administrative records, and it urges other executive branch agencies and Congress to give their support to such a policy.

Any proactive policy has some risks associated with it, but the panel believes that the risks are justified by the potential benefits. Clinging to the twentieth century census model in a twenty-first century data collection environment could well prove to be even more risky.

6

Alternatives for Long-Form Data Collection

Early chapters of this report primarily concern new methodologies for producing the census counts—the official population totals used in reapportionment, redistricting, and the allocation of federal program funds. Attention in this chapter is given to alternative methods for collecting the detailed sociodemographic data that since 1960 have been gathered by distributing a census "long form" to a national sample of households.

Sampling was first used to gather additional information (or content) in 1940; in preceding decades, all questions were asked of all households in the census (Goldfield, 1992). In 1990, as in other recent censuses, the long form contained questions about education, occupation, income, journey to work, ethnicity, and housing. The long form is completed by a sample of census respondents; in 1990, the national sampling rate was one-sixth of all households, although the fraction was as large as one-half in some small jurisdictions. The long form includes all content that is contained in the short form completed by all other households. The 1990 long form contained a total of 33 questions for each household member and 26 questions about the housing unit; for the short form, the respective numbers were 7 questions per household member and 7 housing questions. The long form thus requires considerably more information from a given household than does the short form.

Some advocates of census reform have questioned the collection of this additional information as part of the decennial census. One current argument is that the accuracy of the decennial population figures would improve and census costs would decline if long-form data collection were eliminated, reduced, or displaced in time from the effort to enumerate the population. Others have suggested that some of the data gathered in the 1990 census could be collected through alternate methods, such as sample surveys or tabulations of administrative records (see Chapter 5), and made available for use in a more timely manner (see, e.g., Sawyer, 1993; U.S. House of Representatives, 1993). Still others have challenged the quality of data collected on the long form, noting the high rates (relative to the decennial short form) at which this information is gathered indirectly, either by imputation or from someone outside the household, particularly for minority populations (see, e.g., Ericksen et al., 1991).

These four criticisms of the decennial long form—effect on population coverage, cost of collection, quality of data, and infrequency of supply—are important factors to weigh in evaluating alternative data collection vehicles. (We interpret the call for more timely data to be a request for more frequent supply, and we reserve use of the word *timeliness* to mean the speed with which results are published after data collection has been completed.) We discuss these considerations further in subsequent sections. First, however, we pause to briefly comment on the merits of the first two arguments—that the long form has negative effects on census coverage and cost.

A comparative analysis of mail return rates from the 1990 census suggests that dropping the decennial long form would yield a trivial improvement in overall census coverage (Keeley, 1993). Further study would be useful, but, at present, there is also no evidence that differential coverage would be reduced by eliminating the long form. The presence of the long form therefore does not appear to diminish to any meaningful degree the accuracy of the decennial population totals used for reapportionment, redistricting, and resource allocation. Adoption of the one-number concept and integrated coverage measurement in the 2000 census would, in any case, compensate for any small impact the long form might have on coverage.

The potential cost savings associated with eliminating the long form from the decennial census should be weighed against the costs of alternative methods of gathering comparable information. The decennial long form meets a wide range of user needs, often mandated by law, for information on the characteristics of small geographic areas and subpopulations (see Bureau of the Census, 1994a, for a review of the legal status of census content). Such information can be used, for example, in allocating federal program funds, and distributing a longer census form to a national sample of households has historically been regarded as a cost-effective means of providing the required data.

Two contradictory pressures in census reform—one to obtain better information more frequently and the other to reduce the respondent burden of the decennial long form—have lent support to two proposed alternatives for long-form data collection: continuous measurement and matrix sampling. In the sections that follow, we address these two proposals under which the long-form data burden might be reduced or eliminated from the census enumeration while the means to collect comparable sample data for small areas and subpopulations is retained. The Census Bureau is conducting ongoing research on these alternative methods, and we review the results of that work to date.

CONTINUOUS MEASUREMENT

There have been proposals in the past that collection of small-area sample data, such as those typically provided by the census, be conducted throughout the decade, rather than once every 10 years. Kish (1981, 1990), Horvitz (1986), and Herriott et al. (1989b) have proposed a variety of data collection schemes that involve this key concept of extending data collection in a more or less continuous fashion. As a part of its planning activities for the 2000 census, the Census Bureau has included an evaluation of this type of process and, on the basis of preliminary research, has indicated a commitment to investigating fully the feasibility of continuous measurement as part of the 2000 census development process (Bureau of the Census, 1993b). Recently, Alexander (1993) proposed a way in which a continuous measurement program might be instituted in conjunction with the 2000 census.

These proposals for continuous measurement share two main features: (1) virtually continuous data collection operations instead of starting and stopping every 10 years, with presumed benefits for data quality through the maintenance of a permanent enumeration staff and improvement through continuous experience and (2) more current small-area sample data throughout the decade (except for the smallest geographic units, for which updates of small-area sample data might be based on a 5- or 10-year moving average of sample data).

A distinguishing feature of the plan currently being developed and evaluated by the Census Bureau is that it calls for continuous measurement to be conducted in connection with a complete enumeration of the population at one point every decade, whereas most earlier proposals would replace the traditional census completely with a continuous measurement program. The present proposal assumes that a decennial enumeration is required in order to meet constitutional requirements. This view is supported by a legal review prepared by the Congressional Research Service (Lee, 1993) and subsequent work by the Panel on Census Requirements (Committee on National Statistics, 1993a). Thus, the objective in proposing continuous measurement in these circumstances is twofold: (1) to reduce the cost and burden of the decade enumeration by removing the need to collect small-area sample data as part of the decennial census and (2) to improve the frequency, timeliness, and quality of small-area sample data.

In the remainder of this section, we describe the Census Bureau's research of continuous measurement and review progress in the development of a prototype system. We examine methodological and operational issues associated with implementation, and we discuss other considerations—such as accuracy, cost, acceptability to census data users, and effect on the decennial enumeration—that are important in evaluating the continuous measurement proposal.

Overview of the Census Bureau's Continuous Measurement Program

Alexander (1993) identified three goals for the Census Bureau's research program on continuous measurement:

1. Determine the basic prototype design for data collection and estimation;
2. Estimate the cost of the operation, or at least give useful upper and lower bounds; and
3. Make general statements about the quality and utility of the data (including coverage and content) from the continuous measurement system compared with alternative systems.

Alexander goes on to identify some decisions that were taken initially in the research process concerning the form of a continuous measurement design:

- The continuous measurement prototype will include a complete year-zero (i.e., end-decade) enumeration for reapportionment and redistricting, rather than a "rolling enumeration."
- The frame for intercensal samples will be the Master Address File (MAF).
- The prototype assumes implementation in time to replace sample data for the 2000 census, rather than waiting for 2010. The development plan is based on the assumption that a decision as to whether to replace sample data from the 2000 census with a continuous measurement operation will be made in 1997.
- The continuous measurement prototype must produce data for most 1990 long-form characteristics for small areas—census tracts/block-numbering areas and block groups—with more or less the same reliability requirements as the 1990 long-form sample.
- The prototype assumes direct sample-based estimates for small areas, rather than relying on model-based indirect or synthetic estimates or administrative records.
- The basic small-area (tract/block-numbering area or block group) estimates will be rolling accumulations (moving averages) of 5 years of data. Current plans call for a 3-year moving average for 1999-2001 (with a corresponding increase in the monthly sample size).
- Data collection will be spread evenly across the year and across the nation.
- The survey will be a separate survey rather than an expansion of any current federal household survey.
- The design will include a combination of mail, telephone, and personal-visit interviews.

The Census Bureau has developed a schedule for implementing a research program on the feasibility of conducting a continuous measurement operation. This plan is shown in Table 6.1, which is extracted from Alexander (1994). It indicates an expanding effort at developing a full system of continuous measure-

TABLE 6.1 Accelerated MAF-Based Continuous Measurement: Data Collection Activities

Fiscal Year	Data Collection Activity	Objectives
1994	Research, planning, outreach only	• Win over a few key federal users • Contact nonfederal users • Remove feasibility doubts • Get commitment to $10 million for 1996 testing
1995	RDD test with 2,000/month total in 3-4 sites, starting November 1994. Convert to split-sample questionnaire test in July 1995. Small mail pretest.	• Get demonstration file of cumulative estimates • Test alternative versions • Get user acceptance of testing/decision process • Get commitment to fiscal 1997 funding and decision process
1996	Address-list-based test with 4,000/month total in 4 sites, starting October 1995.	• Better demonstration file of cumulative estimates • Develop/test field procedures • Get user input and decide whether to proceed further • Decide to eliminate 2000 long form if fiscal 1997 results successful • Get commitment to fiscal 1998-2002 funding conditional on decision process
1997	MAF-based "development survey" for congressional-district-level estimates, full speed in January 1997. Rural sample clustered in PSU.	• Demonstrate actual procedures • Produce actual high-level estimates • Measure coverage, quality of estimates • Close scrutiny of 1995, 1996, 1997 data by all users • Final decision to drop 2000 long form in December 1997
1998	Expand MAF-based sample size; change procedures and questionnaire to fix problems found in fiscal year 1997. Better rural spread.	• Final content determination • Final procedures • Further evaluation of quality • More actual high-level estimates
1999	Full MAF-based system. Complete rural spread.	• Collect small-area data to replace 2000 long form

Note: MAF = Master Address File; RDD = random-digit dialing; PSU = primary sampling unit.

SOURCE: Based on materials provided to the panel by C. Alexander, Bureau of the Census.

ment over the next six years. This plan is characterized by three features: (1) a steadily increasing level of resources over time, from a relatively modest research effort in 1994 to the full system (as currently envisaged) in 1999; (2) a series of decision points at which the results of the research to date and other developments are evaluated and a decision is made whether to proceed with plans for a continuous measurement operation in place of long-form data collection in connection with the 2000 census; (3) parallel efforts at developing data collection capabilities, the estimation system, reliable cost estimates, and user needs.

Expansion of Research and Development

Staff at the Census Bureau have been pursuing research and development of a prototype system for continuous data collection. Proposals for the prototype have undergone several revisions, particularly with regard to such characteristics as sample size and date of initiation. The current proposal (Alexander, 1994) involves a random-digit dialing (RDD) survey starting in November 1994 (fiscal 1995) at three to four geographic sites, totaling approximately 2,000 households per month. The sites may possibly be the same sites as those for the 1995 census test, but this has not been determined.

The Census Bureau plans to use the data from the survey to produce 6- or 9-month cumulations, in the form of data tapes for prospective users, in mid-1995. These data tapes would have the same format as that proposed for the mature continuous measurement program in order to provide users with a sense of what estimates and data products would be available.

In October 1995, the RDD survey would be replaced by an address-list-based test in four sites involving a total of about 4,000 households per month. The sample size corresponds to the level of sampling that these sites would receive under the national system as currently proposed. Experience from actual field operations would be used to refine cost estimates.

The Census Bureau has begun to work with census data users at some federal agencies to study the implications of continuous measurement. In particular, the Census Bureau has established contact with officials at the Department of Transportation and the Department of Housing and Urban Development. Data users in state and local government and in the private sector will also be consulted; such efforts will intensify when prototype data products become available.

Program Milestones

Three key decision points for the continuous measurement program are:

1. October 1995: The Census Bureau could stop before increasing to the proposed level of effort—for example, if cost estimates increase substantially—but the program does not call for a large investment at this stage.

2. October 1996: Extensive data collection would begin in order to provide estimates for congressional districts and to work on remaining problems. Users will have had time to consider the demonstration files from the fiscal 1995 program and some of the fiscal 1996 results. A conditional decision would be made to drop the long form from the 2000 census if the fiscal 1997 program is successful.

3. September 1997: A final decision would be made about whether to retain the long form for the 2000 census or replace it with the continuous measurement program. One possible complication in reaching this decision point is that, in early 1997, the Census Bureau must provide, for congressional review and approval, a list of topics to be included in the 2000 census. It is unclear whether the means of collecting data on these topics must also be determined by early 1997.

If continuous measurement is not implemented for the 2000 census, then the Census Bureau would try to maintain program activities, such as updating the Master Address File, using current survey interviewers. The MAF could serve as a frame for household surveys, such as the Current Population Survey. We note that a decision to use a long form as part of the 2000 census does not necessarily imply that continuous measurement would not be implemented during the next decade.

If continuous measurement is implemented in place of a long form in 2000, then the sample size of the monthly survey would increase from approximately 80,000 households in 1997 to 100,000 in 1998 and, finally, to 325,000 in 1999. In 1997, estimates would be available for states and other large areas. A systematic (and geographically sequenced) sample of households within census blocks would begin in 1999.

Current Initiatives

The Census Bureau has now established a project team to carry out the research on the practical issues in developing a system of estimates obtained from a continuous measurement program. This group will be responsible for the development of the RDD telephone survey at the four test sites and the subsequent transition to an address-list-based survey. The group will examine various aspects of questionnaire and content issues, working with interested parties and advisory panels, evaluating cost components, developing operational systems, developing the survey design and estimation procedure, and evaluating the impact on current household survey programs throughout the federal statistical system.

The panel is impressed by the breadth encompassed in this early thinking in developing the plans to examine the desirability and feasibility of a continuous measurement system. We recognize the need to develop the various aspects of the research effort in parallel. This is essential if an effective continuous measurement system is to be developed. The evaluation of each of the aspects of the system depends on the research efforts in the other areas. To study whether user needs will be met effectively by continuous measurement, we believe that it is imperative that simulated products be provided to users at an early stage in the investigation, and that user comments be solicited to guide the process (see below). These user responses may well influence the requirements for data collection and estimation. Preliminary data collection and estimation procedures must also be in place to develop the simulated products. Thus, all features of the system must be developed in a synchronized fashion.

We emphasize the need to maintain a strong commitment to the principle of synchronized development over time. Some aspects of the research are likely to be easier to develop, to have a clearer path, and to be under the Census Bureau's control to a greater extent than others. A situation could quite conceivably develop in which research into the data collection methods is progressing rapidly and reaching an advanced stage with many decisions finalized, whereas essential research into user needs is lagging and hence not informing appropriately the decisions on data collection methods. Close monitoring will be needed to ensure that uniform and timely progress is made on all fronts.

> **Recommendation 6.1: The panel endorses further research and evaluation of a continuous measurement program. In conducting this work, the Census Bureau should establish, and continually reinforce, a commitment to simultaneous research and development of cost estimation, data collection and processing methods, estimation procedures, and user needs.**

Key Operational Features

The Census Bureau's current prototype combines three main components: (1) continuous updating of a national MAF; (2) a large periodic sample survey to collect intercensal data, using the MAF as a frame; and (3) an integrated estimates program, which produces estimates from the periodic sample survey, using other data sources such as the decennial census, the master address list, and administrative records to enhance the estimates. The data and estimates from the continuous measurement program would in turn be used to enhance estimates from other national household surveys and the demographic estimates program.

In current plans, the intercensal long form (ILF) would sample about 250,000 addresses nationally each month, drawn from all geographic areas. Different addresses would be included each month. The initial sample would be mailed a data collection form. A subsample (possibly all) of the mail nonreturns would be followed up by telephone whenever possible. A further subsample of those who cannot be contacted successfully by telephone (for whatever reason) would be followed up in person.

Annual average estimates would be produced for large geographic areas in which the population exceeds 250,000—e.g., states, large metropolitan statistical areas, and groups of counties. For small areas, such as tracts and block groups, a moving 5-year average would be produced annually using data from the previous 5 years.

The survey frame of mailing addresses would be updated quarterly using Postal Service mail delivery lists and possibly lists from local governments. City-style addresses would be geocoded to the block level. For areas without city-style addresses (rural delivery routes, post office boxes, general delivery, physical description only), additional efforts would be needed (see Alexander, 1993). The extent to which these efforts are needed depends on the extent to which city-style addresses are prevalent in the MAF in 1997. The development of cost-effective procedures for handling such addresses is an important step in establishing the viability of a monthly national ILF survey.

Once the data have been collected, survey weights would be applied. Initially, each household record would be weighted by the inverse of the selection probability. This weight would depend on whether the data for the unit were collected by mail, telephone, or personal visit. These base weights would then be adjusted for nonresponse, as a means of accounting in the estimation system for those nonvacant households that fail to provide data through any of the mail, telephone, or personal-visit modes. For cases of missing item-level data from respondents, imputation would be used to compensate for the missing data. Finally, some type of poststratification would be used to ensure that the survey weights agree, at some level of geography, with accurate independent estimates of the population size. Because the exact nature and benefit of the poststratification procedures are unclear at present, the Census Bureau is evaluating the reliability of the ILF estimates under the conservative assumption that there would be no benefit from such a procedure.

User Support for Continuous Measurement Data Products

Although a change to continuous measurement requires considerable methodological and operational changes, the major question is how well it meets the requirements of small-area data users. Continuous measurement would provide users with more current data (for all but the smallest geographic areas) and with greater frequency than data collected every 10 years. More frequent estimates could be especially valuable to those making decisions about the distribution of funds or who are concerned with measuring characteristics of populations that change considerably during a 10-year period. However, the notion of replacing single-point-in-time data for small areas with 5-year rolling averages may be troublesome for some users. Although some social and economic statistics are collected over long periods of time, most census long-form data users are likely to be unfamiliar or uncomfortable with the concept of moving averages and may have to reexamine their use of the data.

The Census Bureau should therefore proceed vigorously with an outreach program to explain cumulative estimates and to discuss possible applications with current and prospective data users. As noted above, the Census Bureau has begun to work with census users at some federal agencies to acquaint them with the type of data product that would be produced by a continuous measurement program. The Bureau of Transportation Statistics is arranging a small workshop on the potential value of continuous measurement data for transportation planning. Discussions with data users in state and local governments and with private sector users are also planned.

Assessing the potential demand for an innovative data collection system poses a strategic challenge: it may be difficult to interest prospective data users without a data product. Continuous measurement is new and different. Skepticism about its value among long-form data users is understandable and should be anticipated. It is easy for current users of the decennial long form to see what information would be lost by dropping the long form, but the benefits of a new program or new methods may not always be obvious. Simulated data products should be an excellent tool for engaging long-form data users and for measuring potential demand and acceptance of a continuous measurement program.

Simulated data products can be developed from census and current survey data. Also, as mentioned above, the Census Bureau will begin a small random-digit dialing telephone survey of 2,000 households per month in four sites starting in November 1994 and continuing for 6 to 9 months. One purpose of this test survey is to provide demonstration files of cumulative estimates to distribute to census data users. The estimates will be accumulations of cross-section or snap-shot surveys. The RDD survey will be followed in October 1995 by a MAF-based test survey in four sites of at least 4,000 households per month and will provide data users with additional experience using cumulative estimates. The demonstration files are intended to get user reactions to moving averages and to determine the level of demand and acceptance of continuous measurement data. In addition to providing data in the development of simulated data products, the test surveys will also help to identify and define operational issues.

Recommendation 6.2: The Census Bureau should initiate discussions with all potential users of continuous measurement data, including state and local governments and private-sector users. A research program should be developed to answer user questions. The Census Bureau should also develop a program to inform data users of the simulated data products emerging from the test surveys and to get their reactions.

Total Error and Frequency of Data Products

Will data users regard more frequent cumulative estimates as superior or inferior to single-point-in-time data once per decade? Ultimately, the question to be addressed is the extent to which continuous measurement improves accuracy relative to its cost. Because continuous measurement estimates will be based on the same sample size, for each 5-year moving average, as the census long-form sample data estimates were based in 1990, the sampling errors for these two different types of estimates should be comparable. If continuous measurement estimates are subject to so much less bias than once-per-decade estimates, on average across the decade, that their total errors are substantially smaller, then it is likely that continuous measurement will be cost-effective. If the bias that results from outdatedness over time of once-per-decade estimates is modest compared with the standard error of sampling, then continuous measurement will offer little relative advantage.

Clearly the situation will vary with the level of geography and the characteristics being estimated. At broader geographic levels, sampling errors (for 5-year moving averages) will be small; hence, the biases that result from outdatedness will be relatively major. Certain characteristics (e.g., housing characteristics) change relatively slowly over a 10-year period for most geographic areas, and in these cases the benefits of continuous measurement will probably be modest. Conversely, the benefits may be considerable for characteristics that change relatively quickly in many geographic areas in the years after the decennial census. To reach conclusions about the benefits of continuous measurement, it is necessary to weigh the importance of accuracy (i.e., mean square error) across different levels of geography and across estimates of different characteristics.

Recommendation 6.3: The Census Bureau should evaluate the gains in accuracy that may be offered by continuous measurement for estimates of various characteristics at varying levels of geography. In making accuracy assessments, the Census Bureau should take full advantage of simulations, based on existing census and survey data, to provide realistic scenarios for the changes in estimates over time. As part of its outreach program, the Census Bureau should provide long-form data users with accompanying estimates of bias and precision for various geographic levels and aggregations of one to five years of data.

Costs of Long-Form Data Collection

Cost estimates of operating a continuous measurement program and the potential savings from eliminating long-form questions are not yet well defined. Various assumptions about the intercensal long-form survey relating to such matters as the cost of frame maintenance, response rates, follow-up effort required, and the percentage of interviews completed using various data collection modes (mail, telephone, and personal visit) are based on very limited knowledge. The prototype test surveys could be very helpful in refining assumptions used for cost estimates and determining the direct costs of various operations.

The Census Bureau is committed to building a continuously updated Master Address File regardless of the final 2000 census design. As noted in Chapter 2, this activity could conceivably grow into a cooperative effort involving other federal, state, and local agencies. A continuous measurement program would require stronger updating of the MAF. With a traditional decennial census, the computer processing of Postal Service delivery files would be done regularly, probably once every year or two. Some clerical resolution of the Postal Service files for decennial census use is scheduled to begin in 1995 and will continue through the rest of the decade, but some of the updating activity could be postponed until immediately prior to the decennial census. With continuous measurement, MAF updating would be done quarterly. How should the costs of developing and updating the MAF be allocated to continuous measurement, to the census, and possibly to statistical activities of other government agencies? This question needs to be resolved to accurately determine the costs of continuous measurement.

Another important question that must be answered in assessing the feasibility of a continuous measurement program as an alternative to the census long form is the extent to which response rates will be affected by the fact that the program would be conducted in an environment vastly different from that of the census. Response rates are important factors in determining both the costs and data quality of survey and census operations. We emphasize cost considerations in this section; the implications for data quality are mentioned later.

The decennial census is carried out with extensive publicity, generated not only by the public communications activities of the census program (advertising, outreach efforts, etc.), but also by the fact that the census is a highly newsworthy event that attracts a great deal of unsolicited media attention. Such extensive publicity generates a high level of public awareness, which serves not only to stimulate initial mailback response rates, but equally important, to motivate census field staff and make it much easier for them to conduct follow-up activities. Both respondents and field staff are aware that they are participating in the decennial "national portrait," and, even if a general decline may be occurring in the sense of civic responsibility that motivates participation, there is no doubt that the census benefits greatly—in terms of response rates, costs, and data quality— from the publicity surrounding the program.

A continuous measurement program, in contrast, would be conducted in the virtual absence of such publicity. While the launching of such a major new survey could be expected to generate some significant attention, it is highly unlikely that media attention would be sustained, and it would be prohibitively expensive to conduct continuing national and local advertising campaigns in support of the program.

There is little useful evidence now available on which to base estimates of the impact of the noncensus environment on response rates. The tests conducted to date in conjunction with the 2000 census have little direct relevance to this issue, nor do other government or commercial surveys yield much insight. A November 1993 national (long form) census test in Canada, where recent mail-back response rates have been considerably higher than in the United States, produced an initial mail response rate of less than 54 per cent. This test, however, differed in many respects from the proposed program of continuous measurement.

One factor that might have a substantial impact on response rates is whether response to the ILF survey is mandatory, as for the decennial census, or voluntary, as for the Census Bureau's household surveys. It may be useful to establish whether response to the ILF survey could be ruled mandatory under current or revised statutes (Title 13, U.S. Code). A well-implemented mandatory survey might achieve mail return rates similar to those obtained for the redesigned long forms in recent Census Bureau experiments (see Chapter 3).

Clearly at this time it is not possible to assess the credibility of the response rate assumptions used in the current Census Bureau plans for continuous measurement. Consequently, estimates of program cost are subject to a very wide range of uncertainty, as are estimates of data quality (see below); there is no information available on which to assess inevitable differences in response patterns among various important subpopulations.

Estimates of the potential cost savings from eliminating the long form from the decennial census also need to be refined, especially in relation to proposed uses of sampling and estimation that should significantly reduce total follow-up costs in the 2000 census. The consequent reduction in respondent burden is likely to yield a modest increase in mail response rates, thus reducing follow-up costs. The Census Bureau's response improvement research has yielded differential mail return rates of 11-12 percentage points between redesigned versions of the 1990 short and long forms (Dillman et al., 1994). Elimination of long-form items should also make it easier and less costly to collect data during nonresponse follow-up.

However, even when there are substantial differences in response rates between the long form and the short form, dropping the long form will have a mitigated impact on the overall mail response rate, since only a minority of households receive a long form. For example, if the mail return rate were to be 5 percentage points lower than for the short form if only 16 percent of households receive a long form (as was the case in the 1990 census), then the mail return rate would only be $5 \times .16 = 0.8$ of a percentage point lower than the mail return rate that would be achieved if only the short form were to be collected. (In the 1990 census, the long-form and short-form mail return rates were 60 and 66 percent, respectively.) Such a difference could nonetheless yield substantial savings in follow-up costs, depending on the decennial census design.

Recommendation 6.4: The Census Bureau should work to improve cost estimates to determine more accurately the marginal cost of using a

continuous measurement survey in place of the decennial census long-form questions. This work should include a program of research and test surveys to refine assumptions required to estimate costs.

Implications for the Decennial Enumeration

As we noted at the beginning of this chapter, it has been argued that the decennial census could obtain a more complete count of the population if the questionnaire were limited to only those questions needed to satisfy the legal minimum requirements (about which there does not yet seem to be complete agreement). A continuous measurement program, by serving as an alternate source for the long-form information, would thus contribute to a more accurate (and less costly) decennial census.

To what extent does available evidence support this argument? Results of tests conducted as part of the 2000 research program and elsewhere show clearly that, in general, the shorter the form, the higher the mailback response rate.[1] By itself, however, this result does not necessarily imply that dropping the long form would lead to a more complete count. In fact, the panel has seen little evidence to suggest that there would be any significant reduction in net or differential coverage. A recent study (Keeley, 1993), based on the experience of the 1990 census, suggests that the long form had little impact on net coverage and is also likely to have had little effect on differential coverage. It is plausible and reasonable to assume that coverage improvements could be achieved by diverting some of the resources saved from the elimination of the long form to improved coverage and follow-up activities. The extent of such improvement, however, is difficult to estimate, and the panel is not aware of any definitive research in this area.

One could even speculate that dropping the long form from the census might lead to increased underenumeration of some subpopulations. Currently, the Census Bureau can enlist the support of many ethnic and minority groups because the census provides a great deal of useful information about the numbers and characteristics of these groups. Dropping the long form would reduce the amount of information—by eliminating data on ancestry, language, country of birth, and citizenship status, as well as data that permit comparative assessments for such key socioeconomic characteristics as income—and could potentially erode support provided for the census program. Again, there is no direct evidence on which to base estimates of the impact on coverage, but the possibility of a negative impact, especially on differential coverage, should not be rejected out of hand.

---

[1] Experience with the Canadian census, however, shows relatively little difference in mailback rates between the short and long census questionnaires.

In summary, then, although it is possible that the decennial count could be improved by dropping the long form, the panel believes that the extent of such improvement is likely to be small, with little effect on differential coverage. Furthermore, any effects on net or differential coverage would be corrected by the use of integrated coverage measurement procedures in producing the final census population totals.

Regardless of whether the long form is eliminated or reduced in size, however, continuous measurement could have several positive consequences for the decennial census. Operation of a continuous measurement program would improve the ability of the Census Bureau to maintain a continuous presence in local areas over the decade, which would enable those concerned with response and coverage improvement to conduct more effective outreach programs and improve public response to the census. Also, a higher-quality MAF would be available for the decennial census operation because of the more extensive regular updating that would be required to support continuous measurement. A higher-quality MAF should result in fewer missed dwellings and fewer erroneous address inclusions, thus reducing the costs of mail nonresponse follow-up and decreasing the level of undercoverage due to missed housing units.

Data Quality

As noted above, response rates are a major factor in determining the quality of data from census and survey operations. Lower mail response rates (relative to the decennial short form) and difficulties in nonresponse follow-up, especially for minority populations, have been cited as evidence of significant problems in the quality of data on sociodemographic characteristics provided by the decennial long form. In the 1990 census, data were gathered indirectly, either by imputation or from someone outside the household, for 14.4 percent of black non-Hispanic households and 10.2 percent of Hispanic households that were mailed the long form. The corresponding percentages for the short form were 4.9 percent and 3.3 percent, respectively (Ericksen et al., 1991).

In a continuous measurement program, improvements in data quality should result from a greater ability to develop and retain a well-trained field and operations staff, a uniform workload for managing and controlling operations, and more cost-effective use of hardware and software for data collection and management systems. With a continuing operation such as would be needed to conduct a continuous measurement program, repeated opportunities are available to refine and improve the design, field and data processing procedures, survey instruments, and estimation procedures. The continuing presence of an experienced staff and an established operation would lead to a greatly reduced risk (compared with a once-a-decade collection) that a serious unforeseen problem will arise and would introduce efficiencies into the operations that are not possible with a major effort mounted once a decade.

However, as noted in the preceding section on costs, potential improvements in data quality must be weighed against the potential challenges of operating in a noncensus environment. Poor response rates and difficulties in follow-up could result in lower data quality data from continuous measurement. As in matters of cost, large uncertainties prevent reaching definitive conclusions about data quality at this time. Further progress in the Census Bureau's research and development program should provide sufficient evidence on which to make informed comparative assessments of data quality from the decennial long form and from an intercensal long-form survey.

Changes in Survey Form and Content

A concern often raised during discussions of continuous measurement as an alternative to the census long form is that pressures for changes in the continuous measurement content and design throughout the decade (whether through budget reductions or emerging new data needs) would lead to a loss in comparability over time. Although the panel agrees that such pressures are inevitable, we do not believe that they are unmanageable or that the possibility of such problems should weigh heavily in the decision on whether to proceed with the continuous measurement research and testing program.

Significant fluctuations in budget allocations to a continuous measurement program would create serious difficulties for the planned output of such a program, but, should such fluctuations occur, changes in sample size (rather than content) would be the most likely response. Such changes would have an impact on geographic and subpopulation detail and accuracy and would reduce the frequency of the output.

Demands for changes in content would be most likely to take the form of requests for new questions or additional detail on existing topics, and the response to such demands could most easily be handled through the conduct of supplementary surveys.

Other Potential Benefits of a Continuous Measurement Program

In addition to providing data more frequently, a continuous measurement program could potentially offer other direct benefits to the Census Bureau and the federal statistical system.

Supplements to Monthly Collections

A continuous measurement program, conducted on a monthly basis, would provide an excellent vehicle for conducting supplementary surveys—i.e., additional questions on specific topics. Such questions could be asked at the same time as the regular set or could be posed in the form of a subsequent follow-up targeted at households or individuals with particular characteristics as determined by the standard questionnaire. A supplement could be included for one month only, to give estimates for a particular topic of interest at a broad geographic level. The same supplement could be repeated annually or at longer periods to give national and major subnational estimates of change over time. Alternatively, the same supplement could be repeated for several successive months to give estimates at finer geographic levels.

The value of such supplementary inquiries, whether directed at completely new topics or at obtaining deeper insights into topics covered in the regular questionnaire, has been demonstrated clearly in other continuing household surveys in the United States and abroad. The panel believes that careful exploration of supplementary survey capabilities should be included as part of the research and testing plan for the continuous measurement program.

In using the continuous measurement program to collect supplementary data or as a screening device (see below), care would be needed to ensure that the presence of these extra components did not negatively affect the response rates, or change the respondents' answers to the core questions, thus affecting movement over time estimates for these core components.

Sample Frame for Current Demographic Surveys

The Master Address File itself might constitute a high-quality, cost-effective frame for other demographic surveys. The Census Bureau conducts a number of periodic household surveys—for example, the Current Population Survey, the National Health Interview Survey, and the Survey of Income and Program Participation—as well as one-time surveys, and the benefits of having an up-to-date MAF as a sampling frame for these surveys are potentially great. Depending on the legal requirements with regard to the confidentiality of the MAF data, perhaps this frame could be used by other federal statistical agencies for their own surveys (not conducted by the Census Bureau). If Title 13 of the United States Code is amended to permit access to allow sharing of address lists with federal, state, and local officials, as has been proposed (see Recommendation 2.4 of this report and Bureau of the Census, 1994g:March), then not only would the use of the MAF as a frame be possible at a federal level, but also it could be used by state and local agencies for conducting surveys.

Screening Device for New Demographic Surveys

A second feature would be the use of the ILF survey itself as a screening device for rare populations, which would be subsequently surveyed at a later time via telephone or personal visit. This feature would make feasible surveys that otherwise would have prohibitive screening costs. Thus, a continuous measurement program has the very real potential to enhance the data collection capability of the Census Bureau (and the federal statistical system more generally) to include areas that heretofore have not been practical because of cost considerations. It would be difficult to quantify the value of such capabilities and to credit the continuous measurement system with potential cost savings. Nevertheless, this important potential benefit should be recognized when evaluating the prototype continuous measurement system.

Support for Research and Development Initiatives

Continuous measurement would create a more conducive environment for statistical use of administrative records by providing the opportunity for periodic checks on the quality of administrative records to be incorporated in the integrated estimates program.

Summary

The panel believes that the ongoing thorough review of census requirements, costs, and methods presents an opportunity to undertake a full evaluation of the viability and desirability of instituting a permanent continuous data collection program to obtain traditional census data on population and housing characteristics. We believe that the efforts by the Census Bureau to develop a prototype for continuous measurement provide a very promising start to this process. We are especially encouraged that a project team has been established and has begun to carry out work on a program of evaluation for continuous measurement. Our position is that considered judgments about the merits and drawbacks of continuous measurement can be made only after extensive study to describe exactly how such a system would operate, what it would produce, and how much it would cost. The Census Bureau's initiation of a project team, along with a development plan, promises that such information will become available through an active program of research and development.

Much of the interest and discussion surrounding continuous measurement to date has concerned its cost when fully implemented (Committee on National Statistics, 1993c). As we stated in our interim report, this panel is not convinced that continuous measurement would provide a less costly alternative to the traditional long form. What continuous measurement would offer is greater frequency of small-area sample data and, possibly, improved data quality. Benefits for the decennial enumeration of the population might result from the removal of the requirements to collect and tabulate sample data as part of the decennial census operation, but the evidence for such benefits is not well documented.

Many interesting issues surround an evaluation of the merits and feasibility of a continuous measurement program to collect small-area sample data. Many aspects of this program need to be developed and evaluated in concert, and a great deal more needs to be tested and learned on all fronts before rational decisions about the prospects for such a scheme can be reached. In addition to the question of whether a continuous measurement program such as the one proposed has merit over the long term, there are additional questions relating to the feasibility of introducing a continuous measurement program of sufficient quality and scope in time to act as a viable replacement for any small-area data collection (i.e., a long form) as part of the 2000 census.

Another important consideration in judging the merits of continuous measurement is the relationship between the decennial enumeration and statutory requirements for information. A recent review (Bureau of the Census, 1994a) found that legislative mandates exist for most of the items collected on the 1990 census long form, but the statutes do not specify that the data must be collected in the decennial census. The key question is whether the decennial census is the most appropriate vehicle for collecting this information. Considerable research and development must occur to answer that question and thus determine the extent to which continuous measurement might replace, rather than supplement, data collection using the decennial census long form.

Continuous measurement represents a fundamental change in methodology for obtaining data of the type traditionally collected on the decennial census long form. It has implications that extend far beyond issues of coverage, cost, quality, and frequency. In particular, the relationship of a continuous measurement program to other federal government surveys and to state and local governments is a very important topic that lies beyond the scope of the panel's work. Careful evaluation and widespread consideration of its implications will be needed to clarify the merits of this proposal.

MATRIX SAMPLING

The more modest of the two proposed alternatives to long-form data collection is to change the nature of the decennial collection of small-area sample data by using a technique known as matrix sampling to reduce the respondent burden on individual households. In this section, we discuss the general approach and the Census Bureau's plans for research on matrix sampling.

As indicated at the beginning of this chapter, there is concern that the respondent burden imposed by the use the of census long form, as in the 1990 and previous censuses, will give rise to reduced mail return rates in the 2000 census. Matrix sampling is a technique designed to spread and reduce the response burden, while meeting small-area data needs.

Overview of Matrix Sampling

Matrix sampling is a technique to spread the respondent burden associated with collecting a given quantity of data across a larger group of respondents than would be the case without its use. Thus, rather than collecting data on a set of m

data items from n respondents, a group of somewhat more than n respondents is included (generally, severalfold n), with each asked to respond to fewer than m items (generally, substantially fewer). This is done in such a way that the reliability requirements for estimates and tabulations are equivalent (or even superior) to those that would be achieved using n respondents to all items, while collecting just nm total item responses, or perhaps somewhat fewer (so that total burden is in fact reduced, as well as spread).

The use of matrix sampling obviously implies the use of several different data collection forms, each to be administered to a random subsample of the full respondent sample. In any application this increases the complexity of administering the data collection, processing the data, and analyzing the data. To be worthwhile, therefore, a matrix sampling plan must achieve benefits through the increased spread, and possible overall reduction, in respondent burden. Later, we discuss the kinds of circumstances in which these benefits would be realized.

The Census Bureau is considering the use of matrix sampling for the collection of sample data (long-form data) in the 2000 census. By spreading the response burden, this methodology reduces the maximum burden on any single responding household. The aim is to increase the mail response rate for forms containing long-form data, thus increasing the quality and reducing the cost of census data collection.

For this to be successful, it is necessary that the reduction in nonresponse achieve a critical threshold through the reduction in content asked of each respondent. Otherwise, matrix sampling may actually act to increase cost. Suppose that, as in the 1990 census, a proportion p of the household population are asked to complete a long form, with the remaining households completing a short form. Suppose that the short-form response rate is r_s, and the long-form rate is r_l, where $r_l \leq r_s$. Then, the overall response rate is

$$pr_l + (1 - p)\, r_s = r_l + (1 - p)(r_s - r_l).$$

Now suppose that with matrix sampling the proportion of the population asked to complete a form with something other than basic short-form data is kp (where $k > 1$ and $kp \leq 1$), and that the response rate for the matrix sampling forms is r_m, where $r_l \leq r_m \leq r_s$. Then, the overall response rate under matrix sampling is

$$kp\, r_m + (1 - kp)\, r_s = r_m + (1 - kp)(r_s - r_m).$$

Hence, matrix sampling can be beneficial only if

$$r_m + (1 - kp)(r_s - r_m) > r_l + (1 - p)(r_s - r_l).$$

This is achieved provided that $r_s < r_m + (r_m - r_l)/(k - 1)$. Since $r_s > r_m$, the quantity $(r_m - r_l)/(k - 1)$ must be sizable to make the gains worthwhile. In other words, the difference between the response rates for the matrix form and the long form must be more than $(k - 1)$ times as great as the difference between the response rates for the short form and the matrix form.

For example, suppose that instead of using a single long form given to 16.7 percent of households ($p = 0.167$), three different matrix forms were constructed, each containing one-third of the total content of sampled items. Suppose each form is given to 16.7 percent of households, so that overall 50 percent of households receive a matrix form ($k = 3$), with the other 50 percent receiving a short form. Suppose that the mail return rate for the short form is 80 percent ($r_s = 0.8$), whereas the return rate for the long form is 70 percent ($r_e = 0.7$). Then matrix sampling will increase mail response overall provided that the average mail return rate for the matrix forms (r_m) satisfies the inequality

$$0.8 < r_m + (r_m - 0.7)/(3-1);$$

that is, the matrix form response rate must exceed 76.7 percent ($r_m > 0.767$), so that it is almost equal to the short form return rate of 80 percent. If matrix forms were to achieve an overall response rate of 79 percent ($r_m = 0.79$), almost equal to the short form rate of 80 percent, then the overall mail return rate would be 79.5 percent, only a modest increase from the 78.3 percent overall rate that would be achieved with a long form and no matrix sampling.

The example described above would not permit any cross-tabulations to be produced among items from the different matrix forms. This is likely to be such an important requirement that it seems very probable that, if there were to be three matrix forms, on average each would have to include substantially more than one-third of the items. In such a case it seems likely that the return rate r_m is more likely to be closer to the long-form response rate (r_l) than to the short form rate (r_s).

Simply put, to be useful matrix sampling will have to eliminate a very large proportion of the differential response rates between the short and long forms. Current evidence suggests that this is unlikely to happen. Before reviewing the thinking behind the use of matrix sampling for the 2000 census, and considering how to evaluate its possible use, we will review the general circumstances under which matrix sampling is an effective data collection device.

Conditions Favorable to Matrix Sampling

The following conditions lend themselves to matrix sampling:

1. Collection of all data items from a single given respondent is impossible or impracticable or leads to very low response rates.
2. There is interest in statistics that are aggregated across items.
3. There is little interest in cross-tabulations, or at least only a subset of cross-tabulations are of interest.
4. Different sampling rates are desirable for different items.
5. There is a strong relationship among responses to various subsets of the items, which permit reductions in variance through estimation techniques that model (directly or indirectly) the relationships among variables.

Sample surveys to assess the educational achievement of populations often meet with circumstances very favorable to the use of matrix sampling. Often a large pool of test items is developed to cover the full range of materials to be assessed. This makes it infeasible to think of giving the whole battery of test items to a given student. To make the data collection workable, each student must be assessed using a subset of the test. The prime statistics of interest are those that aggregate across the test items. The mean score on a particular item is of much less interest than the mean score on the whole test. Every responding student contributes data to such an estimate. Intercorrelations among test items are of some interest, and the matrix forms are developed so that those of particular interest can be estimated, but they are of less interest than the overall score. Finally, results for the individual test items are generally highly correlated, and this can be used in developing the estimation procedure for the statistics on the distribution of the test scores. A student's achievement on a well-chosen but relatively small subset of the test items is highly predictive of the student's score on the whole test. For an example of the use of matrix sampling in an assessment of educational achievement, see Beaton and Zwick (1992).

It is notable that, of the five conditions outlined above, four of them in general do not apply strongly in the case of census long-form data. The mail response rate for the long form in 1990 was lower than that of the short form, but not greatly so (Keeley, 1993). There is considerable interest in many of the cross-tabulations, not only two-way but also higher-dimensions. In fact, these may well be the statistics of prime interest, both at the small-area level and for larger areas. For the most part, there is little or no interest in statistics aggregated across items. In those areas of such interest, total income derived from components, for example, it would seem very problematic to spread these items across different forms (asking some households to report some components of income and other households to report different components), and even this is of little or no use for statistics other than mean income. Finally, although there may be possible gains in efficiency that can be obtained through estimation procedures that utilize the intercorrelations among the variables, this is not immediately evident and has not yet appeared in the Census Bureau's plans for evaluating matrix sampling.

The one property favorable to the use of matrix sampling in its broadest sense that might apply in the 2000 census is that of having different sample rates for different items. There might be requirements to have some data at a finer level of geographic detail than others (but without the need for full enumeration in either case). In the absence of the other conditions favorable to matrix sampling, such a requirement is probably best served by having a sequence of nested long forms, with each form containing a subset of the items contained on each longer form. As noted in the panel's interim report (p. 36), this variant of matrix sampling has been used in the 1950, 1960, and 1970 censuses.

Matrix Sampling in the 1995 Census Test

The Census Bureau has proposed the use of some form of matrix sample design in its 1995 census test and has identified two purposes for using matrix sampling in the test. The first is to obtain information about the impact of the operational complexities that arise from using several different forms (in addition to the short form) with varying sampling rates. The second is to obtain information about the relative response rates for the different forms. Two alternative plans have been proposed by the Census Bureau in its discussion with the panel. The first plan involves four different forms of the long form. One contains all of the long-form items, and the other three each include all items from two of the three broad areas of interest—social, economic, and housing. One possible implementation of this design calls for 10 percent of those receiving other than a short form to receive the full long form, and 30 percent of such households would receive the other three "medium" forms. It has been proposed that for the 1995 census test, 80 percent of households receive a short form, 6 percent receive each of the three medium forms, and the remaining 2 percent receive the long form. Thus, any given long-form questions will be asked in 14 percent of households.

The second proposal involves a series of nested forms. There would be three forms, in addition to the short form. The longest of these would include the full content to be collected. The second extended form contains a subset of the items on the full form, and the third will be even shorter still, containing a subset of the items from the second form. As indicated above, this variant of matrix sampling has been used in the 1950 and 1960 censuses for housing items and was used extensively for both population and housing items in 1970, albeit with only two different forms. We encourage the Census Bureau to review carefully the history of the use of matrix sampling and to ensure that the information to be obtained from the census test has not actually been well established in the past.

The designs proposed for the 1995 census test may be effective in evaluating the two aspects targeted by the Census Bureau. It is very important that there be a realization both inside and outside the Census Bureau that the information to be obtained from the census test will not be adequate of itself to determine whether matrix sampling is a suitable approach to long-form data collection in 2000. If the use of matrix sampling in the 1995 census test demonstrates its operational feasibility (and its use in three previous censuses suggests that it should be feasible), then a substantial research program is needed to establish the worth of proceeding with it. This is discussed in the next section.

The panel does not think it is likely that the first of the above matrix sampling plans proposed for the 1995 census test will demonstrate substantial improvement in response rates. The small difference between the long- and short-form mail response rates in 1990, and the fact that the three medium length forms require, on average, two-thirds as long to complete as the long form (relatively longer if one includes the short-form data in such reckoning) combine to make it appear unlikely that the medium-length forms will achieve response rates noticeably higher than for the long form itself. The second approach of using nested forms seems much more likely to give useful information about the effect of form length and content on response rates.

Matrix Sampling for the 2000 Census

If the 1995 census test indicates that matrix sampling is operationally feasible, then the panel believes that it is important that the Census Bureau undertake fundamental research on three fronts before the case for using matrix sampling in the 2000 census can be sufficiently established. The three areas in which research is required are: (1) establishing the relationship between form length and content with mail response rates, (2) ascertaining requirements for cross-tabulations, at the small-area level, of the data to be captured on a sample basis, and (3) investigating possible gains in estimation efficiency by using the intercorrelation structure of the data (i.e., composite estimation). The results of this research can be combined with the findings from the 1995 census test and past censuses concerning the operational costs and complexity of matrix sampling.

To establish the relationship between form length and composition and mail nonresponse, a program of cognitive research and experimental studies will be needed. The cognitive research should shed guidance as to which aspects of the long form give rise to total mail nonresponse and the extent to which the length of the form per se is a factor. Experimental studies can be used to evaluate the effect of various proposed forms on mail response rates, although, as with other studies of mail response rates, the interpretation of the findings will be hampered by the fact that the tests are not conducted in the atmosphere of public awareness that surrounds a census.

On the basis of experience both in the census and in other survey settings, one aspect that is likely to have a substantial impact on the long-form response rate is the presence and format of the questions on income. Thus, in investigating mail response rates and matrix sampling, we urge the Census Bureau to research fully the exact requirements for the income data at the small geographic level. It would seem likely that mail response rates might be improved somewhat by ensuring that income is not asked any more often than is necessary. If other data items are required at a finer geographic level than is income, these could be included on a shortened version of the long form that does not include income. That said, and without detailed insight into census data requirements, the panel does not really expect that there will be any data items requiring a finer level of geographic breakdown than does income. If indeed the presence of income questions does prove to be a major determinant of long-form response rates, then it will be important to intensify cognitive and experimental research into the best format for asking income questions, so as to have the least negative impact on mail response rates.

At the same time, the Census Bureau needs to conduct an evaluation of the requirements for cross-tabulations from the 2000 census, especially at the small-area level. The establishment of sets of cross-tabulations that are required, and at what level of precision, will drive and define the determination of possible alternative census forms for use in matrix sampling. Perhaps not all cross-tabulations require the same level of accuracy. This might lead to the development of a long form and one or more medium-length forms containing a subset of items from the long form, the subset being those items for which more precise cross-tabulations are required.

The third avenue of research is to examine the possible development of composite estimation and other techniques that make use of the correlation between two items that are both present on some census forms, but only one of which is available on other forms. These estimators will utilize this correlation to give estimates that are more precise than those obtained by just weighting the data using the inverse of selection probabilities and perhaps poststratifying to some control totals. It would be particularly worthwhile to see if such procedures can be developed that improve precision for estimates of cross-tabulations. If a nested sequence of forms is used, for example, then a stratified (or ratio) multiphase sample estimator might be used to give greater reliability for tabulations of those characteristics included only on the longest of the forms.

All of this research into the effectiveness of matrix sampling makes sense only in the context of a given set of content. Thus, the Census Bureau will be limited in its ability to evaluate matrix sampling appropriately until such time as the content requirements for the 2000 census become reasonably clear. Consequently, the plan to investigate the operational complexities in the 1995 census test, and then proceed to investigate the other aspects of matrix sampling as content requirements become clearer, seems a sound one. Finding sufficient developmental lead time to evaluate fully plans for matrix sampling may be difficult as a result of the dependence on content.

> **Recommendation 6.5: The panel endorses the Census Bureau's plan to investigate the impact of form length and content on mail response rates in the 1995 census test. Even if the operational feasibility of multiple sample forms is confirmed in the 1995 census test, the Census Bureau should not introduce matrix sampling without undertaking further research. Such research should be assigned low priority relative to other decennial census research projects.**

On the basis of the evidence that we have seen to date, the panel judges it unlikely that matrix sampling will present an effective alternative to long-form data collection in 2000. Given that content is unlikely to be increased substantially beyond that of 1990, it does not appear likely that the conditions will exist that are needed to make matrix sampling an effective option for the census. The most likely possibility is that there would be a long form and a medium form containing that subset of the long-form data items for which the most precise cross-tabulations are required.

Recommendations

For the reader's convenience, we present all the panel's recommendations, keyed to the chapters in which they appear.

CHAPTER 1
INTRODUCTION

Recommendation 1.1: In assessing the design innovations included in the 1995 census test or other research and development, the Census Bureau should place great emphasis on cost-benefit analysis as part of the overall evaluation leading to implementation decisions for the 2000 census. Requirements for evaluating new data collection methodologies in the 1995 census test should include information on such characteristics as cost, yield, and gross error that are needed to inform cost-benefit judgments.

CHAPTER 2
PRELIMINARY CENSUS DESIGN ISSUES

Recommendation 2.1: The Census Bureau should continue aggressive development of the TIGER (topologically integrated geographic encoding and referencing) system, the Master Address File (MAF), and integration of these two systems. MAF/TIGER updating activities for the 1995 census test sites should be completed in time to permit the use and evaluation of the MAF/TIGER system as part of the 1995 census test.

Recommendation 2.2: The Census Bureau should continue its research program on record linkage in support of the 1995 census test and the 2000 census. Efforts should include studies of the effectiveness of different matching keys (e.g., name, address, date of birth, and Social Security number) and the establishment of requirements for such components as address standardization, parsing, and string comparators. Existing record linkage technology should be tested and evaluated in the 1995 census test.

Recommendation 2.3: In view of the operational advantages that are likely to result, the panel endorses the proposed change in census reference date from April 1 to the first Saturday in March. Furthermore, we recommend that changing the census reference date from early in the month to midmonth (e.g., the second Saturday in March) be reconsidered if subsequent modifications to the mailout operation would permit all census mailings to be executed within the same calendar month using a midmonth reference date.

Recommendation 2.4: The Statistical Policy Office of the Office of Management and Budget should develop a structure to permit the sharing of address lists among federal agencies and state and local governments—including the Census Bureau and the Postal Service—for approved uses under appropriate conditions.

CHAPTER 3
RESPONSE AND COVERAGE

Recommendation 3.1: A program of research extending beyond the 1995 census test should aim to reduce coverage errors within households by reducing response errors (e.g., by using an extended roster form). This research should also evaluate the impact of these new approaches on gross and net coverage errors, as well as assess the effects on coverage of obtaining enumerations using different instrument modalities (e.g., paper and computer-assisted) and different interview modes (e.g., paper instrument completed by household respondent and by enumerator).

Recommendation 3.2: The Census Bureau should use the 1995 census test and subsequent tests to inform the design of the 800 number call-in system for the 2000 census. The Census Bureau should focus on the public's response to the menu-driven call-routing system, acceptance of the computer-administered interview, possible differential mode effects between a computer-administered interview and one administered by an interviewer, and the technical feasibility of administering interviews using voice recognition and voice recording. The Census Bureau should also develop and implement a monitoring system in these tests to collect operational and cost data on the call-in program.

Recommendation 3.3: The Census Bureau should expand the research program involving the acquisition of telephone numbers for MAF addresses by working with more companies that offer electronic directory services and developing an optimal protocol for matching addresses. If the Census Bureau is able to acquire unlisted telephone numbers for a 1995 census test site, it should carefully monitor the results obtained from calling households with unlisted numbers.

Recommendation 3.4: The Census Bureau should consider developing an extensive network of relations between field offices and local community resources, particularly in hard-to-enumerate areas, and should examine the cost-effectiveness of maintaining this infrastructure in continuous operation between censuses. The Census Bureau should develop and implement pilot programs in conjunction with the 1995 census test in order to gather information about the potential costs and benefits of a large-scale local outreach program.

Recommendation 3.5: The Census Bureau should conduct further comparative studies of hard-to-enumerate areas, focusing on those parts of the country where three phenomena coincide: a shortage of affordable housing, a high proportion of undocumented immigrants, and the presence of low-income neighborhoods.

Recommendation 3.6: In the 1995 census test, the Census Bureau should include a larger repertoire of foreign-language materials than those currently available in Spanish (both written and audio). In addition, the Census Bureau should conduct more aggressive hiring of community-based enumerators (with due consideration of local concerns about the confidentiality of census responses) and should accommodate greater flexibility in the timing of enumeration by personal visit (i.e., permitting contact during evenings and weekends).

Recommendation 3.7: We endorse the Census Bureau's plans to conduct, in the 1995 census test, enumeration at service providers (e.g., shelters and soup kitchens) as a method for counting persons with no usual residence (and possibly migrant workers). The Census Bureau should consider conducting enumeration of streets and other public places on a sample basis at each of the test sites for the purpose of coverage assessment.

Recommendation 3.8: The Census Bureau should undertake a program of research in cognitive anthropology, sociology, and psychology that will contribute to the development of more acceptable racial and ethnic identification questions.

Recommendation 3.9: The Census Bureau should assign overall responsibility for decennial census outreach and promotion to a centralized, permanent office. The Census Bureau should consider expanding the mission of the extant Public Information Office to include this charge. Evaluation of outreach and promotion programs should be conducted by an independent unit within the Census Bureau.

Recommendation 3.10: The Census Bureau should evaluate the costs and benefits of alternatives to the use of the Advertising Council to conduct the 2000 census media campaign. Some alternative options are working directly with local and regional agencies, undertaking paid media research, and supplementing pro bono advertising with paid advertising in hard-to-enumerate localities.

Recommendation 3.11: The Census Bureau should evaluate the programs for state and local cooperation that will be overseen by census advisors in the 1995 census test areas in order to collect from these experimental initiatives those programs most likely to (a) reduce the cost of the decennial census (particularly by improving mail response rates) and (b) reduce the differential undercount. Preservation of the Census Awareness and Products Program should, however, be a high priority, not to be superseded by this new initiative for improving state and local cooperation.

CHAPTER 4
SAMPLING AND STATISTICAL ESTIMATION

Recommendation 4.1: Sampling for nonresponse follow-up could produce major cost savings in 2000. The Census Bureau should test nonresponse follow-up sampling in 1995 and collect data that allows evaluation of (1) follow-up of all nonrespondents during a truncated period of time, combined with the use of sampling during a subsequent period of follow-up of the remaining nonrespondents, and (2) the use of administrative records to improve estimates for nonsampled housing units.

Recommendation 4.2: Differential undercount cannot be reduced to acceptable levels at acceptable costs without the use of integrated coverage measurement and the statistical methods associated with it. We endorse the use of integrated coverage measurement as an essential part of census-taking in the 2000 census.

Recommendation 4.3: The Census Bureau should investigate during the 1995 census test whether the CensusPlus field operation can attain excellent coverage in CensusPlus blocks without contaminating the regular enumeration in those blocks. If substantial problems are identified, CensusPlus should not be selected as the field methodology for integrated coverage measurement in the 2000 census unless clearly effective corrective measures can be implemented within the research and development schedule.

Recommendation 4.4: Whatever method for integrated coverage measurement is used in 2000, the Census Bureau should ensure that a sufficiently large sample is taken so that the single set of counts provides the accuracy needed by data users at pertinent levels of geography.

Recommendation 4.5: The Census Bureau should prepare alternative sample designs for integrated coverage measurement with varying levels of support for direct state estimation. The provision of direct state estimates should be evaluated in terms of the relative costs and the consequent loss of accuracy in population estimates for other geographic areas or subpopulations of interest.

Recommendation 4.6: The panel endorses the continued use of demographic analysis as an evaluation tool in the decennial census. However, the present state of development does not support a prominent role for demographic methods in the production of official population totals as part of integrated coverage measurement in the 2000 census. The Census Bureau should continue research to develop subnational demographic estimates, with particular attention to potential links between demographic analysis and further development of the continuous measurement prototype and the administrative records census option.

Recommendation 4.7: Before the census, the Census Bureau should produce detailed documentation of statistical methodology to be used for estimation and modeling. After the census, the Census Bureau should document how the methodology was applied empirically and should provide evaluation of the methodology.

Recommendation 4.8: The Census Bureau should develop methods for measuring and modeling all sources of error in the census and for showing uncertainty in published tabulations or otherwise enabling users to estimate uncertainty.

Recommendation 4.9: The Census Bureau should vigorously pursue research on statistical estimation now and throughout the decade. Topics should include nonresponse follow-up sampling, coverage estimation, incorporation of varied information sources (including administrative records), and indirect estimation for small areas.

CHAPTER 5
ADMINISTRATIVE RECORDS

Recommendation 5.1: Legislation that requires or authorizes the creation of individual record systems for administrative purposes should not create unnecessary barriers to legitimate statistical uses of the records, including important uses not directly related to the programs that the records were developed to serve. Preferably, such legislation should explicitly allow for such uses, subject to strong protection of the confidentiality of individual information. The panel urges Congress, in considering legislation relevant to health care reform, not to foreclose possible uses of health care enrollment records for the decennial censuses and other basic demographic statistical programs.

Recommendation 5.2: To facilitate statistical uses of new health record systems, the responsible executive branch agencies should invite the Census Bureau and other federal statistical agencies to participate actively in the development of content and access provisions for these record systems.

Recommendation 5.3: The Office of Management and Budget should review identifiers, especially addresses, and demographic data items currently included in major administrative record systems with a view to promoting standardization and facilitation of statistical uses of information about individuals both in these record systems and in new ones that may be developed.

Recommendation 5.4: The Census Bureau, in cooperation with other agencies and organizations, should support a program of research on public views about statistical uses of administrative records in government. The research should focus on public reaction to very specific administrative record use scenarios, rather than on general questions of privacy.

Recommendation 5.5: Research on the production of population estimates from Internal Revenue Service and Social Security Administration records should continue as a joint initiative of these agencies with the Census Bureau and should focus on identifying measures that could serve to reduce coverage differentials and improve geographic precision.

Recommendation 5.6: The Census Bureau should continue its development of a cost model for an administrative record census and should use the model to maintain current cost estimates for several versions of this option as they are developed.

Recommendation 5.7: During the 2000 census the Census Bureau should test one or more designs for an administrative records census in selected areas. Planning for this testing should begin immediately.

Recommendation 5.8: The Census Bureau should plan its uses of administrative records in the 1995 census test and other tests leading up to the 2000 census and in the census itself in a manner that will also provide knowledge and experience of value for a possible administrative records census in 2010 or beyond and for uses of administrative records in demographic programs other than the census.

Recommendation 5.9: In maintaining and updating its Administrative Records Information System, the Census Bureau should give high priority to the acquisition of detailed information about record systems that are being developed to support health care reform at the state level. The Census Bureau should seek early opportunities to obtain and use health enrollment records in one or more states and should plan for experimental uses of these records as part of the 2000 census.

Recommendation 5.10: The Census Bureau should substantially increase the scope of its efforts to use administrative records to produce intercensal small-area tabulations, either through stand-alone tabulations of data from one or more administrative record sources or by combining such data with data from current surveys.

Recommendation 5.11: The panel urges the Census Bureau to adopt a proactive policy to expand its uses of administrative records, and it urges other executive branch agencies and Congress to give their support to such a policy.

CHAPTER 6
ALTERNATIVES FOR LONG-FORM DATA COLLECTION

Recommendation 6.1: The panel endorses further research and evaluation of a continuous measurement program. In conducting this work, the Census Bureau should establish, and continually reinforce, a commitment to simultaneous research and development of cost estimation, data collection and processing methods, estimation procedures, and user needs.

Recommendation 6.2: The Census Bureau should initiate discussions with all potential users of continuous measurement data, including state and local governments and private-sector users. A research program should be developed to answer user questions. The Census Bureau should also develop a program to inform data users of the simulated data products emerging from the test surveys and to get their reactions.

Recommendation 6.3: The Census Bureau should evaluate the gains in accuracy that may be offered by continuous measurement for estimates of various characteristics at varying levels of geography. In making accuracy assessments, the Census Bureau should take full advantage of simulations, based on existing census and survey data, to provide realistic scenarios for the changes in estimates over time. As part of its outreach program, the Census Bureau should provide long-form data users with accompanying estimates of bias and precision for various geographic levels and aggregations of one to five years of data.

Recommendation 6.4: The Census Bureau should work to improve cost estimates to determine more accurately the marginal cost of using a continuous measurement survey in place of the decennial census long-form questions. This work should include a program of research and test surveys to refine assumptions required to estimate costs.

Recommendation 6.5: The panel endorses the Census Bureau's plan to investigate the impact of form length and content on mail response rates in the 1995 census test. Even if the operational feasibility of multiple sample forms is confirmed in the 1995 census test, the Census Bureau should not introduce matrix sampling without undertaking further research. Such research should be assigned low priority relative to other decennial census research projects.

References

Alexander, Charles

1993   A Continuous Measurement Alternative for the U.S. Census. Report CM-10. Bureau of the Census, U.S. Department of Commerce.

1994   Small Area Estimation with Continuous Measurement: What We Have and What We Want. Paper presented at the Annual Research Conference of the U.S. Bureau of the Census, Arlington, Virginia, March 20-23.

Alho, Juha M., M.H. Mulry, K. Wurdeman, and J. Kim

1993   Estimating heterogeneity in the probabilities of enumeration for dual-system estimation. *Journal of the American Statistical Association* 88(423): 1130-1136.

Bates, Nancy, and D.C. Whitford

1991   Reaching Everyone: Encouraging Participation in the 1990 Census. Paper presented at the 1991 annual meetings of the American Statistical Association, Atlanta, Georgia. Bureau of the Census, U.S. Department of Commerce.

Bates, Nancy, Manuel de la Puente, Theresa J. DeMaio, and Elizabeth A. Martin

1994   Research on Race and Ethnicity: Results from Questionnaire Design Tests. Paper presented at the Annual Research Conference of the U.S. Bureau of the Census, Arlington, Virginia, March 20-23.

Bean, Frank D., Barry Edmonston, and Jeffrey S. Passel

1990   *Undocumented Migration to the United States: IRCA and the Experience of the 1980s.* Washington, D.C.: The Urban Institute Press.

Beaton, A.E., and R. Zwick

1992   Overview of the National Assessment of Educational Progress. *Journal of Educational Statistics* 17(2):95-109.

Belin, Thomas R., G.J. Diffendal, S. Mack, D.B. Rubin, J.L. Schafer, and A.M. Zaslavsky

1993   Hierarchical logistic-regression models for imputation of unresolved enumeration status in undercount estimation. *Journal of the American Statistical Association* 88(423):1149-1159.

Bell, William R.
  1993   Using information from demographic analysis in Post-Enumeration Survey estimation. *Journal of the American Statistical Association* 88(423):1106-1118.
Bentley, Colene, and Adele Furrie
  1993   Reaching Out to Native People: Statistics Canada and the 1991 Aboriginal Peoples Survey (APS). Oral presentation given at the Census Bureau Research Conference on Undercounted Ethnic Populations, May 5-7, 1993, Richmond, Virginia.
Beresford, John C.
  1992   Social Security Numbers (SSN) and Design 2000 Census. Bureau of the Census, U.S. Department of Commerce.
Biemer, Paul
  1994   An Integrated Approach to Quality Assurance and Nonsampling Error Evaluation for the ICM-DRAFT. Memo from Paul Biemer to Jon Clark, dated April 26, 1994. Research Triangle Institute, Research Triangle Park, North Carolina.
Biemer, Paul, and Gosta Forsman
  1992   On the quality of reinterview data with application to the Current Population Survey. *Journal of the American Statistical Association* 87:915-923.
Blair, Johnny
  1994   Ancillary Uses of Government Administrative Data on Individuals: Public Perceptions and Attitudes. Paper commissioned by the Panel to Evaluate Alternative Census Methods. Survey Research Center, University of Maryland, College Park.
Bowie, Chester, and Daniel Kasprzyk
  1987   A Review of the Use of Administrative Records in the Survey of Income and Program Participation. SIPP Working Paper No. 8721. (November 1987). Bureau of the Census, U.S. Department of Commerce.
Bradburn, Norman M.
  1993   Alternative Census Methods. Written testimony of Norman Bradburn, chair of the Panel to Evaluate Alternative Census Methods, Committee on National Statistics, National Research Council. Presented before the Subcommittee on Census, Statistics and Postal Personnel, Committee on Post Office and Civil Service, U.S. House of Representatives, March 2.
  1994   Letter to the Honorable Thomas C. Sawyer from the Committee on National Statistics chair, Norman Bradburn. Committee on National Statistics, Commission on Behavioral and Social Sciences and Education, National Research Council, Washington, D.C. (March 28, 1994).
Brownrigg, Leslie A.
  1991   Irregular Housing and the Differential Undercount on Minorities. Paper prepared for the Census Advisory Committee Meetings at Alexandria, Virginia, November 13-15, 1991. Bureau of the Census, U.S. Department of Commerce.
Brownrigg, Leslie A., and Manuel de la Puente
  1993   Alternative Enumeration Methods and Results: Resolution and Resolved Populations by Site. Bureau of the Census, U.S. Department of Commerce.

Bryant, Barbara E.
 1992   Results of the March Simplified Questionnaire Tests and Other Census 2000
         Issues. Written testimony before the Subcommittee on Census and Popula-
         tion, House Committee on Post Office and Civil Service, July 1. Bureau of
         the Census, U.S. Department of Commerce.
 1993   Census-taking for a litigious, data-driven society. *Chance* 6 (3): 44-49.
Bureau of the Census
 1987   Enumeration and Residence Rules for the 1990 Census. Bureau of the Cen-
         sus, U.S. Department of Commerce.
 1992a   Master Address File: Documentation of Requirements. Paper prepared by
         the MAF Requirements Process Action Team (July 1, 1991). Bureau of the
         Census, U.S. Department of Commerce.
 1992b   1990 Census Cost Components. Year 2000 Research and Development Staff
         Memorandum Series, Book I, Chapter 30, No. 4. Memo from Jay Keller to
         Susan Miskura (August 6, 1992). Bureau of the Census, U.S. Department of
         Commerce.
 1992c   Administrative Records and Design Alternatives for the 2000 Census. Design
         Alternative Recommendation (DAR) #2, Year 2000 Research and Develop-
         ment Staff (September). Bureau of the Census, U.S. Department of Com-
         merce.
 1992d   Implementation Test (IT) Mail Response Evaluation Preliminary Report. Pre-
         pared by Census Data Quality Branch, Decennial Statistical Studies Division
         (December). Bureau of the Census, U.S. Department of Commerce.
 1992e   Draft option paper, "USPS Involvement in the 2000 Census." Prepared by the
         Bureau of the Census for the Appropriations Committee, U.S. House of Rep-
         resentatives. U.S. Department of Commerce.
 1993a   Census 2000 Updates. Monthly issue prepared by the Year 2000 Research and
         Development Staff. Bureau of the Census, U.S. Department of Commerce.
 1993b   Design Alternative Recommendation #14, Year 2000 Research and Develop-
         ment Staff (May 17, 1993). Bureau of the Census, U.S. Department of Com-
         merce.
 1993c   Description of the Postcensal Income and Poverty Estimates Program for the
         1990s. The Housing and Household Economic Statistics Division (August
         1993). Bureau of the Census, U.S. Department of Commerce.
 1993d   Potential Cost Savings by Sampling for Nonresponse Follow-up. Year 2000
         Research and Development staff memorandum series, Book 1, Chapter 30,
         #11. Memo from Janice Pentercs to Jay Keller (September 17, 1993). Bureau
         of the Census, U.S. Department of Commerce.
 1993e   Special Census/Administrative Records Research Results for Godfrey, Illi-
         nois. Prepared by the Special Census/Administrative Records Match Work-
         ing Group. 2KS Memorandum Series, Design 2000, Book 1, Chapter 1 of #3
         (October 1, 1993). Bureau of the Census, U.S. Department of Commerce.
 1993f   Results of the South Tucson, Arizona Administrative Records Test. Produced
         by the Special Census/Administrative Records Match Working Group in con-
         junction with the Year 2000 Research and Development Staff. 2KS Memo-
         randum Series, Design 2000, Book 1, Chapter 1 of #4 (November 15, 1993).
         Bureau of the Census, U.S. Department of Commerce.

1993g State and Local Agencies Preparing Population and Housing Estimates. Current Population Reports, Population Estimates and Projections, Series P-25, No. 1063. Bureau of the Census, U.S. Department of Commerce.

1994a The 1995 Census Test: A Plan Based on Census Bureau Research and Critical Review by Stakeholders. Transmitted with cover letter from Robert Tortora. Bureau of the Census, U.S. Department of Commerce.

1994b Results of the Tool Kit Workshops. Prepared by the Interdivisional Tool Kit Working Group. DSSD Census Memorandum Series #D-7 from John Thompson to Susan Miskura (February 7, 1994). Bureau of the Census, U.S. Department of Commerce.

1994c 1995 Test-Experimental Design for Sampling for Nonresponse Followup. Memo from John Thompson to Susan Miskura (March 7, 1994). Bureau of the Census, U.S. Department of Commerce.

1994d Targeted Methods for the 1995 Census Test (March 11, 1994). Bureau of the Census, U.S. Department of Commerce.

1994e Proposed Methodology for a Service-Based Enumeration (SBE) to be Tested in the 1995 Census Test (Draft, March 11, 1994). Bureau of the Census, U.S. Department of Commerce.

1994f A Comparison of Three Different Computer Matchers. 2KS Memorandum Series Design 2000, Book 1, Chapter 1 of #5 (March 30, 1994). Bureau of the Census, U.S. Department of Commerce.

1994g Census 2000 Updates. Monthly issue prepared by the Year 2000 Research and Development Staff. Bureau of the Census, U.S. Department of Commerce.

1994h Interagency Conference on the Statistical Use of Administrative Records: Final Proceedings. (July 15, 1993). Bureau of the Census, U.S. Department of Commerce.

CEC Associates
1987 Decennial Census Residence Rules and Enumeration Principles. Final report for the Bureau of the Census, February 1987.

Causey, B.
1994 An Area-Based Alternative to Synthetic Estimation for 2KS. (January 14, 1994). Bureau of the Census, U.S. Department of Commerce.

Chandrasekar, C., and W.E. Deming
1949 On a method of estimating birth and death rates and the extent of registration. *Journal of the American Statistical Association*, 44:101-115.

Childers, Danny R.
1993 The Impact of Housing Unit Coverage on Person Coverage. Housing Unit Coverage Study (HUCS) Results Memorandum Number 2. Distributed with cover memo from Ruth Ann Killion to Thomas C. Walsh (June 24, 1993). Bureau of the Census, U.S. Department of Commerce.

Choldin, Harvey
1994 *Looking for the Last Percent: The Controversy Over Census Undercount.* New Brunswick: Rutgers University Press.

Choudhry, G.H.
1992 Changing the Date of Census Day. Social Survey Methods Division, Statistics Canada (August).

Citro, Constance F., and Graham Kalton, eds.

1993 *The Future of the Survey of Income and Program Participation.* Panel to Evaluate the Survey of Income and Program Participation, Committee on National Statistics, National Research Council. Washington, D.C.: National Academy Press.

Citro, Constance F., and Michael L. Cohen, eds.

1985 *The Bicentennial Census: New Directions for Census Methodology in 1990.* Panel on Decennial Census Methodology, Committee on National Statistics, National Research Council. Washington, D.C.: National Academy Press.

Clark, Jon R., Don A. Dillman, and Kirsten K. West

1993 Influence of an Invitation to Answer by Telephone on Response to Census Questionnaires. Proceedings of the American Statistical Association, Survey Methods Section, August 1993.

Clogg, C.C., D.B. Rubin, N. Schenker, B. Schultz, and L. Weidman

1991 Multiple imputation of industry and occupation codes in census public-use samples using Bayesian logistic regression. *Journal of the American Statistical Association* 86:68-78.

Clogg, Clifford C., and Christine L. Himes

1993 Comment: Uncertainty in demographic analysis. *Journal of the American Statistical Association* 88(423):1072-1074.

Coale, A.J.

1955 The population of the United States in 1950 classified by age, sex, and color—A revision of census figures. *Journal of the American Statistical Association* 50: 16-54.

Collins, LaVerne Vines

1994 Options Paper on Cooperative Ventures with State, Local and Tribal Governments. Paper prepared for the March 1994 Census Advisory Committee for the Design of the Year 2000 Census and Census-Related Activities for 2000-2009. Bureau of the Census, U.S. Department of Commerce.

Committee on National Statistics

1978 *Counting the People in 1980: An Appraisal of Census Plans.* Panel on Decennial Census Plans, Committee on National Statistics, National Research Council. Washington, D.C.: National Academy Press.

1992 Letter Report to the Bureau of the Census from the Panel to Evaluate Alternative Census Methods, Committee on National Statistics, Commission on Behavioral and Social Sciences and Education, National Research Council, Washington, D.C.

1993a *Planning The Decennial Census: Interim Report.* Panel on Census Requirements in the Year 2000 and Beyond, Committee on National Statistics, National Research Council. Washington, D.C.: National Academy Press.

1993b *A Census That Mirrors America: Interim Report.* Panel to Evaluate Alternative Census Methods, Committee on National Statistics, National Research Council. Washington, D.C.: National Academy Press.

1993c Letter Report to the Bureau of the Census from the Panel on Census Requirements in the Year 2000 and Beyond, Committee on National Statistics, Commission on Behavioral and Social Sciences and Education, National Research Council, Washington, D.C.

Czajka, John L., and Allen L. Schirm
  1994   Using IRS Administrative Records for Population Estimation: A Technical
          Appendix to Sailer, Weber, and Yau (1993). (January 13, 1994). Mathematica
          Policy Research, Inc., Washington, D.C.

Darroch, John N., S.E. Fienberg, G.F.V. Glonek, and B.W. Junker
  1993   A three-sample multiple-recapture approach to census population estimation
          with heterogeneous catchability. *Journal of the American Statistical Associa-
          tion* 88(423):1137-1148.

de la Puente, Manuel
  1993   Why Are People Missed or Erroneously Included by the Census: A Summary
          of Findings from Ethnographic Coverage Reports. Report Prepared for the
          Advisory Committee for the Design of the Year 2000 Census Meeting, March
          5. Bureau of the Census, U.S. Department of Commerce.

Dillman, Don A., Jon R. Clark, and James B. Treat
  1994   Influence of 13 Design Factors on Completion Rates to Decennial Census
          Questionnaires. Paper presented at the Annual Research Conference of the
          U.S. Bureau of the Census. Arlington, Virginia, March 1994.

Duncan, George T., Thomas B. Jabine, and Virginia A. de Wolf, eds.
  1993   *Private Lives and Public Policies: Confidentiality and Accessibility of Gov-
          ernment Statistics.* Panel on Confidentiality and Data Access, Committee on
          National Statistics, National Research Council. Washington, D.C.: National
          Academy Press.

Ericksen, E.P., L.F. Estrada, J.W. Tukey, and K.M. Wolter
  1991   Report on the 1990 Decennial Census and the Post-Enumeration Survey. Re-
          port submitted by members of the Special Advisory Panel to the Secretary of
          the U.S. Department of Commerce (June 21, 1991).

Ericksen, Eugene P., and Joseph B. Kadane
  1985   Estimating the population in a census year: 1980 and beyond. *Journal of the
          American Statistical Association* 80 (389):98-109.

Fay, Robert E., and John H. Thompson
  1993   The 1990 Post Enumeration Survey: Statistical lessons, in hindsight. *Pro-
          ceedings of the 1993 Annual Research Conference.* Bureau of the Census,
          U.S. Department of Commerce.

Fienberg, Stephen E.
  1992   An adjusted census in 1990? The trial. *Chance* 5 (No. 3-4): 28-38.

Freedman, D.A. and W.C. Navidi
  1986   Regression models for adjusting the 1980 census. *Statistical Science* 1(1): 3-
          17.
  1992   Should we have adjusted the U.S. census of 1980? *Survey Methodology* 18:1-
          74.

Freedman, D.A., and K. Wachter
  1994   Heterogeneity and census adjustment for the intercensal base. *Statistical Sci-
          ence.* Forthcoming

Freedman, D.A., K.W. Wachter, D.C. Coster, D.R. Cutler, and S.P. Klein
  1993   Adjusting the census of 1990: The smoothing model. *Evaluation Review* 17:
          371-443.

Freedman, D.A., K. Wachter, R. Cutler, and S. Klein
  1994   Adjusting the census of 1990: Loss functions. *Evaluation Review*. Forth-
          coming.
Fuller, W.A., C.T. Isaki, and J.H. Tsay
  1994   Design and Estimation for Samples of Census Nonresponse. Paper presented
          at the Annual Research Conference of the U.S. Bureau of the Census, Arling-
          ton, Virginia, March 20-23.
Gerber, Eleanor R., and Nancy Bates
  1994   Respondents' Understanding of Residence Terminology in Cognitive Research
          and the Living Situation Survey. Paper presented at the Annual Research
          Conference of the U.S. Bureau of the Census, Arlington, Virginia, March 20-
          23.
Goldfield, Edwin D.
  1992   Innovations in the Decennial Census of Population and Housing: 1940-1990.
          Paper prepared for the Committee on National Statistics, Commission on Be-
          havioral and Social Sciences and Education, National Research Council.
Green, Samuel, Jr., and Harry A. Scarr
  1993   USPS-Census Cooperation in Planning for the 2000 Decennial Census of
          Population and Housing. Letter of Transmittal from the U.S. Postal Service
          and U.S. Census Bureau to members of the House Appropriations Subcom-
          mittee, November 5, 1993.
Greenberg, Tom
  1993   Results of the Income Permission Question from the August 1993 Test. (De-
          cember 1993 Draft). Labour and Household Surveys Analysis Division, Sta-
          tistics Canada, Ottawa, Ontario.
Hansen, M.H., W.N. Hurwitz, and M.A. Bershad
  1961   Measurement errors in censuses and surveys. *Bulletin of the International
          Statistical Institute* 38, II.
Herriot, R., C. Bowie, D. Kasprzyk, and S. Haber
  1989a   Enhanced Demographic-Economic Data Sets. SIPP Working Paper No. 8905.
          (April 1989). Bureau of the Census, U.S. Department of Commerce.
Herriot, R.A., D.V. Bateman, and W.F. McCarthy
  1989b   The decade census program—A new approach for meeting the nation's needs
          for sub-national data. *American Statistical Association Proceedings, Section
          on Social Statistics*. Alexandria, Va.: American Statistical Association.
Himes, C.L., and Clogg, C.C.
  1992   An overview of demographic analysis as a method for evaluating census cov-
          erage in the United States. *Population Index* 58: 587-607.
Hoag, Elizabeth
  1984   Estimating Annual Migration for California Counties Using Driver License
          Address Changes. Paper presented at the annual meeting of the Population
          Association of America, Minneapolis, Minnesota, May 1984. Population Re-
          search Unit, Department of Finance, State of California.
Hogan, Howard
  1992   The 1990 Post-Enumeration Survey: An overview. *The American Statisti-
          cian* 46(4):261-269.

1993   The 1990 Post-Enumeration Survey: Operations and results. *Journal of the American Statistical Association* 88(423):1047-1060.

Horvitz, Daniel G.

1986   Statement to the Subcommittee on Census and Population, U.S. House of Representatives (May 1). Research Triangle Institute, Research Triangle Park, N.C.

Internal Revenue Service

1993   1990 Taxpayer Opinion Survey Final Report. Conducted for the Internal Revenue Service by Schulman, Ronca, and Bucuvalas, Inc., for the Commissioner (Planning and Research), Research Division.

Isaki, C.T., J.H. Tsay, and Y. Thibaudeau

1993   Evaluation of Two Sample Design Options for Sampling for the Count. 2KS Memorandum Series Design 2000, Book 1, Chapter 12, #1 (May 12, 1993). Bureau of the Census, U.S. Department of Commerce.

Kalton, Graham, Daniel Levine, David Marker, and Laura Sharp

1994   Methods to Enumerate Persons With No Usual Residence Using Sampling and Estimation: Final Report. (January 14, 1994). Westat, Inc., Rockville, Maryland.

Kearney, Anne, Roger Tourangeau, Gary Shapiro, and Lawrence Ernst

1993   Coverage Improvement from Experimental Residence Questions. Unpublished manuscript, dated 31 August 1993. Proceedings of the 1993 Annual Meeting of the American Statistical Association, Section on Survey Research Methods.

Keeley, Catherine

1993   Could the Census Bureau Reduce the Undercount by Not Using a "Long Form?" (September 10). Bureau of the Census, U.S. Department of Commerce.

Keller, Jay, and Carol Van Horn

1993   What Will the Next Census Cost: The Use of Cost and Operational Modeling in the Examination of Alternative 2000 Census Designs. Paper presented at the 1993 annual meetings of the American Statistical Association. Bureau of the Census, U.S. Department of Commerce.

Kim, J., R. Blodgett, and A.M. Zaslavsky

1991   Evaluation of the synthetic assumption—1990 Post-Enumeration Survey. *American Statistical Association Proceedings, Section on Survey Research.* Alexandria, Va.: American Statistical Association.

Kish, L.

1981   *Using Cumulated Rolling Samples.* No. 80-52810. Washington, D.C.: U.S. Government Printing Office.

1990   Rolling samples and censuses. *Survey Methodology* 16:63-71.

Knott, Joseph J.

1994   Proposed Uses of Administrative Records in the 1995 Census Test. Memo from Joseph J. Knott to Susan M. Miskura, dated January 5, 1994. Bureau of the Census, U.S. Department of Commerce.

Kulka, R.A., and M.F. Weeks

1988   Toward the development of optimal calling protocols for telephone surveys: A conditional probabilities approach. *Journal of Official Statistics* 4: 319-332.

Lee, Margaret M.
  1993   *Legal Issues for Census 2000.* Congressional Research Service Report 93-177-A. Washington, D.C.: U.S. Government Printing Office.
Leggieri, Charlene A.
  1994   Development of a Master Address File as a Base for the 2000 Census. Paper presented at the Annual Research Conference of the U.S. Bureau of the Census, Arlington, Virginia, March 20-23.
Leyes, John
  1990   An Administrative Record Paradigm: A Canadian Experience. Paper presented at Seminar on Quality of Federal Data, May 23-24, 1990. Statistics Canada, Ottawa, Ontario.
Long, John F.
  1993   Postcensal Population Estimates: States, Counties, and Places. Technical Working Paper Series, Report No. 3 (May 1993). Bureau of the Census, U.S. Department of Commerce.
Louis Harris and Associates
  1993   Health Information Privacy Survey 1993. Conducted for Equifax, Inc., by Louis Harris and Associates, New York.
Mahler, Sarah
  1993   Alternative Enumeration of Undocumented Salvadorans on Long Island. Prepared under joint statistical agreement 89-46 with Columbia University. Bureau of the Census, U.S. Department of Commerce.
Marks, Eli S., W. Seltzer, and K.J. Krotki
  1974   *Population Growth Estimation: A Handbook of Vital Statistics Measurement.* New York: Population Council.
Martin, Elizabeth
  1992   Preliminary Research and Evaluation. Memorandum No. 112 (January 20). Bureau of the Census, U.S. Department of Commerce.
Miskura, Susan
  1993   Definition, Clarification and Issues: One Number Census. Bureau of the Census, U.S. Department of Commerce (April 14).
Mulry, Mary H., and B.D. Spencer
  1991   Total error in PES estimates of population (with discussion). *Journal of the American Statistical Association* 86:839-844.
  1993   Accuracy of the 1990 census and undercount adjustments. *Journal of the American Statistical Association* 88(423):1080-1091.
Ogden Government Services
  1993a   U.S. Bureau of the Census Technology Assessment of Publicly Available Data Collection Technologies for the Year 2000. Deliverable 4, p. 75, April 1993. Bureau of the Census, U.S. Department of Commerce.
  1993b   U.S. Bureau of the Census Technology Assessment of Publicly Available Data Collection Technologies for the Year 2000. Volume 1, p. 17, October 1993. U.S. Bureau of the Census, U.S. Department of Commerce.
Redfern, Phillip
  1994   Precise identification through a multi-purpose personal number protects privacy. *International Journal of Law and Information Technology* 1(3):57-55.

Robinson, J.G., B. Ahmed, P. Das Gupta, and K. Woodrow
   1993   Estimation of population coverage in the 1990 United States census based on demographic analysis. (with discussion). *Journal of the American Statistical Association* 88(423):1061-1079.

Robinson, J.G., B. Ahmed, E.W. Fernandez
   1994   Demographic Analysis as an Expanded Program for Early Coverage Evaluation of the 2000 Census. Manuscript presented at the 1994 Annual Research Conference, Bureau of the Census, March 21-24, 1994.

Romero, Mary
   1992   Ethnographic Evaluation of Behavioral Causes of Census Undercount of Undocumented Immigrants and Salvadorans in the Mission District of San Francisco, California. Ethnographic Evaluation of the 1990 Decennial Census Report #18. Paper prepared under Joint Statistical Agreement 89-41 with the San Francisco State University Foundation. Bureau of the Census, U.S. Department of Commerce.

Rubin, Don B.
   1987   *Multiple Imputation for Nonresponse in Surveys*. New York: John Wiley and Sons.

Sailer, Peter, M. Weber, and E. Yau
   1993   How well can IRS count the population? *1993 Proceedings of the American Statistical Association, Survey Research Methods Section*. Alexandria, Virginia: American Statistical Association.

Sawyer, Thomas C.
   1993   Rethinking the Census: Reconciling the Demands for Accuracy and Precision in the 21st Century. Transcript of Congressman Sawyer's statement at the Census Bureau Research Conference on Undercounted Ethnic Populations, May 5-7, 1993, Richmond, Virginia.

Scarr, Harry A.
   1994   Report to Congress on the Status of the Year 2000 Decennial Census Planning Efforts. Testimony given on January 26, 1994, before the Subcommittee on Census, Statistics, and Postal Personnel. Report transmitted with letter from Ronald H. Brown.

Schirm, A.L., and S.H. Preston
   1987   Census undercount adjustment and the quality of geographic population distributions (with discussion). *Journal of the American Statistical Association* 82: 965-990.
   1992   Comment on "Should we have adjusted the U.S. census of 1980?" *Survey Methodology* 18:35-43.

Schwede, Laurel
   1993   An Empirical Exploration of Residence Rules: The Living Situation Survey. Proceedings of the American Statistical Association, Survey Methods Section, August 1993.

Seber, G.A.F.
   1982   *The Estimation of Animal Abundance and Related Parameters*. Second Edition. New York: Macmillan.

Singer, Eleanor
   1994   The Appeals and Long Form Experiment (ALFE): The Short Form Debriefing Analysis. Final Report.

Singh, R.P.
   1993   2000 Census: Coverage Measurement Prototype Methodology. (December 15, 1993). Memo from Rajendra Singh to John Thompson. Bureau of the Census, U.S. Department of Commerce.
Spencer, B.D.
   1980   Implications of equity and accuracy for undercount adjustment: A decision-theoretic approach. *Proceedings of the Conference on Census Undercount* 204-216. Bureau of the Census, U.S. Department of Commerce.
Standish, Linda D., R. Bender, M. Michalowski, and A. Peters
   1993   Administrative record comparison (ARC): Report of demographic comparisons with the 1991 Canadian census. *Proceedings of the 1993 Annual Research Conference*, Bureau of the Census, U.S. Department of Commerce, Washington, D.C., pp. 144-165.
Statistics Canada
   1987   *Population Estimation Methods, Canada.* Ottawa: Statistics Canada.
   1994   Permission from Respondents to Link Data with the National Population Health Survey. (April 6, 1994).
Statistics Canada and Bureau of the Census
   1993   Challenges of measuring an ethnic world: Science, politics and reality. *Proceedings of the Joint Canada-United States Conference on the Measurement of Ethnicity*, April 1-3, 1992. Washington, D.C.: U.S. Government Printing Office.
Sweet, Elizabeth M.
   1994   Roster Research Results from the Living Situation Survey. Paper presented at the Annual Research Conference of the U.S. Bureau of the Census, Arlington, Virginia, March 20-23.
Thompson, John
   1993   Integrated Coverage Measurement and Sampling for Nonresponse Followup. (December 13, 1993). Paper presented at the meeting of the advisory committee for the design of the year 2000 census and census related activities for 2000-2009.
Treat, James B.
   1993   1993 National Census Test: Appeals and Long-Form Experiment, Appeals or Short-Form Component., DSSD 2000 Census Memorandum Series E-62.
U.S. Department of Commerce
   1991   The Decision of the Secretary of Commerce on Whether a Statistical Adjustment of the 1990 Decennial Census of Population Should Be Made for Coverage of Deficiencies Resulting in an Overcount or Undercount of the Population. *The Federal Register*, Docket 91281-1181, July 15.
U.S. Department of Health and Human Services
   1976   *The Objectives of the SSA.* OHR/EC Publication No. 029 (7-76). Washington, D.C.: U.S. Department of Treasury.
U.S. General Accounting Office
   1992   *Decennial Census: 1990 Results Show Need for Fundamental Reform.* Washington, D.C.: U.S. Government Printing Office.

U.S. House of Representatives
1993   Report of the House Committee on Appropriations. (June 24, 1993). H.R. 2519, Departments of Commerce, Justice, and State, the Judiciary, and Related Agencies Appropriations Act, 1994 (Pub. L. 103-21).

Vobejda, Barbara
1994   Civil rights groups protest lack of racial data on medical form. *The Washington Post*, March 14:A17.

Weeks, Michael F.
1988   Call scheduling with CATI: Current capabilities and methods. Pp. 403-420 in R.M. Groves et al. (eds.), *Telephone Survey Methodology*. New York: John Wiley and Sons.
1992   Computer-assisted survey information collection: A review of CASIC methods and their implications for survey operations. *Journal of Official Statistics* 8:445-465.

Weeks, M.F., R.A. Kulka, J.T. Lessler, and R.W. Whitmore
1983   Personal versus telephone surveys for collecting household health data at the local level. *American Journal of Public Health* 73:1389-1394.

Weeks, M.F., R.A. Kulka, and S.A. Pierson
1987   Optimal call scheduling for a telephone survey. *Public Opinion Quarterly* 51: 540-549.

Wolter, K.M., and B. Causey
1991   Evaluation of procedures for improving population estimates for small areas. *Journal of the American Statistical Association* 86: 278-284.

Wright, Tommy
1993   CensusPlus: A Sampling and Prediction Approach for the 2000 Census of the United States. Unpublished manuscript. Bureau of the Census, U.S. Department of Commerce.

Zaslvasky, Alan M.
1993   Combining census, dual-system, and evaluation study data to estimate population shares. *Journal of the American Statistical Association* 88(423):1092-1105.

Zaslavsky, Alan, and G.S. Wolfgang
1993   Triple system modeling of census, Post-Enumeration Survey, and administrative list data. *Journal of Business and Economic Statistics* 11:279-288.

APPENDIX

Biographical Sketches of Panel Members and Staff

NORMAN M. BRADBURN is the Tiffany and Margaret Blake distinguished service professor in the Department of Psychology and the Harris Graduate School of Public Policy Studies at the University of Chicago, as well as senior vice president for research at the National Opinion Research Center. He is an authority on nonsampling errors in surveys and has written extensively on questionnaire design. He has been active in the developing field of research applying cognitive psychological principles to the study of response errors in surveys. He received B.A. degrees from the University of Chicago and Oxford University and M.A. and Ph.D. degrees in clinical and social psychology from Harvard University.

ROBERT M. BELL is a senior statistician and head of the statistics group at the RAND Corporation. He has worked on a number of different projects, mainly in health and education. His areas of expertise include survey design, survey analysis, and general experimental design issues. He received a B.S. degree in mathematics from Harvey Mudd College, an M.S. degree in statistics from the University of Chicago, and a Ph.D. degree in statistics from Stanford University.

GORDON J. BRACKSTONE is assistant chief statistician responsible for statistical methodology, computing, and geography at Statistics Canada. His professional work has been in survey methodology, particularly the assessment of the quality of census and survey data. He is a fellow of the American Statistical Association and an elected member of the International Statistical Institute. He received B.Sc. and M.Sc. degrees in statistics from the London School of Economics.

CLIFFORD C. CLOGG is a demographer and statistician at Pennsylvania State University. He is a former chairman of the Committee on Population Statistics of the Population Association of America and a member of the Census Advisory Committee; he was the coordinating and applications editor of the *Journal of the American Statistical Association*. His areas of specialization are categorical data analysis and social statistics. He received a B.A. degree from Ohio University, and an M.S. degree in statistics and M.A. and Ph.D. degrees in sociology from the University of Chicago.

THOMAS B. JABINE is a statistical consultant who specializes in the areas of sampling, survey research methods, and statistical policy. He was formerly statistical policy expert for the Energy Information Administration, chief mathematical statistician for the Social Security Administration, and chief of the Statistical Research Division of the Bureau of the Census. He is a fellow of the American Statistical Association and a member of the International Statistical Institute. He has a B.S. degree in mathematics and an M.S. degree in economics and science from the Massachusetts Institute of Technology.

KATHERINE S. NEWMAN is a professor of anthropology at Columbia University. She specializes in cultural analyses of work and mobility in the suburban middle class and in inner-city communities. She has written extensively on the topic of downward mobility and is currently engaged in a study of minority youth in low-wage, service-sector jobs in the Harlem section of New York and Oakland, California. She has a B.A. degree from the University of California, San Diego, and M.A. and Ph.D. degrees in anthropology from the University of California, Berkeley.

ANU PEMMARAZU is a senior project assistant with the Committee on National Statistics, National Research Council. She is also currently working with the Panel on Statistical Methods for Testing and Evaluating Defense Systems and previously worked on the Panel on the National Health Care Survey. She received a B.S. degree in mathematics from the University of Maryland, College Park.

D. BRUCE PETRIE is assistant chief statistician of the Social, Institutions, and Labor Statistics Field at Statistics Canada. He is responsible for social statistics, which includes the census of population, demography, education, health, justice, labor, and household surveys, including Canada's equivalent of the Current Population Survey. He has a bachelor of commerce degree from Dalhousie University and an M.B.A. degree from the University of Western Ontario.

PETER A. ROGERSON is professor and chair of geography at the State University of New York, Buffalo. His areas of specialization include internal migration, mathematical demography, and estimates and projections. He was formerly a research trainee at the Census Bureau in the Census Bureau/American Statistical Association program on economic-demographic modeling. He received a B.A. degree from the State University of New York, Albany, an M.A. degree from the University of Toronto, and a Ph.D. degree in geography from the State University of New York, Buffalo.

KEITH F. RUST is an associate director at Westat, Inc., and formerly was with the Australian Bureau of Statistics. He is the director of sample design and statistical operations for the National Assessment of Educational Progress, as well as the sampling coordinator for the Third International Mathematics and Science Study. His work deals mainly with educational surveys; he has expertise in the areas of variance estimation and inference for complex samples. He is a member of the Committee on National Statistics, the editorial board of the *Journal of Official Statistics*, and the faculty of the University of Maryland-University of Michigan Joint Program in Survey Methodology. He received a B.A. degree from Flinders University of South Australia and M.S. and Ph.D. degrees in biostatistics from the University of Michigan.

NORA CATE SCHAEFFER is professor of sociology at the University of Wisconsin, Madison. Her areas of expertise include respondent behavior and interviewer-respondent interaction. Her past research has concentrated on a number of different areas in survey methodology dealing with nonsampling error, both nonresponse and response errors of various kinds. She is on the editorial board of *Public Opinion Quarterly*, *Sociological Methodology*, and *Sociological Methods Research*. She has an A.B. degree from Washington University and a Ph.D. degree in sociology from the University of Chicago.

EDWARD A. SCHILLMOELLER is senior vice president of the A.C. Nielsen Company, where he directs all statistical operations and activities of the media research division. His work includes both continuous and ad hoc household surveys of television audiences. His interests are sample design and survey methods. He received a degree in mathematics from Iowa State University and an M.B.A. degree in statistics from the University of Chicago.

DUANE L. STEFFEY is a study director with the Committee on National Statistics, National Research Council. He is on leave from San Diego State University, where he is an associate professor of mathematical sciences. He has published research on statistical methods, particularly on hierarchical Bayesian modeling, and has engaged broadly in interdisciplinary research and consulting. He received a B.S. degree and M.S. and Ph.D. degrees in statistics, all from Carnegie Mellon University.

MICHAEL F. WEEKS is director of Survey Research Associates, Inc., a wholly owned subsidiary of Battelle Memorial Institute. His areas of expertise include survey methods and operations. In particular, he is interested in survey methods aimed at reducing nonsampling error and making survey operations more efficient and more cost-effective. He is on the editorial board of *Public Opinion Quarterly.* He received a B.A. degree from Davidson College and an M.A. degree from the Episcopal Theological Seminary of the Southwest.

ALAN M. ZASLAVSKY is an associate professor of statistics at Harvard University. His research interests include methods for estimating and correcting census undercount, applications of hierarchical Bayes methods, microsimulation modeling, and missing data. He has an A.B. degree from Harvard College, an M.S. degree from Northeastern University, and a Ph.D. degree in applied mathematics from the Massachusetts Institute of Technology.

MEYER ZITTER is an independent demographic consultant and was formerly with the Bureau of the Census. He was chief of the Bureau's population division in the year leading to the 1980 census and later served as assistant director for international programs. He is a fellow of the American Statistical Association and a member of the International Statistical Institute and the International Union for the Scientific Study of Population. He received a B.B.A. degree from City College of New York.